The Science Book

The Science Book
Sara Stein

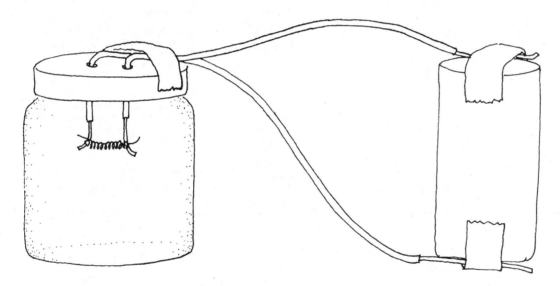

Workman Publishing, New York

A Media Projects Incorporated book

Library of Congress Cataloging-in-Publication Data:

Stein, Sara.
  The science book.

  Includes index.
  SUMMARY: Examines various principles and phenomena of biology, physics, and chemistry through discussion and observation of familiar surroundings—one's own body, home, pets, siblings, food, yard, etc.
    1. Biology—Juvenile literature.
    2. Science—Juvenile literature.
    [1. Biology. 2. Science.]
I. Title
QH309.2.S74 500 79-64786
ISBN 0-89480-121-X
ISBN 0-89480-120-1 pbk.

Cover illustration: Creston Ely
Photographs: Sally Anderson-Bruce
Illustrations: Sara Stein
Photograph on page 152 by Kathryn Abbe
Photograph on page 254 by Erika Stone

Workman Publishing Company, Inc.
708 Broadway
New York, New York 10003

Manufactured in the United States of America

First Printing January 1980

20 19 18 17 16 15

Dedication

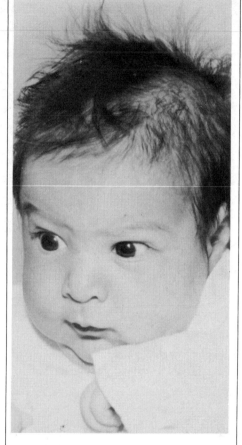

To Lincoln

Contents

Part 1 Outsides

Pests

Pets

People

Part 2 Insides

Protistas

Plants

Animals

Part 3 Invisibles

Touches

Noises

Sights

Tastes & Smells

Charges

Thoughts

Introduction

This has been the hardest book to write that I have ever written. It was hard because many of the things I felt I understood, I really didn't; every time I thought I had an answer, I found another question; and I never really got to the bottom of anything.

That bothered me for a long time. But now I realize that's the way writing a science book ought to be. Because science itself is like that: never really finished, and never really right.

Most people think of scientists as specialists in right answers. Scientists it seems know better. What seemed right yesterday may be proven wrong today; what seems right today may be proven wrong tomorrow. Scientists take time to observe things and to think through ideas that explain what they notice. This is not different from what every child does. When a three year old notices that leaves and clouds move on windy days, he fits an idea to the observation: that leaves and clouds make wind when they move. For the child, that is today's truth. Tomorrow the leaves may fall, the sky may look clear — yet the wind still blows. The child, like the scientists, abandons his first idea and tries another. As long as people keep noticing, ideas will keep changing.

Making sense

All humans, day-old babies and grown-up scientists, can't help but make sense of things in another way, too. You can't look at a quilt without seeing a pattern, listen to a song without hearing a melody, handle a coin without feeling a shape, or stop moving without knowing you are still. These kinds of sense — pattern, shape, motion — seem very different from ideas. They are not made up in our heads, but exist outside ourselves, right and real. Yet an optical illusion is a pattern you see that isn't there; there is no sound of the sea inside a shell; and even as you stand stock still, you are hurtling through space with unimaginable speed.

What appears to be, no matter how sensible, may not be what really is. And here is where a scientist goes farther in his thinking than most of us.

Inside the book

The Science Book begins at home and stays there. The living specimen for scientific study are molds and roaches, geraniums, cats, and humans. The dead specimen are logs and lamb chops, leather, and lettuce. Laboratory apparatus isn't more complicated than a flashlight or a jelly jar. Even the chemicals will be familiar and homey: vinegar, bleach, your own saliva.

The book is divided into three sections, *Outsides, Insides,* and *Invisibles. Outsides* deals with what you can notice about the animals that live in your home — pests, pets, and people — without looking inside them. In one way, you may have already observed a lot in this section. You have seen moths circling lamps, cats rubbing against ankles, kids throwing stones at cans. Nothing new there. But what you haven't seen is a moth navigating across the night sky by moonlight, or a cat in the wild marking its territory with its scent, or a hunter a hundred thousand years ago killing dinner with a stone. With the observations suggested here, and with some new ideas too, you'll see and understand a little of what these animals are like — *really*.

Inside insides

Insides is about what you can't observe directly without cutting a plant or an animal apart. That may sound like something you'd rather not do; luckily, the cutting has already been done for you. Wood is cut up trees; vegetables are cut up plants. Meat is cut up animals.

You can also make indirect observations about insides. You can feel your own bones, though they are hidden beneath your skin, and hear your own intestines at work, though you will never see them. You can observe the effects of what is happening inside a yeast, mold, or bacteria, although most of these organisms are too small to see the outside of without a microscope. Logs rotting, bread rising, and milk turning to cheese are all results of some creature's digestion. That's *really* why a log gets mushy, bread fills with air, and cheese tastes sharp.

Making sense of senses

Invisibles gets even closer to the question of what things are really like. When you feel a cat rubbing against your ankles, is the cat really touching you? When you smell cheese, how do you know which smell it is? And what is a smell, really? And even as you read these words, what is really happening in your eyes — and in your brain?

Everything that comes at you from outside yourself is made of bits of stuff too small to see, powered by energy that isn't even made of stuff. What really happens when you touch, hear, smell, taste, see, and think is invisible.

That doesn't mean you have to take someone else's word for the small bits of stuff called molecules, or for the energy that powers them. You detect the differences between a molecule from bacon and one from a banana when you sniff them. You've always been able to tell molecules apart. You cut up starch molecules when you munch a banana. That's something you can test. You release your own electrical energy when you hit your funny bone. You can certainly feel that. And you absorb packets of light energy when you read this page. That's what you really see. These invisible events are familiar too.

Take your time

The Science Book is supposed to last for years — I don't mean that it is well made, on good paper with a strong binding — but that it contains a lot of information that you will want to know about but don't have to read or experiment with immediately. Take it easy — that way you can enjoy what is fun for you this year, and still have plenty left for next year. Also, not everyone will be equally interested in everything. I like bedbugs myself, but can ignore batteries. You can, too (or the other way around). Or, you can be a mad scientist, doing every experiment, game, test, and invention in the book without understanding why they work. Hot air balloons and dogs that do tricks won't suffer the least from being misunderstood; nor will your pleasure be less for not understanding them.

But I think something will happen even if you don't work at it, even if you don't memorize, test yourself, study, or build your vocabulary. And that is a way of thinking — the scientists's way of thinking — will creep up on you. You will begin to wonder: what are things *really* like?

Outsides

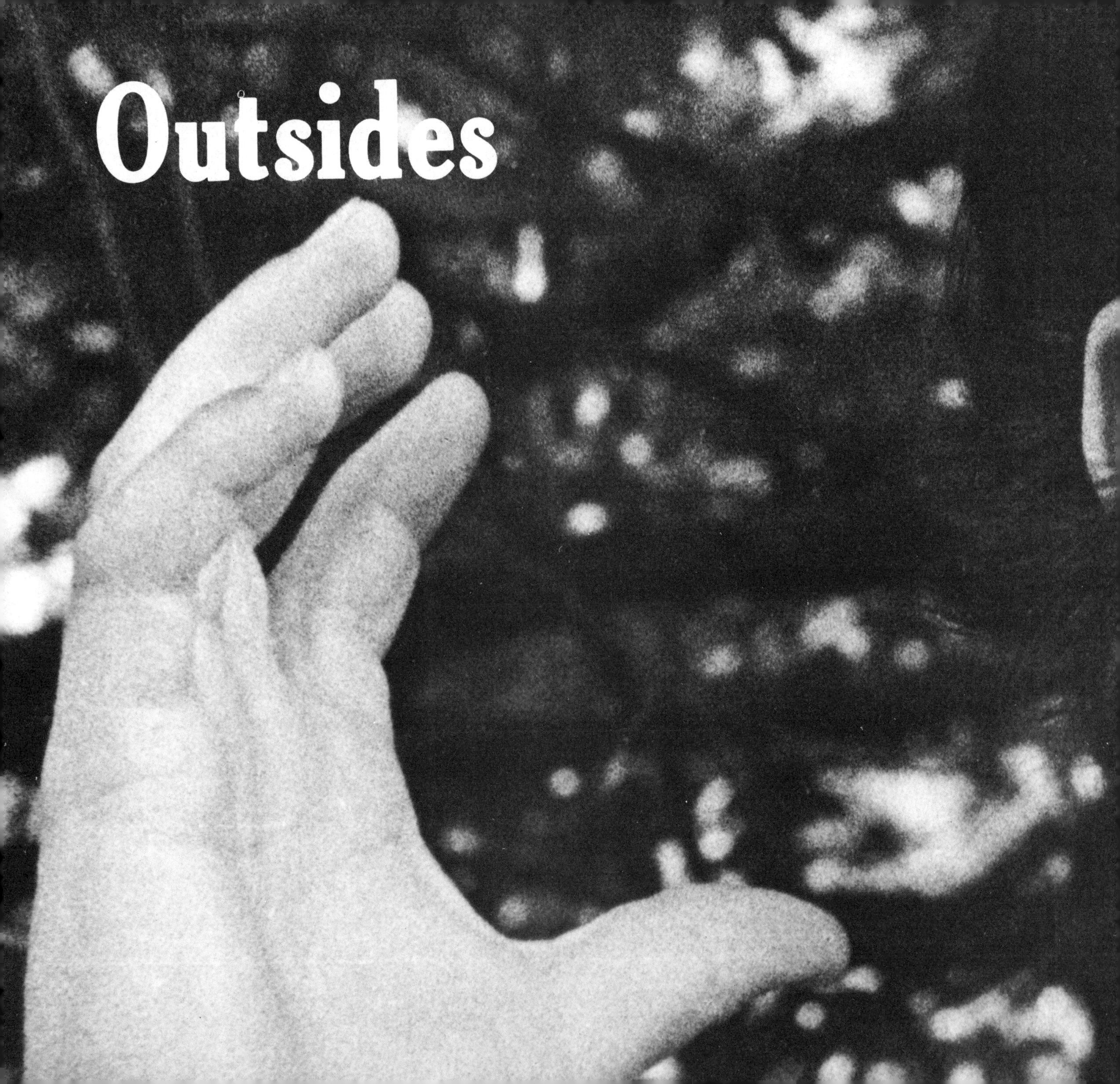

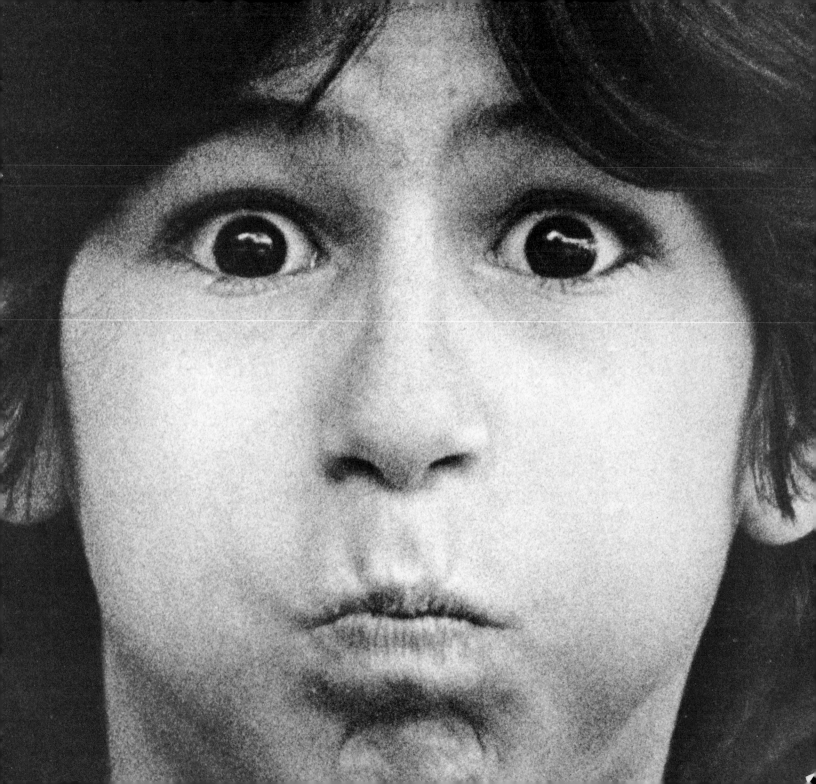

Outsides:

Within the walls, cockroaches snuggle together to sleep with their babies safely on their backs. Between the cracks, fleas await the return of their pet dog — in time for breakfast, they hope. The spider, whose web you dusted away yesterday, has just finished a night's rebuilding. Behind the furnace, a mouse nurses ten newborn pups born in a nest woven from sofa stuffing and shredded sock. A fly, newly hatched from your flower pot, tests out its wings as it follows the smell of jam to the kitchen. Home for the day, the cat rubs its scent onto the lamp before settling down for a nap on the hall table. The dog bows good morning to you as you bend to attach its leash.

And so the morning begins among the creatures who share your home. The night shift is retiring from hours of foraging under sinks and within the fibers of carpets. The day shift, including the humans who thought the house was theirs alone, is coming on. But before the business of the human day begins — before the mousetrap is set, the fly swatted, the cabinets sprayed, the webs dusted again, and the cat and dog dismissed as too familiar for us to notice much — wonder for a while about all these other lives. What are all these creatures doing here? Why do some bite the dog, others gnaw the walls, or spin their webs, or rub the lamp, or bow good morning to us? And what might they think of us? What kind of animal are we? Through a quarter of a million years of evolution, all these creatures who once lived their independent lives have come to live in familiarity with one another in a place we all call home. The stories and ideas that follow will introduce you to them, and to yourself.

Morning as usual

Pests

Why the bedbug bites

At three o'clock one morning in early September, I awoke with a fiercely itching belly. Curious as well as uncomfortable, I switched on a light to take a look. There, in the center of a large, red, swollen patch of skin, was a bedbug. I squished it, placed it on the bedside table, scratched some more, and went back to sleep.

In the morning, I checked its identification in *Webster's International Dictionary*. The illustration was definitely my bedbug's first cousin. I taped the tiny corpse next to its relative, and called my doctor for instructions in bedbug extermination. "Mrs. Stein," he told me patiently, "there hasn't been a bedbug in our neighborhood for thirty years."

Armed with this helpful remark, I stripped the bed and sprayed it and every surface or crevice within a yard of it. We never found another bedbug. That's the end of the story, but not the beginning. If "our neighborhood" had no bedbugs, how come I had one? Little by little, we pieced the circumstances together.

Bats but no belfry

During the preceding month, we had all gone to Maine while my husband stayed home to do some work on the house. We were trying to sell it, and it needed some sprucing up. One night, I got a frantic phone call from him. The house was filled with bats; he was beating the air with

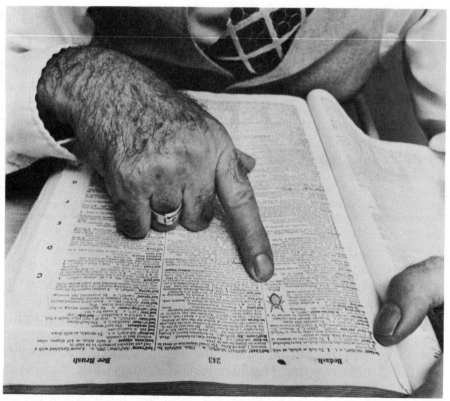

At the top of the dictionary page, above the picture of the bedbug, is an actual bedbug taped in place.

Itchy bites

Flea bites are often in rows of three or four. They are hard bumps, not flat like mosquito bites. They itch intensely, sometimes for a whole week.

Fleas don't actually bite at all. They pierce the skin and suck blood through two very narrow "straws" at their mouth. But blood is quite thick. So, to thin the blood and keep it flowing from the puncture, fleas inject a blood-thinning saliva into the tiny wound. It is flea saliva that is an irritant to us and it stimulates the swelling and itching we call a "bite."

If this sort of thing interests you, you can let a mosquito land on your arm and watch a similar procedure. The mosquito's mouth parts are somewhat different, but the long tube through which it sucks is easy to see, and the technique of injecting the blood-thinning saliva is the same. As the mosquito, who may take a moment or two to find the spot it prefers, pierces your skin, you probably won't feel anything. But when you are able to see the mosquito's belly filling up with blood, the spot will begin to prickle slightly, and by the time the meal is finished, the bite will have begun to swell and itch.

his arm at that very moment; they wouldn't go away; and what was he to do about it? "Where had they come from?" I asked, though I had already guessed. We had harbored a colony of bats in an unused chimney flue for many years. The flue led to an upstairs bedroom where it had originally been intended for a small woodburning stove. We had never gotten around to connecting the stove, and had stuffed rags into the round flue opening in the wall. Thinking the rags an unsightly way to greet potential buyers, my husband had pulled them out just that day. The bats, who usually left their home at night through the top of the flue, discovered the new exit and tried it out. When he saw bats issuing by the dozen from the bedroom, he quickly slammed the door — a wrong move, for now the bats had no way of getting home again. I advised opening the bedroom door. Sure enough, by morning the bats were all chirping in their chimney, and the flue could again be stuffed to keep them there.

A change of name

The accidental association of bats and humans began when Neanderthal man first moved into caves where bats had long preceded him. On the whole, they neither bothered nor benefited one another. But the association definitely benefited another creature, a small bug who lived among the bats and dined upon their blood. This insect, which up until then had not known another food, found it possible, in time of need, to drop upon the cavemen down below and dine among them. Over the years, though it could still get along with bats, the creature became so adapted to man, and so common a nighttime visitor, that what had once been exclusively a "batbug" became known as a bedbug.

And so history had simply repeated itself in our house.

. . .And why the flea usually doesn't

Any mammal that lives in a permanent residence can get fleas. That includes rabbits, who live in burrows; mice, who live in nests; foxes, who live in dens; and humans, who live in houses. But each animal has its very own species of flea. If your dog has fleas, they are most likely dog fleas. If your cat has fleas, they are most likely cat fleas. But, although there are human fleas too, you are not likely to have any. You'll see why when you hear more about fleas.

Fleas join their host for dinner, but once they have filled themselves with blood, they don't necessarily stay on the animal. If the animal is in its usual resting spot, its fleas hop off to take their rest in the same area. In your home, that area might be the chair where your cat usually naps, or your dog's bed, or the carpet at the side of its master's bed. When a flea is hungry again, it simply waits for its animal to come "home." Then it hops aboard for another meal. Fleas have never been able

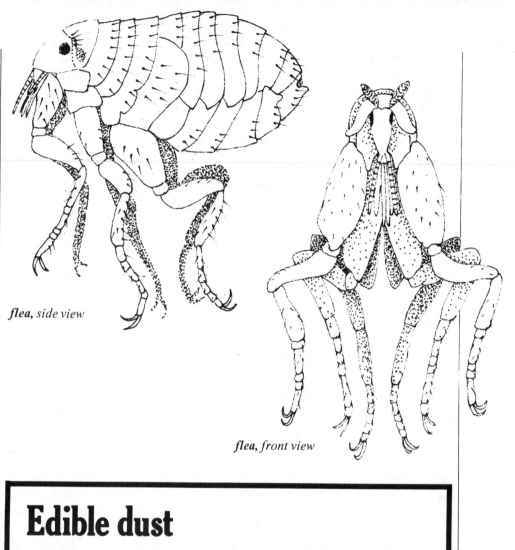

flea, side view

flea, front view

Edible dust

To discover what sorts of food your family may make available to flea larvae, brush up dust from near a dog's bed or from the floor where you snack in front of the TV set. Look at it through a hand lens or magnifying glass (page 193). You will often be able to find crumbs of food, animal and human hairs, even cotton or woolen threads from clothing or furniture. Compared to the tiny size of the larvae, half a thimbleful of dust may provide a feast for an army.

to adjust to wandering animals like buffalo and antelopes. No matter where the fleas had jumped off, when it was time for dinner again, their animal had long since gone.

A home for fleas

Female fleas lay their eggs on their animal. Though they only mate once, they can store the sperm and use it to fertilize eggs many times during the rest of their six-month life. The eggs, laid one or two at a time, are round and smooth; they drop through the host animal's hair to the ground wherever the animal happens to be. (The black, gritty stuff on the skin of a flea-infested pet is droppings, not eggs.) And since most of a pet's fleas hop on while the animal is in its resting spot, most of the fleas' eggs land there as well. The eggs hatch into hungry larvae, which is what the immature, wormlike form of an insect is called. The larvae don't yet have the complicated mouth parts adults use to suck out blood. Instead, they eat the organic debris ordinarily found within the cracks of floorboards and in the fibers of carpeting — animal hairs, adult flea droppings, cookie crumbs. Both the eggs and the larvae are so small people don't notice them.

The two-week-old larvae spin cocoons — again too small to notice — and go through a pupal stage inside the cocoon, during which they change both inside and outside from larvae to adults. They emerge as mature fleas. If all has gone well, their parents' animal is right there waiting for them.

Better than nothing

But what if the dog has met up with a skunk and been banished to the garage? Or what if the tomcat is off on a prolonged journey through the neighborhood? That's the only time you'll be bitten by another animal's fleas. Desperate for food, and deprived of its preferred dog or cat, the flea will dine on your less tasty offerings.

As to human fleas, you will find them making do these days with pigs and badgers. They have become victims of our modern, technological society. Gone are the complicated, seldom-washed clothes whose many dirty folds and pockets they used to love to live in. Gone are the hair and straw and corn husk mattresses where the larvae could not only live, but eat as well. Instead, here are the cleaners and laundromats, the synthetic fabrics and stuffings, the simple clothes — and the vacuum cleaners. These days, more flea eggs are disposed of in the vacuum cleaner bag than live to adulthood.

American cockroach

Commensal cockroaches

Commensal means literally "one who eats at the same table." Scientists use the word to describe an animal who has adapted to live with another kind of animal in order to share some benefit that animal can provide. Cockroaches are commensals of man. Unlike fleas and bedbugs, they are not after our blood — only the shelter of our homes and the nourishment of our leftovers. You don't have to like your commensals (which include rats and mice), but you are not likely to get rid of them altogether.

Ancient roaches that closely resemble our modern ones were already common insects long before the existence of human beings or other mammals — long before the dinosaurs, for that matter, or trees and flowers. Three hundred million years ago, roaches scavenged for dead food on the floors of treeless forests thick with gigantic ferns, horsetails, and club mosses that

German cockroach

grew to a height of a hundred feet. In tropical forests of the modern world, most cockroach species still live as they always have, eating the remains of plants and animals they come upon.

But that is not all they can eat, and that is why some roach species have been able to move in with us so comfortably. Cockroaches can eat soap, paper, leather, glue, fabric, paint, hair,

Oriental cockroach

and toenail clippings — as well as any human foods we leave around for them. If worse comes to worst, they can go for months with no food at all.

A success story

Their incredible success can be blamed on other facts about them too. Roaches are nocturnal (active at night), and so escape any predators that hunt by day. They emit a nasty smell that all but a handful of nocturnal predators avoid. We can smell them, too, in a house that is heavily infested. Their six strong legs can propel them rapidly away from an enemy. Even if you think you have a roach right under your raised and ready foot, the two pointed sense organs at the rear of its body will detect vibrations from your movements, and the roach will be elsewhere by the time your foot slams down. When you are sure you have a roach cornered,

it will defy you by scuttling into a crevice so narrow that only a creature with an unusually flattened body could squeeze through. Occasionally, a winged roach will startle you by flying away when it is cornered.

A cockroach's large eyes may not be able to make out the features of your face, but they don't miss the slightest movement. It's possible a roach you touch not only feels your finger but tastes it, too. Those super-long, gracefully waving antennae can smell substances at a distance, and also taste by touch. Roaches always taste their food before they eat it, a behavior you can observe. The antennae will seek out, say, a crumb of bread, then lovingly stroke it before moving in to feed upon it.

Roaches are virtually indestructible in other ways. You can chill a roach in your freezer, warm it up, and watch it scurry happily off. (Don't do this with-

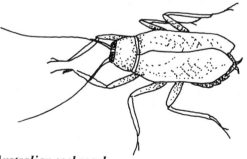

Australian cockroach

out permission from an adult.) You can send it into outer space under conditions people can't take. You can't even get rid of roaches with an atomic bomb. They can survive a hundred times the radiation that kills a human.

Insecticides seldom work for long. The first time an insecticide is used to exterminate a population of roaches, most of them die. But not all. A few roaches out of the hundreds or thousands sprayed will prove to have a natural resistance to the poison. These few survive, breed, and repopulate your home — this time with roaches that have inherited immunity to that insecticide.

Cockroaches are smart, too. We once lived in a roach-infested apartment building. The landlord sent the exterminator on alternate months. He would come to us in October, a neighboring apartment in November, back to us in December, and so on through the year. At the first whiff of spray, my roaches would simply leave via the crack beneath the baseboard to stay with my neighbor for a while. As the exterminator entered her apartment the following month, my roaches — joined now with hers — marched back again. As far as I could see, this monthly migration was accomplished without a single fatality.

Much more impressive migrations have been observed. Hundreds of thousands of cockroaches, blackening the ground, may march from a city dump into the brand new housing complex just completed nearby. Or they may march across the street from one restaurant to another. No one knows why.

Family life

Cockroaches do seem to enjoy group life. They aren't considered social insects because they don't parcel out the chores or cooperate in any noticeable way. Yet, could you peer inside the walls of a roach-ridden house, you would see them during the day sleeping huddled against one another with their babies on their backs.

Mating is performed during the night, and is quite a lengthy affair. It takes one to two hours. The result is not the usual mind-boggling number of eggs most insects lay, but a modest parcel containing as few as a dozen eggs. The parcel is shaped like a

Roach watch

The light we need for seeing is more light than a cockroach can bear. If you have roaches, haven't managed to get rid of them, and feel you might as well observe them, don't turn on the light; they will only run away. Instead, light the room dimly from some source outside it, and let your eyes become accustomed to the dimness. Or do what is done in laboratories: substitute a red darkroom bulb (available in photography stores) for a regular bulb in the room. The red light is not visible to roaches because they are red color blind, but it is bright enough for you to see by. Sit in a chair to watch so you can keep from making movements that the roaches can detect with their vibration sensors. Leave out some crumbs for your subjects' dinner and sprinkle drops of water. Then watch how they eat, drink, clean themselves, and possibly mate.

purse and is small enough to be carried about by the mother at the tip of her abdomen. Most roaches carry their eggs until just a few days before they hatch. Then they deposit them in a safe place, such as behind the drain pipe under a kitchen sink. The babies that hatch look like smaller versions of their parents, but without wings. They eat the same diet as adult roaches, shed their skins several times as they grow, and, at the last shedding, emerge with wings.

Fascinating as all this is, it is unlikely to change the crawly feeling most of us get when we see roaches scurrying for cover as we turn on the kitchen lights to make ourselves a nighttime snack. Your family might be consoled to hear that, regardless of the fact that a roach might well have visited a sewer or garbage dump — in the process, picking up germs as various as tuberculosis and staphylococcus — they don't provide a hospitable environment to any human disease. It might be dumb to eat a roach, but you are not likely to catch anything from having them around. When a roach gets dirty, it cleans itself as thoroughly as a cat, paying special attention to its antennae by pulling their entire length through its mouth parts.

The case of the flies

One expects houseflies in the house toward the end of the summer. One even expects them in the still-balmy weeks of early fall, despite constant screams to shut the door. But one year, we still had flies by the end of September, and still more by the first weeks of October. In fact, there were more each day, and though we killed off dozens with a swatter in order to eat breakfast in peace, there were dozens more by dinner. At first, they congregated downstairs, convenient to the kitchen. But by the end of the month, they had invaded every room in the house. We went to bed and got up with flies, took our baths with flies, played the guitar with flies. When there had been several hearty frosts, we looked up at the living room ceiling one day to see not dozens but hundreds of flies. We could no longer hope they were sneaking in from the frost-covered fields. They were

Some people go to extremes to rid the house of flies.

Fly and worm farms

Fruit flies and mealworms make excellent food for hard-to-nourish terrarium animals such as tree frogs, salamanders, baby snakes, and toads. They can be raised at home on your own farm.

The fruit flies that will be your parent stock must be caught during the summer.

You need:
>   a wide-mouthed jar, with a top
>   an overripe banana

Put a small bit of the overripe banana in the bottom of the jar. If fruit flies are around (they can easily get through screening), they will come to eat the banana in the jar. When you see a half dozen or so flies hovering in the jar, put the lid on. Now place the jar in the refrigerator to chill, while you get a breeding barn ready. When the flies are chilled, they will be unable to fly; you can open the banana jar and shake them into the barn. Here's how to make the barn.

You need:
>   one or more medium-sized glass jars (depending on how many flies you have — one is enough at first)
>   a square of cloth and a rubber band for each jar, to make the top
>   paper towels
>   a package of dried yeast
>   fruitfly mush, made by cooking together the following ingredients:
>>   ¾ cup water
>>   1 ½ tablespoons molasses
>>   2 ½ tablespoons Cream of Wheat or Farina
>>   1 pinch salt

Place a half-inch of the mush in the bottom of each jar. If there are leftovers, store in a jar in the freezer. Sprinkle the

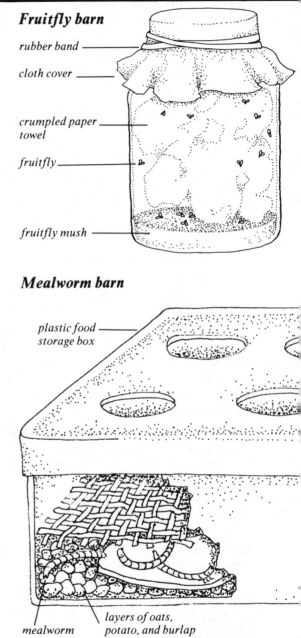

Fruitfly barn

rubber band
cloth cover
crumpled paper towel
fruitfly
fruitfly mush

Mealworm barn

plastic food storage box
mealworm
layers of oats, potato, and burlap

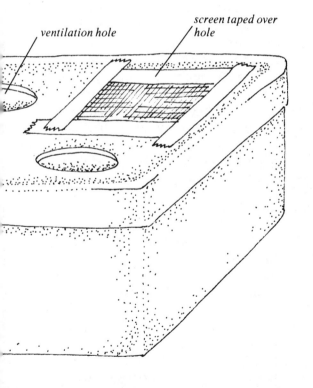

ventilation hole

screen taped over hole

surface of the mush with the dried yeast. Place a piece of crumpled paper towel in each jar. Add the chilled flies. Cover each jar with a square of cloth, held in place with a rubber band. Each jar is a fly barn that will last about six weeks. Moisture can be added occasionally in dry weather by sprinkling water on the cloth. After six weeks, new mush must be made and the flies transferred to clean barns.

Fruit flies live for about a month. They lay their eggs in the same mush they eat, and new flies hatch out about every ten days. To feed fruit flies to pets, chill the barn, put it in the glass-covered terrarium, and remove the jar top.

To raise mealworms, you can start either with some you have found in old flour or other cereals at home, or with a few bought from a pet store.

You need:

a rectangular, soft plastic food storage box with lid
window screening
freezer tape

Cut holes in the lid of the plastic box as shown for ventilation, and cover each with a small piece of window screening, sealed around the edges with freezer tape.

Mealworm food can be rolled oats (uncooked oatmeal) with slices of raw potato added for moisture. The barn is arranged in layers, which are separated by a piece of burlap or some other cloth that is woven loosely enough so that there are spaces between threads for the mealworms to burrow through. Arrange the layers like this: a quarter-inch of oatmeal, topped by two very thin slices of raw potato, followed by a dozen mealworms, covered by a piece of burlap. Repeat until the box is filled. The barn should be kept at room temperature.

Mealworms are the larvae of a small beetle. Before long, the mealworms you put into the barn originally will shed their skin and become pupae — a stage in between larva and adult. The adult beetles will lay eggs within the burlap layers.

After a month or six weeks, it is time to clean the box out and replenish the food supply.

breeding indoors. We stopped screaming and started thinking.

One thought that strangely appealed to my husband was that they were coming through the heating ducts. But that theory didn't work, because flies must be maggots (fly larvae) before they are flies, and maggots must have organic matter to eat. Heating ducts, even if a fly could get into them to lay eggs, are unlikely to harbor dead animals or rotting garbage.

Unwelcome strangers

One detail stuck in my mind as we continued to swat 40 or 50 flies a day, and wash their remains from walls and ceilings. Most were ordinary houseflies, but many were of a second species — a smaller, faster moving fly that was vaguely familiar. Then the answer came to me: the smaller flies were stable flies. They had no business being in the house at all. Stable flies smell out nourishing barnyard manure in which to lay their eggs. Only the smell of manure could have brought them to us.

In June, I had fertilized our large pots of houseplants before putting them outdoors for the summer. I used dried manure. During the late summer, both houseflies and stable flies had been attracted to the scent of manure in the potting soil, and had laid their eggs there.

Normally, the eggs would have lain dormant (not developing) over the cold winter and hatched only when the weather became warm again, but we brought the plants inside during September, and offered them an artificial spring. The eggs hatched, the maggots found enough manure in the soil to thrive and grow. The result was an invasion of flies. The solution? Insecticide sprayed directly on the soil.

A family spider

Spiders aren't insects. They are arachnids, closely related to ticks and scorpions who, like them, have eight legs and no antennae. (Insects have six legs and a pair of antennae.) What is good about spiders is that they capture and eat flies, moths, and mosquitoes around the house. What is bad about them is that the most common house spiders are responsible for the cobwebs people are forever trying to get rid of.

Cobwebs are mostly found in corners between the ceiling and the wall or where one wall meets another. Although not obvious when new, they collect dust more easily than they do prey, and soon are dangling, fluttering masses of dirty strands. Removed one morning, they may reappear the next and, too often, they are up so high that getting rid of them is a real nuisance. Yet you seldom see the spiders that are working as hard to maintain their home as you are to maintain yours. They are too small to notice easily even if they are in the web. And usually they are not. These tiny spiders tend to hide behind their webs or in a crack beneath it until vibrations in the web tell them an insect has been caught. Vacuuming the webs may suck the spiders up as well. But just dusting the cobweb leaves the spider free to start its home all over again.

Spider art

Classic spider webs, the ones that are drawn for Halloween, are rarer than cobwebs inside houses. Most spiders who weave them prefer the outdoors. The long strands that radiate from the center of such a web are spun from glands at the spider's rear before the rest of the web is woven. These strands aren't sticky;

A circular reason

Moths fly in circles around a light because they can't tell the difference between the light and the moon. Before man came along with his torches, campfires, candles, and light bulbs, moths had no trouble using the moon to navigate in a straight course at night. The moon was then the only large bright light in the night sky.

As you know if you stare at the moon while walking or driving in a straight course, you need never shift your gaze to keep the moon in sight. It is only when you turn from that course that you must look about again to relocate the moon in the sky above you. The moon appears to follow you only because it so far away (nearly a quarter of a million miles). The distance you may cover is so tiny in comparison with the moon's distance from you that your angle of vision appears not to change at all. By fixing your eye on its light, and not moving your head or your eyes at all, you can maintain a straight course just as a moth can.

But try to achieve the same guidance from a nearer source of light and you will see the difficulty a moth gets into. The only way now to keep the light fixed in one position (be sure not to move your head or your eyes) is to circle it.

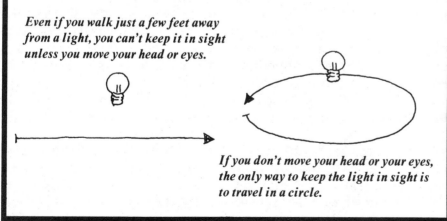

Even if you walk just a few feet away from a light, you can't keep it in sight unless you move your head or eyes.

If you don't move your head or your eyes, the only way to keep the light in sight is to travel in a circle.

the spider must walk only on nonsticky strands or it would be caught in its own web.

Once these radial strands which anchor the web in place are finished, the spider weaves strands back and forth or spirally from radial to radial. Some of these are coated with droplets of sticky stuff. These are the strands that trap insects.

Spiders produce other types of strands, too. One is used to spin a bag around the spider's eggs to protect them. Tear an egg bag open to see how fine and strong the strands are. Another kind is used to bind up a victim so it can't harm the spider as it is eaten. All these strands are liquid as they come out of the spider, but solidify as they hit the air.

Recycled webs

Manufacturing so much material from its own body is a drain on a spider. For the sake of efficiency, spiders eat damaged portions of web, recycle the material, and spin more from it. If you slightly damage a web, you will see that, by the following day, not only is it repaired, but any dangling strands you left have been neatly eaten away.

You may be able to feed a spider and watch how it deals

with its victim. Catch an insect that is the spider's size or slightly smaller. Hold it with tweezers and place it very gently on a sticky portion of the web. Let go. At the first movement of the insect, the shaking strands inform the spider that prey has been trapped. It judges the probable identity and size of dinner by the rhythm and violence of the shaking. (A male spider courting a female informs her of his identity to avoid being eaten by "throwing" a strand over her web on which he then drums. She recognizes the special rhythm is that of a male spider and not her dinner.)

Definitely dinner

If the spider decides the shakings are safe food, it rushes upon the insect, and spins bonds to hold it tightly. But it does not then begin to chew up the insect. Fangs pierce the body, and through them is injected a chemical that liquifies the insect's soft insides. The spider then delicately sips its dinner, sucking the insect shell quite empty. You can remove dead, bound corpses from spider webs, open them up, and see there is nothing left but the hard outer skin.

Ratty facts

Rats are animals people can't get along with and would have problems getting along without. If some mysterious force were to suddenly lift the entire rat population from the earth, medical research would come to a screeching halt. These animals, who for thousands of years have shared our homes and meals (a balanced diet for a rat is nearly identical to a balanced diet for a human), stand in for us in research that covers basic nutrition; the causes of insanity, cancer, and birth defects; the effects of radiation, high noise levels, crowded living conditions, and space travel; the improvement of intelligence, curiosity, and memory; and the treatment of diabetes, epilepsy, cancer, and heart disease.

We not only invite rats to dinner to test products that may eventually appear in supermarkets, but have even asked them over for a drink. When scientists make alcohol available to rats, rats behave like social drinkers who enjoy getting together for a cocktail before dinner. The result of the rat's accidental similarity to ourselves is that rats die for us by the thousands.

It is hard to feel thankful to a wild rat. The brown, or Norway, rat from which our docile laboratory and pet rats were bred is ill-tempered, destructive, and germ laden. It will attack if cornered and will kill to eat. Because its two lower incisors (front teeth) continue to grow throughout its life, the rat must gnaw continually, to keep its teeth worn down. Rats bite chunks from wood as easily as you bite into an apple; they can even chew through metal pipes and cables.

Living rent free

A rat's favorite home is a human home. In cities, even the best kept houses may harbor rats from time to time. But open garbage pails are an invitation rats can't refuse. Grain, even bags of bird seed, is the country rat's favorite snack. Colonies live inside walls, beneath floors, in attics, and in basements: They carve an entry from outside, or find natural openings through cracks and drains. Once inside, they chisel passages through the house's structure so that eventually they can move freely through walls, into kitchens, drawers, and cupboards. They chew not only for passage, but for nesting materials too. A single rat in a single night can shred several square feet of carpet.

Inside the walls, rats lead an orderly, peaceful life. They live in a hierarchy: the rat with the highest status eats and drinks before the others, chooses the best nesting place, and occupies the largest territory. Each of the other rats takes its turn and occupies its territory according to its status in the group. When arguments do occur, they are settled by a ritual wrestling match, which ends with the rat of higher status lightly biting the neck of the other. Such ritual ways of handling problems are very common among aggressive animals. Ritual fights protect the participants from serious injury. Normally, parents stay with one another to defend their nest, and their babies nest close by even after they are grown. Family groups thus form "tribes" within the colony as it grows, and the hierarchy within the family may be much less strict. Each member of the colony recognizes every other member; and any member of the colony will attack or even kill a strange rat who attempts to move into their home territory.

Lots of mouths to feed

Rats reproduce quickly and abundantly. Females give birth to their first litter of as many as a dozen pups when they are less than three months old. On the very day they are born, the mother breeds again. In three weeks, the first litter will be weaned, and the next litter born. Within two months, the first litter will be breeding as well. Given sufficient food and space, a single pair of rats could theoretically multiply to a colony of over 50 thousand within one year.

This is one reason we have not been able to get rid of rats even though an individual rat only lives a couple of years. But other reasons are to be found in rat behavior and intelligence. Rats have a built-in nervousness about open spaces and bright light. If they must cross a room, they scurry close to the wall. They can usually avoid even this

This nutritious rat dinner consists of a peanut, a barbecued chicken wing tip, lettuce, peas, and carrots.

29

chance of exposure by chewing access from beneath and behind food storage areas. And most of their activity is at night. A colony of rats may have made itself at home in your house for months before it is even discovered.

So let's say at that point you set a trap in the potato bin where teeth marks in the potatoes clearly show where rats are feeding. Rats memorize every detail of their territory. When they see something new, they are extremely curious. In fact, being allowed to investigate something new is so pleasurable to rats that such rewards provide nearly as strong motivation as food rewards in rat learning experiments. But as curiosity grows, so does caution. Picture the rats stretching their noses toward the trap, sniffing it, backing off, edging toward it again, until one is overcome by interest, puts its nose to the trigger, and is trapped. That is the first — and probably the last — rat you will catch. The rats know about the new object: they know to avoid it.

Avoiding bellyaches

Rat reaction to new foods — or poisons disguised as food — is even more instructive. Rats will not stuff themselves on any-

Raise a rat with a high IQ

In an effort to discover whether the stimulation provided human babies could have an effect on their later intelligence, baby rats have been raised in both boring and interesting environments. Those raised in empty cages with neither companions nor playthings, were less curious and less able to learn in adulthood than rats raised with friends and toys.

If you want smart pet rats, raise two of them together (make sure they are the same sex). Give the babies all sorts of things to play with in their cage: small milk cartons to climb into, twigs to climb on, even a swing. Every day, take them out and let them explore your room, play on your toy trucks, look into your drawers, investigate your sneakers. (You won't have trouble getting them back again. Pet rats don't run away, and they like to explore their owners too.)

The illustrations here show toys you can make to teach a pet rat special skills. The maze is built of pieces of cardboard glued together with white glue inside a small gift box. A rat can learn to go directly from the door to the food room without going into any of the other rooms. The cart is made from the axles and wheels of a toy car taped to a small block of wood. Another block of wood is glued on top with white glue. The cart is connected to a string tied to a dollhouse-sized bucket of food. A rat can learn to push the cart to lower the food so it can eat. Learning toys like these work best, of course, if the rat is not allowed to eat during the night before.

When rats who have had the advantages of toys, learning devices, and freedom to explore grow up, they will be more intelligent than laboratory rats. But they will still not be as smart as wild rats. It seems the brightest rats of all are those raised in an outdoor area where the natural adventures of burrowing in the soil, balancing on branches, hiding behind rocks, and getting along with a whole tribe of fellow rats excite their intelligence more than any man-made inventions.

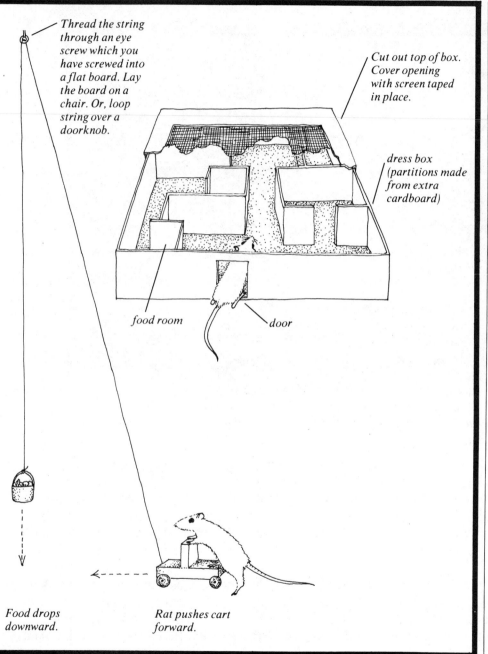

Thread the string through an eye screw which you have screwed into a flat board. Lay the board on a chair. Or, loop string over a doorknob.

Cut out top of box. Cover opening with screen taped in place.

dress box (partitions made from extra cardboard)

food room

door

Food drops downward.

Rat pushes cart forward.

thing they are not familiar with. Instead, one or two of the colony will nibble a tiny bit. Then, over the next few hours or day, their companions watch for signs of distress. If the rats do not become ill, caution is dropped and the food is certified good. But should anything happen to the rats who tried the new food, the colony will refuse to eat it. How rats communicate such information to one another is not understood. But there is no doubt that the rat is man's most intelligent enemy.

Rat math

This is how to figure out how many rats a single pair could in theory produce in a single year. Assume there are 12 babies — six males, six females — in every litter. The original mother rat produces a litter of 12 every three weeks. When the six females from each litter become 12 weeks old, they too become breeding females and produce litters of 12 every three weeks. At first, before many females are of breeding age, the population climbs slowly, but as more and more females begin to breed, the population skyrockets.

Rats will soon chew to bits wooden playthings, such as the ladder here. The piece of log will last much longer, and the swing, made of a can and two lengths of chain, is a permanent toy. The branch from an apple tree is one more new object to investigate.

In the table, the first column shows a year's time in three-week intervals. Figure that all the females are in step with one another, so each interval marks the birth of a new group of babies, there are 17 generations in the year.

The next column shows how many breeding females there are at each interval. For the first three weeks, there are no breeders because they are only counted when they actually give birth (three weeks after they mate). For the next 15 weeks, there is only one breeder, the original mother. During 12 of those 15 weeks, the females in the first litter are growing up. Then another three weeks is required for pregnancy. Then they give birth and are counted as breeders along with the mother.

The third column is the number of females born that day. The number is always six times the number of litters born that day. The next column is the total number of females, and includes breeders, juveniles, and newborns. The last column is the total number of rats in the colony, and so includes the males: six in each litter born plus the original father.

Incredible rat statistics

DATE	BREEDING FEMALES	FEMALES BORN	TOTAL FEMALES	TOTAL RATS
January 1	0	0	1	2

The first litter is conceived. The female in the original pair of rats will be considered a breeder when she gives birth.

DATE	BREEDING FEMALES	FEMALES BORN	TOTAL FEMALES	TOTAL RATS
January 22	1	6	7	14

The first litter is born. From now on, a new generation is born every three weeks. Each litter has six females and six males.

DATE	BREEDING FEMALES	FEMALES BORN	TOTAL FEMALES	TOTAL RATS
February 12	1	6	13	26
March 5	1	6	19	38
March 26	1	6	25	50
April 16	1	6	31	62

The babies born on January 22 are now old enough to conceive.

DATE	BREEDING FEMALES	FEMALES BORN	TOTAL FEMALES	TOTAL RATS
May 7	7	42	73	146

The six females born on January 22 now give birth to their first litters. From now on a new group of females joins the breeders every three weeks.

DATE	BREEDING FEMALES	FEMALES BORN	TOTAL FEMALES	TOTAL RATS
May 28	13	78	151	302
June 18	19	114	265	530
July 9	25	150	415	830
July 30	31	186	601	1202
August 20	73	438	1039	2078
September 10	151	906	1945	3890
October 1	265	1590	3535	7070
October 22	415	2490	6025	12,050
November 12	601	3606	9631	19,262
December 3	1039	6234	15,865	31,730
December 24	1945	11,670	27,535	55,070

In just three more weeks the total number of rats would leap to nearly 100,000. See if you can figure out the exact number.

Good riddance

Here are some sensible ways of dealing with annoying household pests.

spider mite
magnified

Plant pests: For those who don't want to use pesticides, there are other ways to rid your plants of aphids, red spider mites, and scale. Red spider mites, for instance, can't cling well to the plant. Put the pot in the kitchen sink, tip it, and spray its leaves hard with lukewarm water from the sink spray.

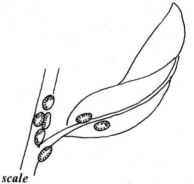

scale
actual size

Scale doesn't look like an insect, and it isn't — at least on the surface. The scale itself is a covering secreted by a nearly invisible insect beneath. Rub the scales to detach them. The pressure of your fingers will crush the insects beneath their scales. If there are lots of scales on stems and leaves, you can use a soft toothbrush dipped in soapy water to rub them off.

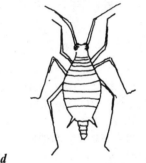

aphid
magnified

For aphids, a visit by lady bugs is a nonpesticide solution. Provided you can find some, each lady bug can eat as many as 34 aphids in a day. Lady bugs are sold by the gallon in some agricultural areas.

Ticks: Ticks breathe through pores in their skin. To remove a tick that has dug into you, put a drop of cooking oil or mineral oil on it. The oil will clog its breathing pores. Within minutes, the tick will decide it has a

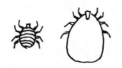

tick
before and after a meal

worse emergency on its hands than a hungry tummy, and will loosen its grip. Then just pick it off.

Oil alone will probably not kill a tick. For quick extermination, drop ticks into a small amount of alcohol. You can use rubbing alcohol or liquor.

Moths: Rabid moth murder by pesticides is a clear case of overkill. The moths that circle your lamps on summer nights do not chew on woolens.

The villains to blame for "moth-eaten" clothing are either the larvae of a tiny moth you may not notice at all or a crew of very common beetles called dermestes. Adults of both insects lay their eggs in organic substances. The moth may prefer wool, but the beetle is less particular. It will lay its eggs in fur coats, leather-bound books, pressed flowers, stuffed moose-heads, and butterfly collections. The greedy larvae that hatch from the moth or beetle eggs are responsible for all those holes.

The best way to protect yourself is mothballs. Within a sealed chest or clothing bag, the fumes from mothballs kill any eggs, larvae, or adult insects that may already be there (the fumes are toxic to humans at that strength, too). When the container is not sealed, the fumes aren't strong enough to kill, but they smell even worse to moths and beetles than to you, and the insects won't enter the area to lay eggs.

Fleas: Fleas live in your floors, carpets, and furniture as well as on your pet. And where there are fleas, there are flea eggs. Using flea soap, spray, or powder on your pet will only kill the fleas that happen to be interested in a meal that day. To kill the others, you have to also spray any area where your pet usually naps. If your home is literally hopping with fleas, a pesticide bomb is better — but you have to leave the house while it works. And that's not all. Sprays won't kill flea eggs. Within three weeks, treat your pet again, and spray the house again to get rid of flea larvae which have hatched.

Cockroaches: Each time a house is sprayed for cockroaches, a few of them will turn out to be resistant to that particular poison. Those few will repopulate your home. The only strategy that has a chance of working is to use a

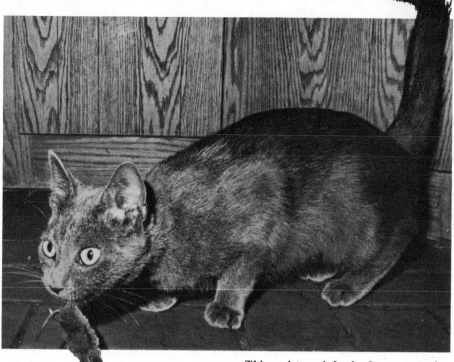

This cat's specialty is shrews, not mice.

variety of different pesticides, at intervals of several months placed along areas where you have seen roaches.

A sequence recommended by exterminators is this: First, keep everything clean — the less food there is around, the less roaches will like your home. The basic insecticide to use is diazenon (few roaches have become immune to it so far). Malathion or a roach tape would be the exterminators' next choice. As with other pesticides, these may be harmful to humans as well as roaches and should be used with caution.

As the roach population dies off, prevent new ones from moving into your apartment by stuffing steel wool into any openings around pipes where they enter through walls — under the kitchen sink, for instance — and under baseboards where they may enter from other apartments. Finally, in any home without pets or babies, sprinkle boric acid crystals (available in drugstores) under sinks and counters as repellent.

Mice: To trap mice, watch where they run, notice where they eat. They may eat in drawers or cabinets. You'll see piles of droppings, and perhaps telltale evidence like a small round hole in the bottom of the dog-food bag. Mice run along walls or below counters where they feel protected. They have a horror of wide open spaces. Set traps in their eating spots, and at the beginning and end of each run (for instance, where a mouse emerges from a wall or cabinet, and where it reenters). You don't have to bait the traps at all. Mice are such creatures of habit, and do everything in such a nervous rush, that they will stumble into the traps by accident.

If you would rather bait a trap, a mouse's favorite foods include peanut butter, raw bacon, and chocolate candy. Cheese will do, too, because it contains the fat mice prefer.

Rats: Forget trying to catch rats in traps. They're usually too smart for that. But you can use a cat. Any old cat will not do — you have to get a ratter. Only a kitten whose mother has brought rats home for dinner will grow up to be a ratter. Kittens raised by nonhunters don't learn to kill their prey, no matter how enjoyable they find the game of pounce-and-bite. What's more, kittens learn which foods are yummy and which are icky by what mama has fed them. Kittens fed on birds consider that their proper food; they may not hanker after rodents. (Humans are much the same. If you've never been fed roasted grubs or snake steaks, chances are you find these delicious foods icky.) So, if you are seeking a cat to rid your home of rodents, make sure the mother brought such live prey home for dinner.

Bee-brained

Many people think of bees as pests because they sting, but nobody should try to get rid of bees because most flowering plants depend on them to fertilize their seeds. What's more, bees are remarkably intelligent.

When a honeybee discovers a patch of nectar-filled flowers, she flies back to her hive to tell other bees where to find it. Within a short time, dozens of other honeybees have followed her instructions and arrived to harvest the nectar. (If you are patient, you can see this for yourself, using as bait a large bowlful of newly opened and freshly picked flowers on the

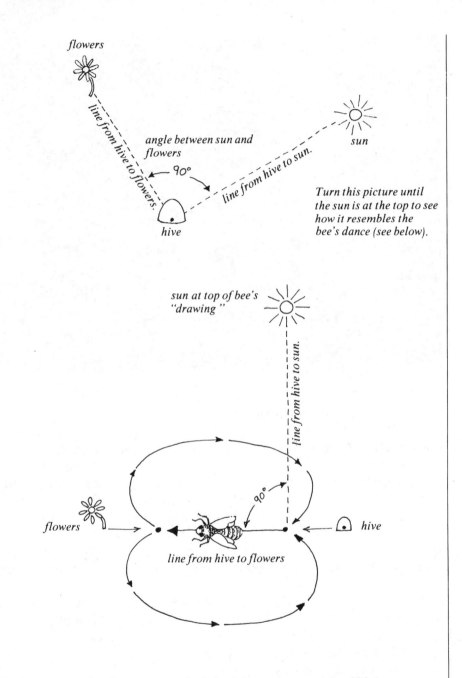

Turn this picture until the sun is at the top to see how it resembles the bee's dance (see below).

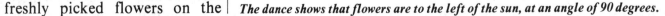

The dance shows that flowers are to the left of the sun, at an angle of 90 degrees.

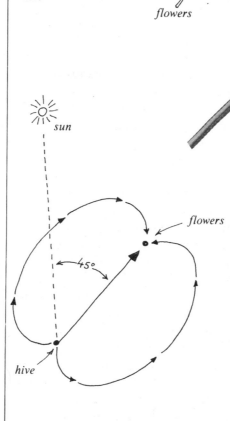

This dance shows flowers are away from the sun. Reversing the direction of the straight run would show they were toward the sun.

Flowers are to the right of the sun at angle of 45 degrees in this dance.

windowsill.) The instructions are coded in a dance that the discoverer performs on the wall of the hive. Other bees gather around to observe and imitate her movements. During the dance, the bee hums to indicate a rich source of nectar, is more quiet if the find is a poor one; she may dance longer for a good find, not so long for a poor one. But two vital pieces of information are given by the shape and speed of the dance itself: the distance the flowers are from the hive and the direction in which to fly.

Honeybee boogie

The dance is in the form of a squashed figure eight: two loops with a straight run between them. If the flowers are close by, the bee dances quickly around the figure eight. As she dances along the straight part, she also wags her abdomen quickly. The farther away the flowers are, the slower she performs the figure eights and the slower she wags her abdomen. The message is very accurate up to a mile from the hive — the farthest bees usually travel.

The code for direction is more complicated. The discoverer notes the position of the flowers, the hive, and the sun as though all three were on the surface of a map. She memorizes the pattern they form as though lines connected the hive to the flowers, and the hive to the sun. The honeybee then is able to reproduce the angle between these two lines in her dance.

Back at the hive, she puts the map on the wall, so to speak, so that it is now vertical, with the sun at the top. Then she performs her dance, with the beginning of the straight run standing for the position of the hive, the end of the straight run standing for the position of the flowers, and the speed of the dance and wags standing for the distance between. The slant of the run stands for the angle between sun and flowers. If sun, hive, and flowers all fall along a straight line, the direction of its straight run shows whether the flowers are toward the sun, or away from it.

If they are not on a straight line, the slant of the straight run indicates the angle to the right, or to the left, of the sun. The honeybee's drawing is accurate to within a few degrees.

Pets

You belong to kitty

Most of the actions and gestures your pet cat uses in its life with you are adapted from actions and gestures a cat would need and use if it lived in the wild.

In the wild, each cat patrols a territory in which it lives and hunts. A solitary animal, it prefers not to meet other cats whose territories might overlap. To warn others of its whereabouts, it marks its area by its own scent: in the case of the male, by spraying landmarks with urine. But both sexes also mark their area by rubbing oil from certain glands against landmarks. The oil glands are behind their ears, along their lips, and to each side of the base of their tail. When your cat rubs against you, it is marking you with its personal scent. You could call this affection, but it is more like slapping a label on you. The label reads: this object belongs to kitty. Any other cat coming along and reading the marker would know to which individual it belongs, what sex that individual is, and how long ago it passed that way. Pet cats mark their humans, their furniture, and even their cans of cat food. The most ecstatic rubbing carefully utilizes all three oil gland areas, beginning with the lips, then behind the ear, and finishing up with the tail.

Purposeful play

Kitten play is hunting practice. Whether your kitten is playing pounce-and-bite with a ball of paper on a string or with a grasshopper in the wild is all the same to it. Each maneuver in the game is designed to practice part of a sequence of movements that, as the kitten grows, should end up putting a square meal in its belly. Crumpled paper on a string is a favorite toy simply because it most closely imitates the movement and sound of a mouse or bird in grass or dry leaves.

First, it rustles. Then it moves — suddenly, jerkily. Although a cat can hear all the sounds and see all the sights around it, it is geared to stiffen with attention if the sound is rustling, if a movement is jerky. Both are signs of prey. What follows is nearly automatic. The kitten crouches. Then it creeps. If the paper is only twitching slightly, it may stop and shift its weight from side to side, preparing to pounce. Or it may make a dash for it, pouncing forelegs first with claws unsheathed to pin its prey to the ground.

What happens next depends on the seriousness of the game. And the seriousness of the game depends on whether the "prey" is edible and the cat is hungry. A kitten may practice biting the paper ball, or it may pretend the ball is attacking it and roll on its side to fight it off by kicking at it. Or it may just bat the ball around and continue chasing it. But let's say the game is for real: the prey is a mouse and the cat is really hungry. Then, that first pounce is followed by a killing bite — and the game is quickly over.

No fun for mice

For most of our pet house cats, hunting never goes beyond playfulness. Even if it does catch a mouse, it toys with it, batting it about, picking it up in its mouth or chewing on it, then letting it go to chase, bat, and maul it some more. Ultimately the mouse expires, but more or less by accident. Such apparent cruelty is actually a short circuit in the cat's behavior. Only the stimulus of hunger triggers the cat to inflict a killing bite that severs the spinal cord between two vertebrae in its prey's neck. If it isn't hungry, the bite is just any old bite, and the cat soon lets go again.

Give it a try

Knowing all this helps you play better with your kitten. To see how a cat is programmed to react to twitchy movements, wiggle your toes under the bedclothes when your cat is sharing your bed. To see how rustling noises are endlessly inviting, open out a grocery bag and watch your cat's antics as it tries to catch its own noises inside the bag.

Wildly yanking a paper ball on a string will not entice your pet nearly so much as twitching

A cat marks its dinner as well as its people.

Cat close-up

Cat whiskers are sense organs. Since they stick out to both sides and in front of the cat's face, they extend its sense of touch to as much as several inches beyond its body. They may help the cat judge the width of tight spaces before it attempts to squeeze through, or even tell it which way the wind is blowing. More important, though, whiskers cause a blinking reflex. When a twig or other hazard brushes a cat's whiskers, it blinks its eyes, thus protecting them from damage. You can try this yourself using a pencil or fingertip to lightly brush against your pet's whiskers.

Cats use their claws mainly for grabbing and holding prey rather than for inflicting injury. Were cat's claws exposed as dog claws are, they would wear down to a short, dull end that would be neither sharp nor curved enough to hook into prey. So the cat has a skin sheath on each toe into which the claw is retracted when the cat's toes are bent. So long as the cat is relaxed or walking about, its toes stay bent and the claws stay hidden. But when the toes are straightened, as when a cat reaches to swipe at prey, strong cords called ligaments, which are attached to each claw, pull the claws downward out of their sheaths. You can watch how the claws emerge from their sheaths by pressing gently along the tops of your cat's toes to straighten them.

In a dark room, shine a flashlight into your cat's eyes. The glowing red, green, or yellow is light bouncing back at you from a layer of cells at the back of the cat's eye that works much like a bicycle reflector.

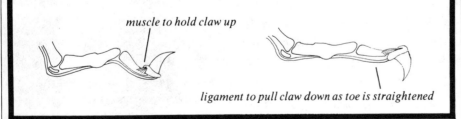

muscle to hold claw up

ligament to pull claw down as toe is straightened

it slightly. And a quiet toy will not entice as strongly as a rustling one. Twitching, then letting a paper ball stay still, then twitching again, will let you see clearly each of the different steps a cat uses in hunting. You can also simulate a bird instead of a mouse with the same paper ball and string. Lift it off the ground for short flights to see your kitten leap and swipe in the air. A ping-pong ball is best for watching the acrobatics a kitten practices for hunting erratically dodging prey. Each swipe of a paw as the ping-pong ball skitters and ricochets stops its motion and sends it in the opposite direction — a maneuver that would quickly tire a mouse.

Plump toys don't lead to cuddling

Plump, soft toys like a thick cotton sock (or your hand) are apt to trigger fighting behavior in your kitten. As it pounces on the sock, it feels it rubbing against its belly — not a place a cat would want a rat to be. Instantly, front claws hug the sock close, rear claws scratch furiously at it, and teeth sink into what would be a live prey's vulnerable throat.

Even when you can't see the cat, you can see its reflecting eyes.

Poodles as wolves

If a dog were to be raised in the wild, it would behave very much like a wolf. Scientists are quite sure the first dogs were wolves; even today wolves domesticate easily, if raised by humans from very early puppyhood. In fact, some scientists claim dogs and wolves are not separate species at all. This seems an amusing notion when you look at a toy poodle next to a 180-pound wolf. However, if you've heard the frequent stories of family pets who join into packs that prey on deer and livestock in winter, and even occasionally attack humans, the smile fades. The way your plump puppy behaves, from its nuzzling nose to its wagging tail, comes about because of the way wolves live in the wild.

A social animal

Unlike cats, who prefer to avoid one another, wolves (and dogs) are extremely social. They have to be. The prey they hunt is as least as large as, and often much larger than, themselves. The hunt is highly organized. The pack leader is always up front, but the rest of the dogs move here and there to carry out maneuvers from straightforward running down of the prey to traps and ambushes. Each day's hunting party does not include all the members of the pack. Pregnant and nursing females, older wolves, or ones who don't feel well that day stay home. The hunters will feed them by regurgitating (vomiting) food when they come home, even if the day's catch was not really enough to go around. Self sacrificing behavior is an everyday matter among wolves. They will subject themselves to danger to protect a weaker or injured member of their pack. On the other hand, they will fight, sometimes to the death, an intruder who is not from their home pack.

Bowing is a dog's way of asking to play ball.

Each individual wolf's greatest devotion and affection is given to the leader, who is already recognized and obeyed by a pup from the time it is only six months old.

You have only to imagine the way hunting people lived long ago to see how easily the first dogs fit into our lives. We, too, hunted in packs, obeyed a respected leader, cooperated in chases and ambushes, lived in related groups or tribes, protected and fed one another, and resisted invasions of our territory. Now take it one step further to the toy poodle living in the suburbs. By the age of six months, it has likely chosen its pack leader or master. This person is not necessarily the family member who has fed it, but is more likely the one who has disciplined (or trained) it. Its happiest moments are when its whole pack-family prepares for an outing — even if that is merely a walk. During the outing, it does its job by making short forays into the bushes or onto the neighbors' lawns, snuffling excitedly along the ground, digging into any hole, barking at a squirrel in a tree, making frantic dashes after the neighbor's cat. It is neither as disciplined nor as effective as a mature wolf or a trained hunting dog, but the poodle is using all its inherited hunting behaviors.

Ready to hunt

An impressive wolf ritual, which is used to psych the pack up for the hunt and to coordinate their movements, can be recognized in the way most dogs behave when it is time to take them out for a walk. As you

Shake the bunny

Wolves and dogs kill small prey, like rabbits, by fiercely shaking them until their necks break. That behavior is behind the common puppy game of tug-of-war. Knot a hand towel to make a nice, limp "rabbit". When your puppy grabs hold, let it do the shaking while you hold on tight and move the toy back and forth a little to keep the game interesting. When your pup lets go momentarily toss the toy a few feet away to encourage it to learn the game of fetch. Don't chase to get the toy back. Just sit where you are until your pet tires of shaking and chewing its bunny, and brings it back of its own accord to renew the game.

Shake the bunny toy

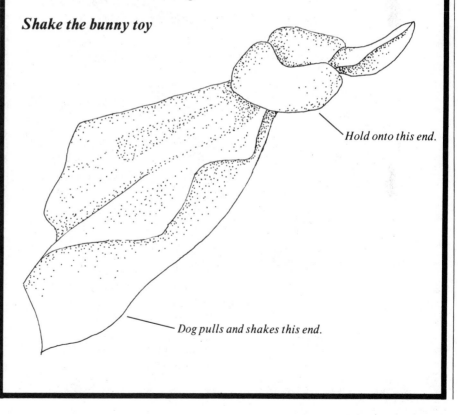

Hold onto this end.

Dog pulls and shakes this end.

Dog talk

Dogs use their tails, ears, lips, hair, and overall posture to tell other dogs their state of mind. You can use a portion of their gestural code to figure out the likelihood that you will be bitten by a dog that is threatening you.

A respectful threat

Lips are not drawn far back, ears are up, and tail is held high. The dog is threatening to bite — and is not at all afraid of you. If you approach closer, you will probably be bitten.

A nervous threat

Lips are drawn back farther and ears are held lower. The tail would be lower too. This dog is threatening to bite, but it is also afraid of you. You are in less danger from this dog than the first one.

A desperate threat

With lips drawn back and downward, ears flat to head, and tail low, this dog is very angry and frightened (it might be cornered or tied up so it can't run away, or defending puppies or family). This dog is sure to bite if you take another step toward it.

make your way to the closet where the leash is kept, the dog bows, bounces back up, bows again. If you were to lean down at this point, it would also nuzzle your face or lick you. As you put on your coat, the dog begins to dash in small circles, coming back each time to repeat the bow and nuzzle. If you are unresponsive or overly slow, it may bark (high-pitched, like a puppy, not a low, warning bark) and perhaps paw at you or at the door. If all of this were to happen outdoors, and if you were to be replaced by a pack of wolves, the bowing, pawing, nuzzling, and yipping would become more and more excited and the circular dashes would become larger and larger until, as though at a signal, the whole pack would take off simultaneously on that day's hunt — just as you, finally, step out the door.

Adapting to adulthood

Most animals adapt their infant behaviors to express themselves as adults. For instance, the nuzzling and licking that your puppy treats you to when you get home from school is the way a puppy gets its mother (or other adult) to regurgitate food after it is weaned, but before it is old enough to hunt.

Bowing is a puppy's invitation to play. Later, both bowing and nuzzling are used to greet returning members of the pack or family.

Another bit of puppy language is the belly-up position. Newborn pups urinate and defecate only when their mother stimulates them by licking their bellies and beneath their tails. They are usually turned belly up by the mother's muzzle and tongue in the process. As they get older, they turn belly up and let out a few drops of urine whenever they feel threatened by the roughness of another animal. Adults respond to the signal as though it clearly said, "Don't hurt me; I am only a puppy." Pet dogs use the gesture two ways: when they are punished, to tell you that you are clearly their master and to acknowledge that they did something wrong; and to get you to stop scolding or hurting them. They also use it to say, as they would to one another in the wild, "I'm a cute puppy; pet me."

Going to the dogs

Once you see how dogs have adapted their wild behaviors to fit in with human life, you can also see how humans have learned dog ways. Listen to a person calling her dog: if she is inviting the dog to play, a higher voice, like a puppy's will be used. When disciplining, a deeper voice, like the low, warning bark or growl of an older wolf, will be used. To get her dog to follow, the master may make a short dash in the right direction or "bow" by placing or clapping hands to knees. A bouncing motion or short dash may be used to indicate direction. If the master wants to cuddle, she may descend to the floor and roll sideways to invite it. If the dog lies down too, the master may roll the dog over to pet its belly, just as mama used to. When greeting the dog, she will respond to its upraised muzzle by nuzzling its face with a hand, or by letting the dog jump up, and lowering her face to its muzzle for a lick or two. Wolves weren't the only ones who learned to adapt their natural behaviors to a different species.

Nell's babies

Puppies begin their social learning at birth. These observations were made on our dog, Nell, and her second litter of puppies. The observations begin the night she went into labor. Keeping this kind of journal helps you notice how animals behave.

First day

Nell refuses dinner, goes outside briefly, then upstairs to the whelping box that was prepared for her three days before. She climbs into the box, lies down, and, for the next seven hours, pants peacefully as labor progresses. The first pup is born at 5:00 A.M. Nell nips at the fluid filled sac which still surrounds the pup. She pulls the sac off, then licks the puppy's face. The puppy breathes. Nell ignores the puppy for the next few minutes, while the pup lies unmoving where it was born, apparently stuperous (very deeply asleep). Then, without any signal we can detect, Nell turns her face to the puppy again and licks it vigorously, working from the face back. She rolls the pup belly up and bites through the umbilical cord. She eats the placenta, then turns her attention to the cord again, shredding it by pulling it between her front teeth until only an inch remains. As she continues to lick the puppy in face-to-tail strokes, the pup responds by moving toward her face. The reciprocal actions guide the pup forward to her belly. There, it noses upward against the grain of the fur until it finds a nipple. The moment it grabs the nipple, its forepaws straighten, it begins pushing and relaxing its forepaws against the mammary gland (an action that stimulates the milk pores to open). Smell and touch alone must guide the pup because its eyes and ears are sealed shut.

About 10 minutes after the first puppy is born, labor begins again. Nell hunches herself around in a circular fashion, but without standing up. The first pup is able to continue nursing as the second is born. This time, when Nell guides the puppy forward, it overshoots the mark and ends up between her paws. She growls and snaps at it, sending it sprawling and crying. But then Nell licks it again, guiding it now in the opposite direction, around the outside of her front legs, back to her belly where the second pup, too, finds a nipple. Discipline has started early.

The next six pups are born at intervals of 10 to 45 minutes over a total of more than five hours. During that time, the puppies intermittently nurse and fall asleep. If they are nursing, the arrival of the next pup never disturbs their activity. The pups sleep in a heap together. If one is separated, it cries, and Nell guides it back to the group by licking again. Occasionally, the licking is especially thorough. The pup is held between her two front paws, sometimes even under one of them. Her nuzzling turns it over on its back, and we can see that, as the pup's belly and anal area is licked, it urinates and defecates. Nell does not leave the puppies for the next 12 hours, or nearly 20 hours since she last went outside.

Third day

The puppies are now three days old. We changed the old bed pads in the box, which had gotten wet during birth, but have not yet changed the green blanket that was also in the box. We take the blanket to wash it. The puppies cry in distress, become very active, and pull themselves along on their bellies, snuffling loudly. From this time on, we give them two green blankets and only remove one at a time for washing. They seem to recognize the smell and feel of "home," and act distressed when it is changed.

End of first week

During the first week, we occasionally rearrange the pups as they suckle to see what will happen. They do not go for the nearest nipple, but seem to rearrange themselves according to a pattern. The plump belly nipples are preferred, and the largest pups appear to have staked these out as their own. If a strong pup empties the milk on one nipple, it may purposefully push a weaker pup off another nipple.

End of first month

At about a month, the puppies' ears and eyes open. They now totter along with their bellies off the ground, and begin to play. We can make out bowing, pawing, nuzzling, nipping, tail wagging, and even mounting (mating) behavior. Besides crying, the pups now growl and bark. They do not bark when Nell does, however. Just the opposite: they become still and silent when she barks. They do not mind being handled in the box, but lose all playfulness and may cry if they are taken out. They show little enthusiasm for humans.

End of fifth week

By five weeks, the pups climb out of their whelping box. They begin to explore, but not more than 15 or 20 feet from the box. The green blanket is now folded into one corner of the box, and the puppies go to it to sleep. They urinate and defecate without the stimulus of licking.

Nell nurses the pups less frequently and for shorter periods. We have started feeding them solid foods. Nuzzling and licking begin to lead to play. Nell paws a puppy as she licks, and now allows it to approach her head in order to nip at her lips and neck. She plays lying on her side or, sometimes, belly up and, at these times, she allows nursing as well. Now it is the pup who approaches her to nip from behind who is snapped at. By six weeks, Nell nurses standing up — not a comfy position for the pups — and shortly walks away. But she continues to allow nursing during play.

The pups are now put out-

Nell and her puppy, Jud. Though Jud is a year old, he still turns belly up to his mother.

doors on the grass when they awaken, and every 20 minutes between naps. Several puppies begin to go to the door just before they urinate. If we are fast enough, they urinate outdoors.

Outside, Nell is more watchful of her puppies than inside. She escorts them — and they follow her — within an area less than 30 yards from the back door. She does not take them all the way around the house, or on her various paths to woods and pond. When a puppy strays beyond the area she has demonstrated, she guides it back by nuzzling.

Nell does not interfere with her puppies' meal. But as soon as the puppies leave, she takes it over. If a puppy comes back for more, she growls and snaps at it. The same is true if a puppy approaches her own dish, even if the dish is empty.

Nell invites her puppies to play more often than they invite her. She bows, paws, and flops on her side. The puppies do the same with one another, but they also tear after one another without preliminary formalities, biting and growling ferociously. This they never do with Nell. The cat also plays with the puppies. Her invitation is different. She lies on her side and extends one paw upward. The pups pile on her; she wrestles in the fighting manner of cats, or runs off to stalk, chase, and pounce. One day, we notice a pup inviting the cat to play. It does not bow, but turns on its side and raises a paw.

Ten weeks old

By the time the puppies are ready to go to other homes, at 10 weeks, their allegiance is obviously to the human race. Since six weeks, they have become less and less interested in their mother, more and more interested in people. They no longer cry to get out of their pen when Nell comes by, but set up a storm when they hear our footsteps. Tired from play, they heap themselves on our feet to sleep, although Nell is only a few feet away. Hungry, they no longer go to Nell, but bounce back and forth between us and the food cupboard.

Outside, one day, nine weeks after the puppies' birth, I go with them for a walk around the meadow. For the first time, they go beyond the bounds Nell taught them, and follow after me. Nell goes down to the pond. They watch for a moment, but turn away. It is already humans they will follow through their lives.

Changing ways

Wolves, successful as their social, organized, hunting life has been for many thousands of years, are now nearly extinct in most of the areas they once inhabited; coyotes, a near relative, are doing quite well; dogs are doing better than either.

No matter what adjustments a species makes to the food, living space, and competition from other animals in the area in which it lives, it can never arrive at a final "best" way to survive. Wolves had beaten the competition from other meat-eating animals by becoming larger and developing a cooperative life style so that they could attack, kill, and share the largest prey. Now these clever strategies are spelling disaster to the species. The spread of human civilization into once wild wolf territories has shrunk the large spaces a wolf pack must occupy to find sufficient food. Man has also killed off many of the large animals wolves are adapted to killing. And should they kill the new food animals that farmers and ranchers provide — sheep and cattle — they only earn themselves death by trap, gun, or poison. Though wolves in a pinch eat frogs — even insects and berries — they are physically too big to survive on such small game.

Coyote survival

Coyotes have taken a different strategy. They have taken advantage of their small size to hunt mostly small prey such as prairie dogs, rabbits, and rodents. Occasionally, they cooperate in very small groups to attack lambs, but even such medium-sized animals are not their basic diet. The alertness needed to capture small, quick, usually shy prey has made the coyote equally quick, shy — and amazingly elusive. Even with bounties offered for each dead coyote, ranchers have found coyotes elude traps and guns quite easily. Coyote numbers are "controlled" (not increasing), but they are not becoming extinct.

Domesticated dogs

The dog's strategy — to become useful and likeable to humans — has over the long run proved the most successful of all. Humans feed dogs, breed them, care for them, use them for sports, keep them as pets. There are certainly many more dogs in the world than wolf and coyote

Trick training

As you probably know, it's easy to train a dog to shake hands because pawing to invite attention is a natural behavior anyway. All you have to do to make it a trick is say, "Shake hands," when the dog is doing it anyway, and then, praise it for its intelligence. Before long, the command, shake hands, will be connected with pawing, and your dog will have learned a trick.

Try the same technique with other doggy behaviors that seem appealing. If your dog circles excitedly before going outside, use a command like "Turn around"; or if it bows, tell it to "Bow"; and if it stands to look out a window when it hears the family car, ask "Where's Daddy?" (or whatever is usually appropriate) to make it look out the window at your command.

relatives combined.

To succeed so well dogs must have changed considerably since man first associated with them tens of thousands of years ago. A domesticated wolf can be used in hunting, but it so hostile toward strangers that it must be kept penned. The tamest adult wolf will leave its human home to mate and hunt with other wolves if it is allowed that freedom. The physical changes that have occurred are easy to see: few dog breeds resemble wolves. Changes in behavior can only be guessed, but they are just as real.

Over millions of years our

planet has changed continually. In order to survive everything on it has had to change too. Such change is called evolution. Evolution happens when individual animals with particular bodies and behaviors die off because they are not suited to the demands of their lives; and other individuals with slightly different bodies and behaviors succeed in living and reproducing young who are like themselves. Humans did the selecting with dogs. We chose the more friendly reliable individuals to breed with one another. We bred for curly coats or whiskery faces, or

whatever struck our fancy. But usually accident, not purpose, is the driving force of evolution.

White moth changeover

This is an unusual but true story of an evolutionary process happening almost right before our eyes. Because the change is simple it is making a species different very quickly. Early in this century there was a species of white moth that, when resting, settled itself flat on the white bark of a birch tree. This matching of wing color to resting behavior was sensible: birds could not see the moths to eat them. Every once in a while, through an accidental change in chemical instructions, an individual moth would produce the dark pigment called melanin (it is the same pigment that colors all shades of human skin). Such dark-winged moths did not survive. No longer disguised against the white tree, birds spotted them easily and gobbled them up.

In cities however, the color of birch bark began to change as

Roosters, with their plumes and colors, are too showy to stay near the nest while the eggs are being cared for. The plain hens get that job.

more and more factories sent black soot into the air. The soot accumulated on the bark, staining it quite dark. When a moth with melanin-colored wings appeared in this city environment, its darkness kept it safe. The white moths, which showed up easily against the dark trunks, were gobbled up instead. Melanin-producing moths survived and reproduced. The result is that today these once-white moths have changed; now they are all dark.

Physical changes

In the case of the white moths changing to dark ones, a physical characteristic — color — evolved. Behavior can evolve too. The ancestors of these moths, tens or even hundreds of thousands of years ago, may not have had a preference for birch trees. Those that rested on non-matching bark, however, would have been eaten more frequently than those that rested on matching bark. Just as chemical information guides the manufacture of a pigment, chemical information guides moths to their resting place. Both bits of information are inherited. Both evolve.

The question of which change came first as a creature evolved is often like asking whether the chicken or egg came first. Did the elephant happen to have a droopy nose, which then became an advantage to an individual elephant who used it to nudge leaves toward its mouth? Or did the elephant happen to nudge food toward its mouth, which then became an advantage to an individual elephant who had a droopy nose?

The answer is, some of both. Scientists look at physical characteristics in order to understand how behavior evolved, and at behavior in order to understand how physical characteristics evolved.

Fancy males

Birds are a good example. Male and female peafowl look very different from one another. Males are gorgeously colored, fancifully feathered. Female plumage is mottled brown; the hen has no crest or fanning tail. With sparrows, however, you can't tell the sexes apart by looking at their plumage. Feathers of both male and female are a streaky brown. The differences in behavior that have evolved hand in hand with these differences in plumage are easy to see during breeding season. After the peacock has courted a peahen with his brilliant displays and mated with her, his job is done.

Minding the kids

The peahen takes on all the work of parenting. But both sparrow parents work to build the nest, guard it, and later feed the babies. The mottled brown peahen, sitting on her nest on the mottled forest floor, is well camouflaged. So are the brown streaked sparrows against their twiggy backgrounds. During the time the eggs are incubated (kept warm) little more than camouflage can protect them from egg-eating snakes, other birds and mammals. Were the brilliant peacock to participate in parenting, his bright color would spell doom to his offspring. The way birds are colored controls the way they must behave, and the way they behave sets limits or gives freedom to the way they may be colored. The behavior of newly-hatched peafowl and sparrows has to be in step with the evolution of their species.

Sparrow babies are hatched with their eyes sealed, their bodies naked, too weak to even stand. Sparrows remain helpless, requiring warmth and constant feeding, until their feathers are grown enough for them to fly, about three weeks after hatching. With two parents taking turns hunting for food and guarding the nest, they can afford these weeks of helplessness. Peafowl babies, with only one parent, could not survive that way. They hatch covered with warm down like chickens, eyes open, able to stand, run, and peck for insects on the forest floor. Sparrows and peafowl have evolved along quite different paths, but each has developed a workable way to keep their species going. With sparrows, the most devoted, best camouflaged parents raise the most number of broods successfully over their lifetimes. Parenting skill and humble disguise is the sparrow strategy for survival. With peafowl, the largest and most brilliant male attracts a whole group of females, and fathers the greatest number of broods. Physical prowess and personal beauty is the peacock strategy for survival. Neither method is necessarily better than the other. The ways in which all creatures have woven together their colors, shapes, skills and habits into workable solutions for getting on in the world are literally uncountable. Anything you notice about an animal's shape, strength, looks, or habits will give you clues to its species' evolutionary strategy.

People

The human animal

Humans are among the most recently evolved, and perhaps most rapidly evolving animals on earth. Right now, our kind is in the process of evolving fewer teeth. Many individuals never get their four wisdom teeth at all. They lack the tooth buds from which they could grow. In those who do grow wisdom teeth, they don't break through the gum until adulthood. We are also losing our little toes, and possibly what is left of our smallish amount of hair. In the three million years that have passed since our large jawed manlike ancestor (complete with all four wisdom teeth) began to walk the earth on his two hind legs, our face muscles have become more complicated, our hands defter, our tongues more mobile, our mouths of different shape, our brains larger, and our childhoods longer. For at least the last 40 thousand years of this drastic and rapid evolution (and probably a great deal longer) we have been able to use our facial muscles to express our feelings, our hands to fashion tools and clothing, our tongues and mouths to speak, our brains to think ideas, our childhoods to learn all these things anew in every generation.

The luxury of childhood

Of all these wonderful changes, perhaps a long childhood is man's greatest invention. A cockroach has no childhood at all. True, a cockroach is hatched small and must grow large, but all the information it will ever need is within it from its beginning. No parenting is required. A kitten has a scant few months of childhood. Within half a year, usually sooner, it must learn all it needs to know in order to survive on its own. There is time to learn finishing touches, but most of the information a cat needs is already

Most children practice being parents from early childhood.

there as inherited chemical instructions when it is born.

With at least 12 years in which to learn human behavior, with a gigantic brain in which to store vast amounts of information, including language, writing, music, mathematics — all used to communicate information — and with the technology to spread ideas around the world at the speed of light, humans have less need of inherited knowledge than any other animal. Although in fact we inherit more instructions than any other creature — including such remainders from ancient history as appendixes, a fear of falling, and perhaps even a dislike for snakes — we've been freed from the slowness of ordinary evolution. Our inheritance still dictates the smaller number of muscle cells a girl may have but that does not stop girls from becoming welders and astronauts. Our inheritance still dictates a boy's slower development of speech, but that does not stop him from becoming a nurse or kindergarten teacher. We are the first animal that has ever been able to wish a future, and plan how it can come to be. We are free to change more rapidly than any evolution the world has known.

Totems

Hunting peoples often feel the tribe they belong to is descended from a special animal that protects and understands them. It is called a "totem." Modern humans, both children and adults, often choose a totem animal, too, to keep them safe, and get them through such trying times as exams or trips to the dentist. This collection began with two stuffed frogs when the owner was two years old. They "protected" him in his early years. Now both the collection and the owner have grown but he still has a special feeling for frogs and toads. Somewhere in this grouping is a real live toad. Can you find it?

When a baby is born, what do you say?

The first question humans ask about a newborn baby is: "Is it a girl or a boy?" If humans treated or even thought about both sexes in exactly the same way, there would be no reason to ask the question; the answer would make no difference in how we behaved. But in fact, careful study has shown that from the moment of birth, humans treat female infants differently from males. We speak more often and for longer periods to girl babies; and newborn girls encourage us to talk to them more often and for longer than newborn boys by gazing at our faces, looking into our eyes. This unlearned behavior of newborn human females, and unconscious behavior of adult humans toward female babies, should make us curious about what has been handed down to us in our evolution.

Human males, no matter whether they are large or small in build, do have many more muscle cells than human females. These extra muscle cells, which give males their greater strength, are not earned in sports or feats of endurance, but are part of inherited instructions for how to make a human male. Physical differences between the sexes is part of our evolution, too.

A reason for everything

There is no reason to suppose such differences in behavior and in strength are accidental nonsense. They must, at least originally, have given humans a workable strategy for survival. We don't have to look to the dawn of history to see what that strategy was. In all the simpler human societies we know, males use their strength to hunt and, when necessary, to defend their family and village. These jobs may keep them from their homes for many hours, or days, at a time. The female job includes gathering vegetable foods closer to home and caring for the children. In more complex societies it may be considered a bad joke to say that women spend all day chatting with one another, but their ease with speech was at one time very essential as it still is in simpler societies: they, who show such early interest in speech, are needed to spend a great deal of time speaking with children and teaching them all they need to know.

Waves and shakes

The first gesture we teach our babies is to wave bye-bye. Later, children learn to wave as a greeting, to shake hands, to salute, and to signify surrender by hands up. You could call all these gestures "open-handedness"; you would find similar open-handed gestures in every group of humans all over the world, both now and as long ago as we have records. They are used to greet, to part, to bless, and to surrender. How come? To show we mean no harm. When we extend an open hand to another human, we are clearly showing that we carry no weapons. Culture has passed on these traditional gestures from the dawn of human history all the way to the newest baby in your family.

Such a strategy in a hunting creature, who also has an unusually lengthy childhood and an enormous amount of information to learn during it, has been a workable way of life for at least the 40 thousand years since Neanderthal men made weapons used to hunt and Neanderthal women worked near the home cave.

As a baby girl's gaze and a baby boy's muscle cells have been determined by an evolution in which males and females take different roles, so probably has been the urge to ask that human question: Is it a boy or a girl?

Fool the baby

The way animals behave depends on all sorts of inherited actions and learned traditions. It also depends on how they think. Human babies don't think the same way older children think, and so, they can't behave the same way either. By playing games with infants (one in your own family or a friend's baby brother or sister), you can notice strange behavior that can only be understood by supposing strange ways of thinking. Babies are born theoreticians. They know the way the world works. They have theories about what the rules are. The only trouble is that they are wrong.

The first theory babies have about objects is that when they disappear from view, they no longer exist. When a baby is about two months old, lie him on his back in an armchair. Get his attention with a pretty toy. When he's looking at it, slowly move it over his head until it disappears from his view behind the chair. He may stare at the spot where it disappeared for a moment, but then he will lose interest. He won't look around to find it again because he assumes it no longer exists, Fig. a.

Three months later, when the baby is five months old, he is beginning to discard his first theory. Put him in the same armchair, but prop him to a sitting position. Hold a toy just in front of his face, open your hand, and let it drop. He will look for it now in his lap or on the chair in front of him. He has learned that by following the direction of movement with his eyes, he can re-find an object that has disappeared, Fig. b.

But now try this: drop the toy again and catch it with your other hand, covering it so the baby doesn't see it. After glancing down, he will probably look up again at the hand that originally held the toy, hoping it will reappear there. He is not that sure of his new theory yet, Fig. c.

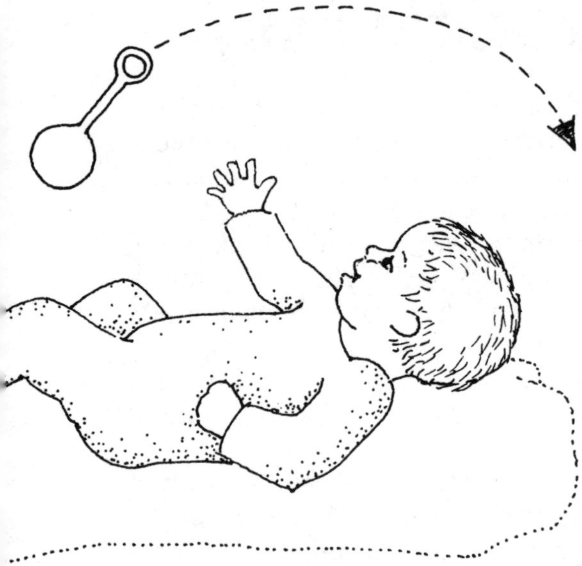

Fig. a

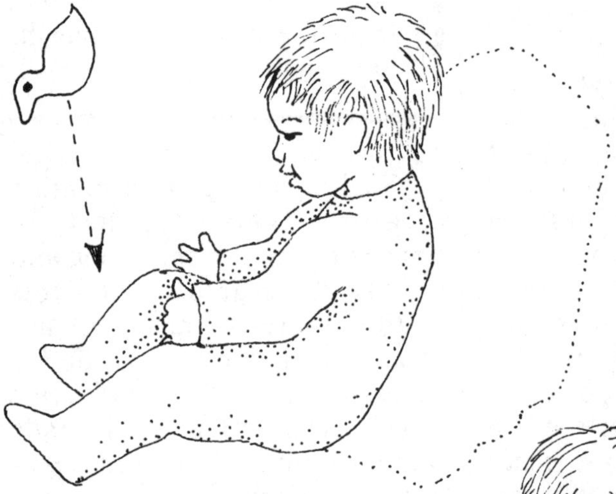

Fig. b

Fig. c

Fig. d

Still, he has not completely understood the rules about objects. Play the toy-under-hand game using a napkin or handkerchief instead of your hand. Repeat it until the baby lifts it to find the toy every time. Now, slowly put the toy under the napkin, and before he can lift it, slowly move it out from under the napkin and slide it under a

By the time a baby is seven months old, he plays more and perhaps crawls and sits. Now he can learn faster and develop more accurate theories. Over the next few months, play this game: entice him with a small toy and, just as he reaches for it, cover it with your hand. At first, he will withdraw his hand, since the toy no longer exists for him. By the time he is nine months old, though, experience will have begun to change his ideas. Now, if a part of the toy still shows, he will believe the rest of it is there too and will lift your hand to find it. It won't be long before he leaps to his next theory: that there is such a thing as "toy under hand," even when it is not visible.

Fig. e

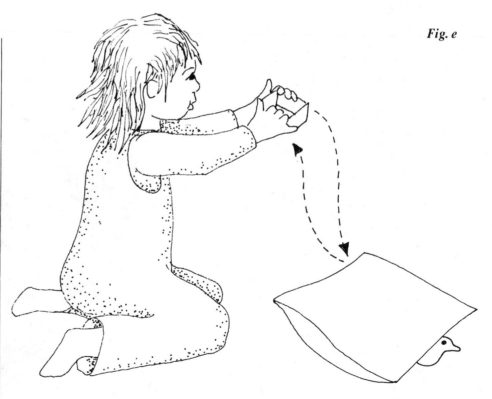

small pillow. Be sure he is watching what you are doing. Where will he look for the toy now? Under the napkin, of course. His theory about the position of a hidden object covers only the first position. He hasn't discovered the rule that objects can change position more than once, and that they will then be found in the last position to which they were moved, Fig. d.

Even by a year and a half, you can still fool the baby with simple now-you-see-it, now-you-don't games. When the baby can find a toy that has been hidden first in one place, then another, try this new game: put a small toy into a small open box. Let him put the toy in and take it out many times, until he understands that part of the game. Then put the toy in its box and the box under a pillow. Before he lifts the pillow, dump the toy from the box, pull out the empty box, and show it to him. He will look and look for that toy inside the box. It will not occur to him to lift the pillow. His theories have advanced, but he has not yet constructed ideas to cover situations he cannot see with his eyes. Logic tells him only this: the toy was in the box the last time he saw it, so it must be there still, Fig. e.

There are ways to see how a slightly older child is thinking. It's not the way you think at all. Take a ball of clay (plasticine or water clay — it doesn't matter which) and offer to play with a child who is of nursery school age (about three years old). Pretend the clay is cookie dough or ice cream. Help the child divide

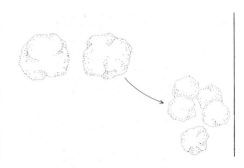

Although both girls have exactly the same amount of food, the food on the right is arranged to make it look like a much greater amount than the food on the left. You can tell by their expressions these girls think this is the case.

the clay into two balls so each of you have the same amount. Check with him to make sure he agrees that each of you have the same amount of ice cream. Now divide your ball of clay into a lot of smaller balls. Ask if you both still have the same amount. Children that young usually think you have more now because you have more pieces.

Now make sausage shapes out of the two amounts of clay. Again, make sure he agrees that both of you have the same amount of cookie dough. Roll yours so it is longer. Who has more cookie dough now? The

child will think you do because your roll is longer.

This may seem remarkably stupid to you, but you yourself once thought this way. Humans have theories about things from the time they are born. A preschool child's theory about amounts of stuff is that stuff is more if it is more pieces, and stuff is more if it is bigger in one dimension, such as length. They haven't had enough experience in their play yet to have devised the theory that amount can't change just by cutting it up or changing its shape. And they can't think of two dimensions at once yet; when they compare two objects, they pay attention to the most obvious difference — length, in the case of a sausage shape. They disregard the fact that while the length is greater, the width has become smaller.

Programmed from the start

Right in your own home, among your own friends and family, you can observe human behaviors that will remind you of certain animal responses — like the rituals by which animals maintain their status in the group; the infant gestures that are adapted to adult needs; the emotions that cause animals to protect their relatives more bravely than strangers; the devotion to "home" that is typical of territorial animals; even the play by which a young wolf prepares itself to join the pack as a co-operative hunter.

High-ranking adults, like top dogs (the leaders of wolfpacks) can take liberties with lower-ranking underdogs, whether those people are subjects, employees, students, or children. Your principal can greet you by ordering you out of the hall, by ruffling your hair, or by saying "Hi there, Sam!" You clearly can't greet him in any of those ways. Your mother's or father's boss may use their first names in greeting; on the other hand, they may have to call him Mister So-and-So. Everyone recognizes a

A toddler paws or tugs at an adult to beg for a cookie. His voice rises too.

top dog by his erect posture, strong handshake, assured voice, and unwillingness to avert his gaze during greetings. In former times, our behavior to the leader of the pack was more doglike than anything. To greet the king, we bowed like any dog.

Even our most disarming gestures and charming ways are more doggy than we think. A dog nuzzles the face of another to express affection. So do we; we call it kissing. A dog uses its high, puppy bark or whine to beg favors of another. Listen to your own voice the next time you try to wheedle a cookie or a gift from a dominant human.

The similarity comes from similar predicaments. Hunting animals have to be aggressive. But if they are as aggressive toward one another as they are toward prey, they would endanger their own lives constantly over any disagreement. So, any potentially dangerous animal whose life depends on cooperation develops behaviors that act like switches to turn off another's aggression. The switches are most likely to be infant behavior that originally triggered protective behavior in adults. A crying baby switches on, in adults, an urge to comfort and protect. A crying adult switches off another adult's anger.

Hair raising

Ever feel your scalp prickle? Did you ever wonder why? It's to make you look bigger so your enemy will be frightened of you. Hair raising is an automatic gesture triggered in many animals (dogs and gorillas, for instance) when they are frightened. The trouble with you, though, is that you don't have fur to raise and the muscles for raising the hairs on your head and neck are not as strong as they once were, so the ploy doesn't work. If only you were a furry gorilla, you could try it out on the bully down the street.

Built in altruism

People like to think that altruism, or the willingness to sacrifice ourselves for the sake of others, sets us apart from other animals. But you can find self-sacrifice, even to the point of death, among bees or porpoises or coyotes. We can't help being altruistic any more than they can. Nature has built it in by the accidental arithmetic of survival.

Here's an example: imagine a wolf pack, on the verge of starvation, thousands of years ago. The hunt has been meager; several members of the pack are already weakened by lack of food. The pups are begging them to regurgitate so they can eat. Depending on the strength of inherited behavior, some of the parents will regurgitate to their pups and others will keep the food for themselves. The self-sacrificing wolves may slowly die of their generosity while the more selfish adults will live. But here comes the arithmetic. The pups of the self-sacrificing parents have a better chance for surviving the period of starvation even if their parents eventually die, while the pups of the selfish parents, even if their parents eventually live, will tend to die off. Since each pair of adults is raising about six pups, and they in turn will have more pups that inherit the self-sacrificing behavior which enabled them to survive into adulthood, altruism will increase in the population, while selfishness will decrease it. Over very long periods of time, wolves, humans, and many other animals have, thereby, become "good."

How it works

The arithmetic of altruism only works if we are more self-sacrificing toward our immediate family or other relatives than toward people who are not related to us. We are protecting, after all, not ourselves, but our genes (those tiny structures that carry inherited characteristics from one generation to the next). Protecting those who are unrelated may not help the spread of altruism because the animal saved may not have the genes that promote altruistic behavior. If this argument is true, we should discover that wolves, or humans, more bravely defend their pups, or children, than their pack, or village; and they defend their pack, or village more bravely than "foreigners." So we do and so do wolves.

Wolves are fiercest when their own pups are threatened, slightly less so when their own tribe of blood relatives is threatened, and make no move at all to protect a foreign wolf or other animal. Human parents cannot help themselves from dashing into traffic or leaping into the surf to rescue an endangered child. We are less impulsive when it comes to saving strangers.

We are, however, likely to get a black eye in a fight that started over an insult to our family, friend, race, religion, or even ideas such as "Freedom" or "The American Way of Life." Our altruism appears to protect ideas, identities, and beliefs as much as relatives. But that is only because our instinct fails to recognize how much the world has changed in the last few hundred years of the millions we have existed.

On a small island where our family spends the summer, life is more like "the old days." Of the graduating class of 15 in the high school, only one or two children, on the average, are not related to any of the others. This used to be true in all communities. Whether a person sacrificed himself to preserve a tradition, a belief, or a way of life, the result would tend to be the survival of his relatives.

No place like home

People also seem more sure of themselves on their own turf. The home team plays best at home: home base and home plate are where it's "safe" to be. When we are uncomfortable, we say we do not feel at home. Home is not only where the heart is, but where our courage resides. Even the worst bully has trouble showing his true colors on the first day in a new school.

Home territories are so dear to us that we even name them after our parents: mother country and fatherland. By that, we mean they are irreplaceable. For we, like dogs, are family animals. It is nearly impossible to consider a mother or a father who has raised us as replaceable (though it happens). We find it quite easy to consider replacing the school principal, and when he or she is replaced we have no special term, such as step principal, for the replacement.

Children's culture

Today, the evolution of human culture is rapidly changing the way we think. Women no longer see their role as one confined to food gathering, homekeeping, and childcare. Men no longer see their role as one confined to fighting, hunting, and providing for the family. No one knows what this will mean in the raising of girls and boys in the future.

Favorite childhood games are usually passed down from child to child. Here an older boy shows his three young friends the fine points of "knock-the-can-off-the-wall."

In spite of the best intentions of adults, however, children appear to have a culture of their own, beginning at about the age of six, and continuing into adolescence. The rules of childhood culture are stricter than those of the adult world. Your parents, for example, may be willing to bend rules in a card or ball game to make the play easier for you. The kids in your neighborhood are less likely to change rules for your sake. Adults expect you to report wrongdoing; other children expect you not to squeal on them. Until kindergarten, children may dress very differently from one another. As the years pass, children allow little freedom in what other kids can wear without being teased and ridiculed.

Passing it on

Childhood culture is not only more rigid than adult culture, it also appears to change less than adult culture from century to century and from one part of the world to another. Games similar to tag, hide and seek, follow the leader, and marbles are played in New England, Kansas, Russia, and among Bushmen and Maori children. Such games are seldom taught by adults; they are handed down from child to child over many centuries. (Think back to from whom you learned such games). In most of the world childhood culture also dictates which games are for males, which for females. In this country, for instance, jacks and jump-rope have traditionally been female games; kick the can, a male game.

Without adult direction, children tend to group themselves by sex: girls with girls, boys with boys. (And their activities when they are with their own sex may differ, too). This behavior made a good deal of sense when the future roles of boys demanded wolf-like skills such as strict obedience, endurance of hard-

Tradition

Old people often complain about young people. They say the young don't value the old ways; apparently old apes feel much the same.

In a colony of macaque apes under study for several generations, a clever young female invented a new way to separate grains of wheat from grains of sand. The apes were fed wheat on the beach near their home. Tradition dictated the wiping of food with hands to remove dirt but the small grains of wheat could not be wiped. Perhaps by accident, perhaps by insight, this girl-ape discovered that if she floated a handful of wheat on the water, the sand would drop away. Then she could scoop up the wheat and chew it without getting grit between her teeth. (Perhaps the salty water added to the flavor, too.) Other youngsters enthusiastically adopted the technique and a full-fledged fad was under way. Soon all the young washed wheat. Very gradually, a few of their mothers thought there might be some sense in the practice and gave it a try. Not so the old folks — or the fathers. Set in their ways, they stuck to the old ways, grit-in-the-teeth and all. Now, generations later, wheat-washing has become a tradition.

But meanwhile, the latest generations have pursued new fads which have occurred to them while standing in the water washing wheat. For example, one decided that, though they are land animals, water was fun to play in — bathing was discovered. Another nibbled at seaweed and found it good. "Health food" was discovered.

In their culture, as in ours, the daring of the young and the caution of the old have a purpose. What if the seaweed proved poisonous over a period of time? Then the reluctance of the mature members of the colony would save them to produce more young. What if other sources of food were to run low? Then the foolhardiness of the young would save them to produce more young. Somewhere between the two extremes traditions are changed at a safe rate.

What must have been normal hairstyles when these photographs were taken would look weird to us today. Family albums often show how quickly traditions of dress and hairstyling change. Yet the tradition that women wear only dresses and skirts and men wear pants changed slowly.

ship, fine physical coordination, and unquestioning cooperation; and the future roles of girls demanded constant verbal communication, shared chores, and child rearing. Segregation and special activities may not make so much sense today.

Sensible or not, behavior handed down since we were hunters is not easy to change. The first step in changing is often to step back and see just what is going on. You might like to keep a journal in which you note the kinds of behavior, both adult and child, that tend to separate males from females.

Here are some things you might look for:
- Different behavior of teachers or parents toward girls and boys
- Games that are "boys only" or "girls only"
- Skills that are considered "masculine," or that make boys popular among boys, and the same for girls
- Behavior that adults criticize among boys, or among girls (crying, disliking or liking rough sports)
- Getting dirty or acting concerned about cleanliness
- Playing with dolls or stuffed animals, dressing up
- Participation in casual physical competitions, such as tossing stones at targets, leaping from heights, risking adult anger for playing "pranks"
- Handling animals such as snakes, frogs, worms and insects
- Reports from parents on infant boy and infant girl behavior they feel "typical" of the sex.

The grasping hand

When you place your finger in a newborn baby's hand, he grasps it tightly. If you brush your finger along the sole of his foot, his toes curl as though his foot, too, would grab hold, if it could. Both movements are reflexes — automatic and unconscious movements, like blinking your eyes when someone punches you, or pulling back your hand from a hot potato. Within a month or so, the grasping reflex will be gone. It seems to have served no purpose.

Newborn monkeys and apes have the same reflex, but with them it serves a vital purpose. From the moment they are born,

When dressing up in masks like this one, children have often frightened themselves if they happen to pass a mirror unexpectedly.

65

their mothers must resume the normal routine of swinging through the trees. For this, they need at least three of their hands and feet, and often the fourth as well. It's up to the infant to hang on, for dear life, to the hair of its mother's chest and belly. That strong reflex, working in both hands and feet, sees to it that the slightest contact with its mother results in a firm grip. Even if an infant were to fall during its mother's acrobatics, the grasping reflex might save the baby's life by causing it to grab at any twig that brushed against its palms or soles.

In monkeys and apes, the reflex persists until the baby has learned to grasp the mother or a branch on purpose. So, such a reflex might once have been necessary to our distant tree-dwelling ancestors. But, why should it have persisted? Millions and millions of years have passed since it was of any use.

Recycled reflexes

Nature just doesn't discard things easily. Often, old ways, when they are no longer needed, are put to new uses. No matter how many times a scientist assures us that a baby holding our finger is only an example of a reflex, we see it differently: as a sign of a bond between the infant and us. The old behavior has acquired a new value: it has become the symbol of a newborn's joining with his kind. The reflex's charm is reason enough for its preservation.

The talking mammal

The human family is bound by strong ties for good reason. We have the longest childhood of any animal on earth, and the most to learn during it. Before you ever set foot through the schoolroom door, you learned from your parents a skill so complicated and advanced that no other animal has invented it or appears capable of developing it on its own. The skill is called spoken language.

Language is much more than communication. All sorts of animals communicate — by clicks, tunes, dances, gestures, and scents. The message may be as simple as, "Hawk coming," or as complicated as, "Me cat, of the female sex, not interested in mating, passed by here within the last few hours." The honey bee, with only a bee-brain, can dance out the message, "Fair to middling source of food, 800 yards from hive, at an angle of 45 degrees." The "words" of animal communication, even the occasion for which the word is appropriate, may be handed down by tradition from one generation to another. Birds raised without others of their species do not learn the full song by which to announce their kind, sex, and individual identity. Details of the song must be learned from the previous generation. Jackdaws utter a rattling word for "jackdaw killer" when they see an animal carrying any limp, black object; but they also learn, from older members of the colony, to cry the word upon the approach of an animal who, long before their time, had been seen carrying such an object.

Human language has syntax, or an order of sounds, from which we derive meaning. "Nub" has a different meaning from "bun," "mother" from "thermo", and "The dog bit Harry" from "Harry bit the dog." The advantage of syntax is another piece of arithmetic. A mere ten words can be put together into 3,628,800 ten-word sentences (although, of course, each language has rules which limit the kinds of sequences that make sense; in our language, "Dog the bit Harry" conveys no meaning).

Ameslan: *fat* *dumb* *want* *car*

When people say "I'm speechless," they often mean "I don't know what to think." Try thinking without forming any words in your mind. Pretty hard. Actually, you can do it; both dreaming and daydreaming are a form of thinking. Music and art also convey images that have meaning to us without the help of words. Even as you read these words, you may catch yourself forming images that help you to understand. As you read a story, you can't help "seeing" the places and people in your mind. But thinking in images alone is like thinking through a fog or at a remote distance. When we want to clearly grasp a meaning, we must use words.

The ape speaks

People have assumed that, without words, animals are basically different from humans. Whether we enjoy being able to insult a dog straight to its face without hurting its feelings, or deeply wish we could explain that we are only leaving it at the vet's office for a single night, the fact that animals don't talk like us had led us to believe that they don't think like us either. Now we are not so sure.

Within the last few years, several chimpanzees and a gorilla named Koko have been taught to speak Ameslan, a language of gestures used by some deaf people. Here's what Koko has to say: Koko has insulted others by gesturing: "Rotten stink" or "dirty toilet." Her worst insult is "You dirty bad toilet." When caught poking a hole in a screen with a stick one day, Koko put the stick casually to her mouth and lied, "I was smoking." Questioned about a bite she had given her trainer the day before (which Koko insisted at the time was only a scratch), Koko apologized: "Bite. Sorry bite scratch. Wrong bite." (Koko also gave as a reason that she was angry.) These are names Koko has made up to speak of objects she has not learned gestures for:

Zebra: "white tiger"

Pinocchio doll: "elephant baby"

Mask: "eye hat"

Grapefruit juice: "frown fruit juice"

As another gorilla was having his picture taken, Koko signed to him, "smile." When someone wanted to know which she liked best of two people she is very fond of, Koko replied: "Not good question." And Koko has several ways to describe herself. When she has been acting bratty, she calls herself "stubborn devil," but in answer to the question "Are you an animal or a person," Koko replied "Fine animal gorilla."

If Koko has a baby (and that is planned when she is old enough), will she teach her baby to speak as we teach our children? She is already attempting to teach a younger male friend and holds conversations with him, though his vocabulary is still limited. And if she does chat with her child, what will they talk about? And if animals speak, and if they tell us, as Koko already has, their feelings, opinions, wishes, and experiences; if they tease, insult, and crack jokes with us, perhaps we will come to see how small the difference between us and them really is.

Odd and sinister

Language allows us to understand all sorts of odd things about how we think. The word "odd," for example. Why should odd, which refers to a number that can't be divided by two, also mean strange? And why does even-handed mean fair? Perhaps since we are symmetrical — two eyes, two ears, two feet — that state of affairs strikes us as right. But on the other hand, the word "right" refers to our imbalance: 80 percent of us are right-handed, 20 percent are left-handed. (That was true of our human ancestors, too, a million-odd years ago.)

We are prejudiced toward the right. Right means correct, true, and straight (right-on means straight ahead). People have rights, can be righteous, or have right-hand men. The guest of honor sits to the right of the host. Unless we are insane, we are in our right minds. Left comes from a word meaning weak; in French, left is "gauche," which also means clumsy, and in Latin the word for left is "sinister." In politics, the right is the safe, conservative side which fears the changes for which the left, or radical side, is pushing. But the opposite of right (straight and true) is wrong, which means crooked. And a crooked person in any language is sinister, or left.

A rat won't learn anything by looking up its name in the dictionary. But, you can find out a good deal about how humans think by seeing what the original meaning of a word is. The word "rat," for instance, originally meant "gnaw," and its original sound probably mimicked the sound of gnawing.

The stupid test

The smartest people can overlook the obvious, as this test proves. Try it out on friends after you test yourself.

1. Circle the largest cross.

2. This rooster is sitting on the barn roof. If he lays an egg, which side will it fall on.

3. This is a one-story house painted all blue. What color is the living room? The kitchen? The bedroom? The stairs?

4. How can the children get across the frozen river to pick the apples on the apple trees?

5. Circle The stupid test.

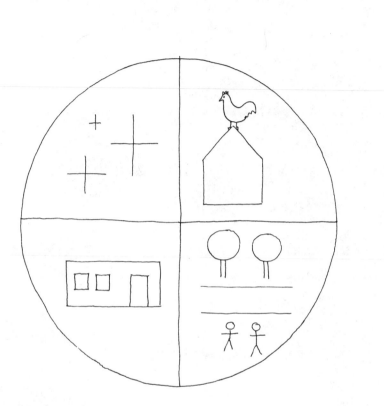

Answers

1. The largest cross is the one that divides the whole test into four parts.
2. Roosters don't lay eggs.
3. A one-story house has no stairs and therefore can't be painted blue.
4. There are no apples on a tree in winter, when the river is frozen.
5. The circle should be put around the entire test not just the title.

Insides

Insides:

It's breakfast time again. In the window, the geranium factory is already cooking with light, to feed sugar to its cells. Mold spores in the jam jar are sending hyphas down to pre-digest their meal. Yeasts in the oven are gobbling away at wheat seed starches, puffing the dough with excreted carbon dioxide. Dad drops some unfertilized chicken ova into melted fat molecules from a cow's mammary gland and sprinkles them with ground dried pepper berries and the evaporated salts of ancient seas, while Mom lays slices of a pig's belly muscle into another pan. Your mouth waters enzymes.

Everybody's ready to eat something — or somebody.

Your kitchen provides food for a multitude. Just how this multitude of living things nourishes itself has to do with how you nourish yourself. Without the one-celled yeast, you'd have neither bread nor beer; without bacteria, there'd be no cheese; without chickens, there would be no eggs; without pigs, no bacon; without cows, no butter. Were the geranium and all its green-plant relatives that produce the pepper berry, the coffee bean, the wheat seeds, and the strawberry fruits not there to make food from soil, water, light, and air, you would have no need of food at all — you'd have no oxygen to breathe.

The way in which animals, plants, and a mysterious group called protistas live, breathe, eat, excrete, and reproduce has everything to do with you.

It's time to meet your mushroom and your cold virus, get to know your bread molds and your houseplants, understand the sex life of a cherry blossom, the skeleton of a chicken, the muscles and organs of the animals you eat — and your own insides.

Morning as usual

Protistas

The first kingdom

Munching on a carrot while romping with a dog — you have no trouble telling the difference between them. Carrots are vegetables. They come planted in the ground and they don't walk around. They stick their green leaves up into the sun and plunge their thick roots down into the soil. Carrots can't nip you; they don't eat other vegetables either. Plants can get along on light, water, air, and soil.

Dogs, on the other hand, are animals. Like other animals, they move about. If they don't eat grass or leaves, or other vegetables, they eat animals. Dogs certainly can't feed themselves from light, water, air, and soil.

Because a dog and a carrot, a fern and a fish, a birch and a bird are so obviously different from one another, people have divided them into two great kingdoms of organisms (living things) — the plant kingdom and the animal kingdom. These two groups are very different from one another, and very different from rocks, sand, water, and metal, which are not alive at all.

Where to put the mushroom

But the world is not made only of organisms as straightforward as a carrot or a dog. In the vegetable department of the supermarket, you are sure to find mushrooms. But mushrooms can't live on light, water and soil. Like you, they eat dead animals and vegetables. They are never green — they don't have the green chlorophyll that gives the plant kingdom its typical color.

Some protozoa (named in Latin for what they were once thought to be: first animals) switch back and forth from animal to plant and back again, depending on which way of life works best at the moment. If there are no dead plants or animals to eat, they produce the

chlorophyll that makes them green. While they're green, they can use light to make food from dirt and water like other plants. But when the eating's good, back they go to an animal existence, eating meat and vegetables. A creature called euglena is listed as a plant (an alga, like the green fuzz in fishtanks) in one book and protozoa in another. No wonder: the euglena swims freely around, waving its tail behind its squishy body, seeing the world in its own way with its light-sensitive eye spot, but it nourishes itself the plant way, with chlorophyll.

Further oddities

And the puzzle of what's what doesn't end with these few oddities. You can't even ask if a virus (an organism that causes, among other illnesses, the common cold) is a plant or an animal; you have to ask whether it is alive, like an organism, or "dead" like a rock. Organisms are made of cells — one or many. A cell has a boundary around it, a sort of jacket. Inside the jacket, the moist cell is equipped with all the cell needs to eat, excrete (get rid of wastes), and reproduce itself. A virus, however, is not a cell. It is dry, not moist. It doesn't carry its own living equipment around with it. In this dry state it neither eats nor excretes. But once a virus invades another organism's cell, it can produce independent and unattached "babies," by substituting its own instructions for the ones the invaded cell carries. A virus is like a brain that can "come alive" by finding a body.

What's included?

There is no way to say whether these strange things are animals or plants or even minerals. So they have been given their own name. They belong to the kingdom protista. The name means, simply, "first."

The first kingdom includes protozoa; fungi, like molds, mushrooms, and yeasts; algae; and "germs," bacteria, and viruses. Numberless, common, living everywhere, the first kingdom may always remain the most mysterious of all. No mushroom has ever left a fossil. No one knows what a mushroom ancestor might have been, or even whether mushrooms have relatives. Maybe euglena is a missing link: a green alga that grew a tail on its way to becoming a protozoa. Maybe viruses are at the beginning of life itself: a long chain of chemicals that could reproduce itself by building a new chain from smaller parts floating in the ancient seas where it originated.

As you clean the algae from your fish's tank, or blow viruses from your runny nose, or pop a mushroom into your mouth, you are touching on one of life's greatest puzzles.

Edible protistas

The largest protista you can eat is a mushroom. The mushroom is only one member of an enormous group. This group includes the yeasts that help humans to make bread and beer; the molds that mildew our basements, flavor our cheeses, and cure our diseases; and the pesky fungi that give us ringworm and athlete's foot. Though no one is positive these are related, they are all called funguses. And they are so different from other forms of life some scientists prefer to put them in a kingdom of their own — neither plant, animal, nor protista.

The part of the mushroom you eat is only the fruiting body. The rest of it is a mass of threads, called hyphas, that reach many feet into the soil. Altogether, the mass of hyphas is called a mycelium.

For most of its life, all there is to a mushroom is the mycelium, hidden deep in the soil. Mushrooms use organic materials like rotted leaves, wood, or other compost for nourishment, and they can only digest these outside themselves. Each hypha secretes (makes and discharges) enzymes into the surrounding soil; the enzymes are chemicals which cut (divide precisely) larger organic substances into smaller pieces. The hyphas can absorb (take in) these smaller bits and distribute the food to the rest of its cells. Only when the mycelium has grown a great deal, and conditions in the outside world seem safe, does it send up its stem and cap.

A closer look

Look underneath a mushroom cap to see the intricate arrangement of flaps. Through the slits between the flaps, spores that can start new mushroom colonies will drop. If you have several ripe mushrooms, try this: lay the caps on paper, some dark, some white. Leave the caps overnight, protected from drafts by a bowl turned upside down (or a cake cover) placed over them. In the morning you will see the dark or cream colored spores that have fallen on the paper. Since they have fallen through the slits, they will form a radial pattern like rays around the center of the mushroom. Each spore is a group of nuclei (the portions of cells that carry all the instructions) identical with those inside the mushroom's other cells so each can only produce an identical mushroom. Each group of nuclei is surrounded by a small amount of moist jelly and a hard jacket. The jacket is so durable that it can protect the nuclei against the harshest conditions of cold, heat, and dryness for many years. A windblown spore will only "come to life" again, producing new hyphas, if it happens upon conditions that are just right.

Lively yeast

The ability of funguses to endure harsh conditions is obvious in yeast, that dry powder or crumbly cake used to make bread full of holes and beer full of bubbles. Nothing about dried yeast cells you buy in the market would lead you to believe they are alive. Yet when you give them a proper environment — moist, warm, and sugary — they leap into action. A single package of dried yeast is millions of one-celled yeasts.

Bread dough doubles in bulk as yeasts excrete carbon dioxide bubbles into it.

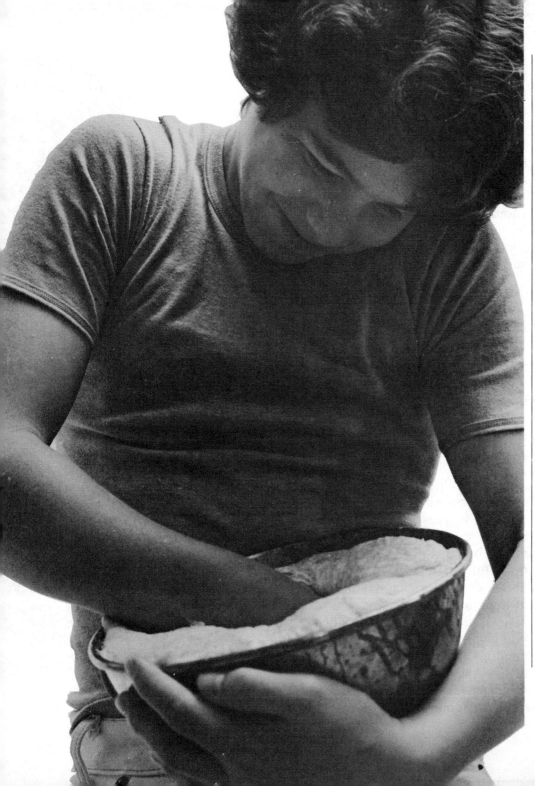

Mix a cupful of warm water with a tablespoon of sugar in a two-cup pitcher. Dump in the yeast and stir. Within 10 minutes, you will see a foam begin to form on the surface of the water. In a few more minutes, the volume of the liquid will expand. In half an hour, it will nearly have reached the top of the two-cup pitcher and will have a distinct "yeasty" smell. This is what is happening: the yeast cells absorb water, which restores their ability to function normally. They begin to digest the sugar in the water and to emit waste products. Two of the waste products are alcohol and carbon dioxide. Carbon dioxide is the bubbles or air-filled foam in the sugar-water mixture; and it is the same gas that forms the holes in bread.

The yeasts themselves are killed by the heat in the oven, but, of course, you eat their microscopic corpses in every sandwich. Alcohol is also in bread when the dough is put into the oven, but it evaporates as the dough cooks. Alcohol made by yeasts stays in beer and wine because the brews aren't heated. When wine is used in cooking, all the alcohol in it evaporates before you eat the final product.

Punching explodes the bubbles.

What puts the head on beer?

Beer bubbles in commercial beer are not the original carbon dioxide excreted by the yeasts. Beer, these days, is usually bottled after the yeasts have used up all the sugar in the brew and have died of starvation. By that time, nearly all the bubbles have escaped. The bubbles are replaced by new bubbles produced by forcing carbon dioxide, under pressure, into the brew when the beer is bottled. Home brewers could tell you why this is a safer method than using the yeast-produced gas. To keep the yeast-produced bubbles in beer, you have to bottle it before all the sugar is gone so that the live yeasts in each bottle can continue, for a while, to produce carbonation after the bottle is tightly capped. But since it's hard to be exact about how many yeasts are left, how long their food supply will last, and therefore, how much gas they will produce inside the capped bottles, the result is an occasional dramatic explosion of beer bottles in the basement.

The dough will be kneaded and shaped into loaves now; the yeasts will raise the dough a second time before the bread is baked.

Ginger beer

Here is a simple recipe for making 12 bottles of your own ginger beer (or ginger ale as it's called these days).

You need:

  2 cups sugar
     Juice from 2 lemons, strained
  6 quarts warm water
  ¼ teaspoon dried yeast dissolved in 1 cup warm water
  1 tablespoon cream of tartar
  4 to 6 tablespoons powdered ginger (depending on whether you like your drink mild, or rather hot)
 12 1-pint bottles, caps, and capper (these are available from companies that sell wine-making supplies)

In a large bowl, mix together the sugar, lemon juice, and water. Stir until the sugar is dissolved. Let the mixture stand until the water is only lukewarm. Then add the cream of tartar and ginger to the yeast mixture, stir, and pour it into the sugar mixture. Stir everything thoroughly.

Using a ladle and funnel, pour the mixture into the pint bottles. Cap them and store on their sides for five days before drinking. As soon as the ginger beer is ready, either drink or refrigerate it as it doesn't keep well at room temperature.

Blue food

Anyone who eats Roquefort, Gorgonzola, or any blue cheese eats molds. Most of the molds that give such cheeses their distinctive taste and decorative streaks are blue. One of the commonest blue molds is bread mold, and it is also one of the most important to human beings. Blue bread mold is one of a family of molds called penicillium, from which the antibiotic penicillin is derived. This chemical, produced by certain penicillium molds, kills bacteria. Many molds, in fact, produce bacterial poisons, and for good reason. Most bacteria live by digesting organic stuffs, and so do molds. Bacteria and molds, like hyenas and jackals, compete for the same food. A mold that can manage to poison surrounding bacteria gets more to eat, thrives, and multiplies. Molds are out for themselves in a competitive world.

We eat untold numbers of bacteria. And not only do we eat them, but we eat foods that they have made for us. Bacteria are

To make as much as five gallons of ginger beer at a time, multiply the recipe, and mix the ingredients in a small, clean garbage pail. Use an aquarium siphon to pour the mixture into bottles.

used to convert milk into cheese, sour cream, buttermilk, and yogurt. You may have seen the word "cultured" on such dairy products. The word on the label means exactly the same as it does in a laboratory: bacteria have been cultured by providing them with the food and warmth they need to multiply into a large colony. The bacterial colony changes the milk chemically in the process of digesting it. Drink the resulting buttermilk and you drink the bacteria, too.

Logs for dinner

Messy, crumbly, loose-barked fireplace logs are those that someone is eating. This sort of log is not the family's favorite as it requires sweeping up after and doesn't burn well. But, if one happens into your home, here are a few of the log-eating creatures you might find in residence.

The first thing you may notice is lichen, a gray, brown, black, or orange flaky stuff on the surface of the bark. Lichen, actually, is not one, but two organisms: an alga living in combination with a fungus. The algal cells use sunlight to manufacture food from water and minerals absorbed by the fungus cells. Their manufactured food in turn feeds the fungus cells. This may seem peculiar to you, but the situation is not unlike that of a cow. Cows don't do all their own digestion: bacteria living in their stomach digest much of their food for them. The difference is that, in a lichen, neither the alga nor the fungus can live on its own. In the partnership we call a cow, the bacteria can live elsewhere. Their cow, however, would die.

Independent fungi grow on the bark of rotting logs. Most of these fruits are shaped like semicircular shelves in various shades of white, beige, gray, and orange. Lift the bark to see the white threads that are their hyphas. Scratch the area with your fingernail. It is usually somewhat mushy because the hyphas have partially digested the wood. The spores from which the hyphas grew got a free ride in through the bark when a beetle bored a hole to lay its eggs. The beetle could hardly help carrying a few spores on its

Invite a mold

Mold spores are microscopic. Though they float in the air all around you, indoors and out, you never see them. But invite a mold to dinner and it will reward you with evidence of its existence that you can feel, see, and smell.

To set up a meal for molds, place various kinds of food, each in a small plastic bag: a slice of orange, a piece of bread (without preservatives), a bit of jelly, a dollop of cream cheese; a spoonful of cooked sweet potato. Blow each bag up and seal it with a rubber band. Keep the bags in a dark closet or cupboard. Several varieties of mold spores, already in the air inside the bags, will discover the meal — you will see them only after the spores have sprouted hyphas, thrust them into the food, and matured sufficiently to send fruits upwards. They may be blue, white, black, even pink, or orange. Look at them carefully through a magnifying lens. You will see a great tangle of hyphas with perhaps round fruits sprouting from them, something like the illustration on page 80. Millions of spores are released from the fruits to begin new wanderings in search of a proper home.

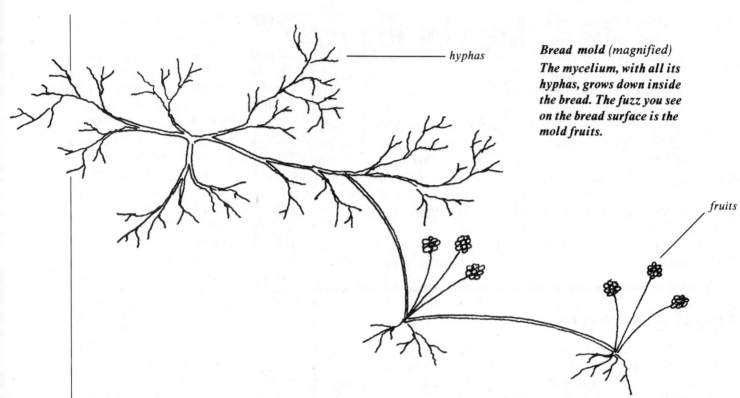

hyphas

Bread mold (*magnified*)
The mycelium, with all its hyphas, grows down inside the bread. The fuzz you see on the bread surface is the mold fruits.

fruits

surface: the small holes you see on the underside of a shelf fungus can release up to seven trillion (7,000,000,000,000) spores into the air.

Beetle clues

Evidence of the beetle is common in the rotting log too. Female beetles of many species bore holes through bark and then chew troughs a couple of inches long along the wood of the trunk. They lay their eggs, at intervals, along the trough, then go back out through the bark.

When the eggs hatch, the larvae chew their way along the wood, eating as they go. Since each larva takes off in a different direction when it hatches in the trough, the pattern you are likely to see, along the log is the original short trough, made by the mother, with longer ones radiating from it. Each radiating trough marks the path of a chewing larva. At the end of the trough, you may find a small deposit of sawdust. This marks the spot where a larva stopped its eating and stayed put while it

became an adult beetle. The sawdust accumulated when it chewed its way out (without eating what it chewed) to take up its adult life.

Because the larvae of wood-eating beetles find wood that has been pre-digested by fungi easier to use than undecayed wood, some beetle species make life easier for their young by carrying a little bunch of spores with them to "plant" beside their eggs. Since the fungus that grows from the spores can use larva excretions as food, both beetles and fungi get more to eat.

More tenants

Unlike beetle larvae, who only tunnel along the surface of the wood, carpenter ants carve out tunnels deep in the trunk itself. Large colonies can chew out so much wood that the log is mostly air; you can lift it with one hand. Get rid of any log that is deeply tunneled since carpenter ants are as happy eating the wood of a house as a log.

Once bark is riddled with beetle holes and undermined by larvae, all sorts of larger creatures can creep in under it. Carnivorous (meat-eating) centipedes, which may be related to a distant ancestor of insects, hang out there to eat the vegetarian beetles. An even stranger creature commonly found in rotting logs is a pill bug (sometimes called a grub, sow bug, or wood louse). It's not a bug, grub, sow, or louse. It's not an insect, either. The pill bug is actually a crustacean, a relative of shrimps,

Sex: the real thing

When we think sex, we think male and female. But that's only because human beings happen to require both a man and a woman for reproduction. Molds don't come in male and female genders, but they do have sex. Each mold can produce two different types of hyphas whose genes are arranged differently from one another. A cell from one type of hypha and a cell from the other type reach out toward one another, touch, fuse, and combine genes. Their offspring, in the form of spores from which new molds will grow, inherit traits from both "parent" hyphas. That's what sex really is: a combining of instructions from two sources, so that offspring are not identical to either source, but a mixture of both. How the mixing is done may be sexy to humans, but all the fuss is only nature's way of getting to the point: mixing genes.

crabs, and lobsters. Pill bugs breathe through gills, even though they live on land. Touch one and it will curl into a "pill" for self-protection. Pill bugs dine off both the rotting wood and any other diners who died at the dinner table.

These few visible lichens, fungi, and other creatures can't

account totally for the mushiness and crumbliness of a rotting log. Invisible bacteria and protozoa are dining by the millions. A rotting log is not softening and falling apart through some vague corruption. It is being digested. What will finally be left of it, if you don't burn it, is soil.

Pillbug

curled into a "pill"

opened out

The people eaters

Athlete's foot, ringworm, and thrush are all fungi that eat people. The fungus involved in athlete's foot eats skin between the toes. Once the fungus sends its hyphas into the skin, the skin flakes. Bacteria move in to take over this new food supply, and they are what's mostly responsible for the fierce itching. Both bacteria and the fungi need moisture to live, so the best treatment for athlete's foot is to keep your feet dry. Soapy water is mildly poisonous to them, too.

Ringworm is not a worm, but a fungus that penetrates into the skin and then spreads outward in a ring. The fungi in the inner area gradually die as new fungi spread around them. There are several poisons (medicines) which kill the ringworm fungus.

Thrush is a malady caused by a fungus called monilia. Babies get monilia fungi rather frequently in their mouths where the colonies look like white patches on the tongue and inside the cheeks. Monilia can also live off the lining of the vagina (the canal through which babies are born), and even the intestines.

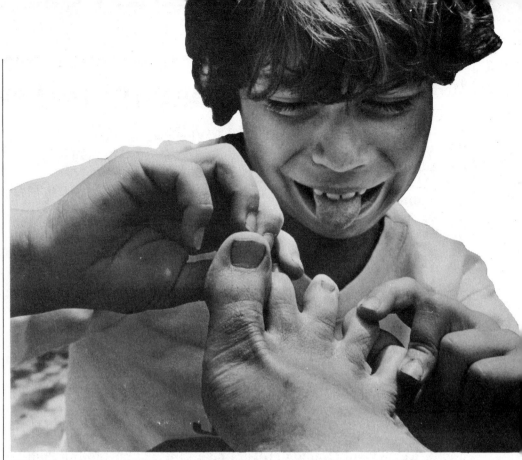

Checking for athlete's foot means looking between your toes for cracking skin.

Hidden competitors

These days a lot of monilia infections are caused by antibiotics. Our bodies are normally inhabited by both fungi and bacteria, both of which compete for the food and living quarters we have to offer. When a person is given antibiotics over several weeks, normal and non-harmful bacteria are killed off along with the ones that are causing illness. The fungi, which aren't harmed by most antibiotics, suddenly find living conditions ideal. Without all those bacteria around, there's plenty of room, plenty of food. Naturally, the fungi take advantage of the situation by multiplying. It's the effects of multiplication that we call "infection." The simplest treatment for monilia infections is to restore the natural ecology of your body by drinking plenty of bacteria — in the form of buttermilk!

Plants

From the ground up

Unlike the confusing protistas, fruits and vegetables are firmly rooted in the plant kingdom. The fruits and vegetables you eat represent all the major plant parts — roots, stems, buds, leaves, flowers, ovaries, and seeds.

Edible roots and stems

Starting at the bottom, onions, garlic, carrots, beets, yams, and potatoes are all portions of root. Look closely at a carrot or beet to see the small feeder roots that still cling to it.

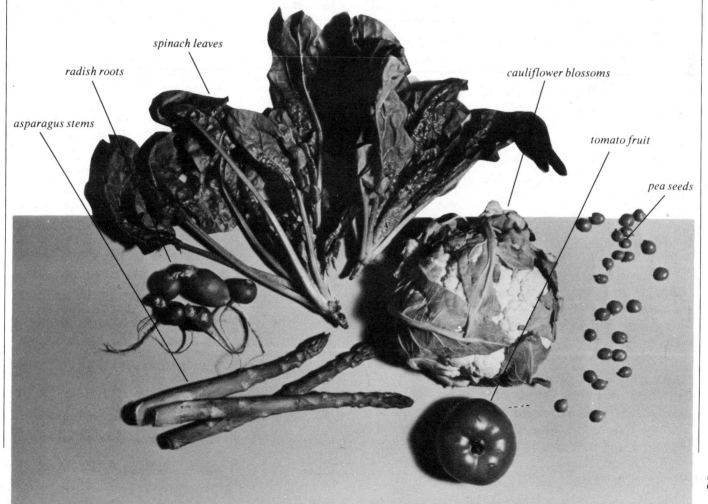

asparagus stems

radish roots

spinach leaves

cauliflower blossoms

tomato fruit

pea seeds

It is no accident that root vegetables are often sweet, like young beets, or starchy, like potatoes. These, and many other plants, store food for their own use in enlarged portions of their roots. If you left a carrot in the ground, the plant would eventually use its stored sugars and starches to produce flowers and seeds.

Moving upward, rhubarb and celery are stems. Asparagus is a young stem; just sprouted from the ground, it has not yet leafed out from the tiny buds at its tip. The stringy portions of a celery stalk are part of the circulatory system of the plant. Each string is actually a tube, made of beadlike cells stacked atop one another, through which the water and nutrients absorbed by the roots, and the sugars produced by the leaves, can circulate through the plant.

Leafy greens

Spinach, salad greens, and cabbages are leaves. They have the same veins through which nutrients circulate as a maple or an oak leaf. The stout walls of the veins hold the leaf open to receive light. The green pigment, called chlorophyll, that gives leaves their summer color, uses light to manufacture food from the water and minerals that have been delivered from the roots. Spinach is dark green because the plant grows in a cluster with nearly all its leaves exposed to the light. When you buy a cabbage in the store, you are buying only the inner leaves that have not yet opened to the light, and therefore have not yet had to produce much chlorophyll. The much darker (and tougher) outer leaves have been discarded. Darker leaves, because they are actively manufacturing food, are always more nutritious than lighter leaves. Romaine lettuce, for instance, is lots healthier than iceberg lettuce.

Flowering vegetables

Were the plant left in the ground, a flower stalk would eventually grow from the center of a head of lettuce or cabbage. Both broccoli and cauliflower, close relatives of cabbages, are these central flower clusters. When you buy them, the flowers are still in bud. But once in a while, broccoli is picked somewhat too late. The small yellow specks among the green are opened broccoli blossoms. Try looking at one through a magnifying glass.

Artichokes are flower buds in a more advanced stage, just ready to open their thistle-like heads into full bloom. They are, in fact, relatives of thistles. Their "choke," or fuzz, growing from the "heart," is the equivalent of thistledown, from which small seeds take off to fly with the wind. The heart itself is an ovary, which contains not only the seeds but the nourishment they will need to mature. The spined leaves protect the ovary. Animals that try to munch the whole flower, instead of delicately removing the leaves one by one, have an unpleasant mouthful.

Ovaries hold the seeds

Many of the vegetables we eat, and all the fruits, are actually ovaries. A plant ovary includes all the structures that the seed needs to complete its development. What we call fruit, as well as what we often call vegetable or nut, is one or more ovaries that stores food for the seeds' nourishment. Botanists call any food-storing ovaries a fruit. Squash, eggplant, and cucumbers, therefore are as much fruits as are apples and oranges. Sometimes a single flower has only a single ovary containing only one seed, like a peach or a cherry. Sometimes the flower has several ovaries, but they fuse together to produce one fruit containing many seeds, like a

nutmeg seed

bay leaf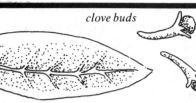

clove buds

black pepper berries

saffron stamens

dill seeds

ginger root

hot pepper fruit

cinnamon bark

thyme leaves

Spicy quiz

You might like to test your family's knowledge (or ignorance) of plant anatomy by quizzing them on the herbs and spices they use. Here's a rundown on what portions of a plant herbs and spices are. Most of them are recognizable if you buy them whole rather than crushed or ground.

Roots: ginger

Leaves: tarragon, basil, oregano, rosemary, sage, thyme

Bark: cinnamon (cut from soft, inner bark that curls as it dries — the curls are short to fit into spice bottles, or ground fine)

Fruit: hot pepper, allspice, black pepper (allspice and pepper are both dried berries; white pepper is the inside portion of the berry after the dark skin has been removed)

Seeds: mustard, caraway, sesame, dill, poppyseed, nutmeg (nutmeg is the dried kernel of a fruit — like an almond or peach pit, it was originally surrounded by the softer portions of its ovary)

Flowers: cloves (they are buds — you can see the pointed sepals and peel the still-closed petals from the round portion atop the stem), saffron (actually it is the stamens only of a certain crocus blossom; the labor involved in harvesting thousands of tiny stamens explains the expense of saffron)

pumpkin. And sometimes the single flower has many ovaries that appear as a cluster, like a raspberry. Each ovary in a raspberry contains a single seed.

Some of the foods we call nuts are ovaries — or were until the outside flesh was removed at harvesting. An almond, for instance, was covered with a thick outer coating similar to, but not as tasty as, a peach. The kernel is the seed. You will find a very similar seed inside a peach pit. A pea is a fruit, too. The pod is the outside of the ovary, and the peas themselves are the seeds. A string bean is similar. In both, the nutrition for the maturing seeds is stored in the fleshy pod walls.

By the time some seeds have stored sufficient food to continue life outside the ovary, they have stored enough to become human foods as well. Peas, nuts, dried beans, and corn kernels are all seeds. Usually we have discarded the rest of the ovary, including pods, cobs, and shells.

The bud scars on the tips of "male" and "female" eggplants.

A tomato argument and an eggplant myth

You can put to rest once and for all that old argument about whether a tomato is a fruit or a vegetable. The rule is, if it's a complete ovary, it's a fruit. So the next time you hear this silly discussion, step in with self-assurance. Yes, the tomato is a fruit, and so are cucumbers, squashes, stringbeans, and pumpkins.

Cooks are often told — by other cooks, by vegetable sellers, by relatives, and total strangers — that if you wish to choose the tastiest eggplants, devoid of bitter flavor and dark seeds, you must buy female ones. You can tell the sex of an eggplant, this advice continues, by looking at the scar at the bottom. If the scar is slit-shaped, the eggplant is male. If it is round, the eggplant is female. Even as I shopped for the eggplants in this picture, another shopper offered that advice. But, since all eggplants are ovaries, they are all female. There is no such thing as a male ovary.

86

The secret life of a cherry

An innocent cherry blossom, blowing in the breeze, may at the very instant you are watching it be involved in sex. Any blossom is actually the sexual part of the plant from which it grows. The pretty petals, like a pretty dress, are only to attract. The flower's perfume, too, is diffused into the wind for the sake of reproduction.

Deep down below the petals is the flower's female part, its ovary. Surrounding the ovary on graceful stalks are the male parts, the stamens. These are topped with anthers that contain tiny grains of pollen, a plant counterpart to sperm. The ovum inside the ovary waits to be joined and fertilized by a grain of pollen. But the pollen on a single blossom, or even on a whole tree of blossoms, may not be mature enough to fertilize the ovum when the ovum is ready to be fertilized. And flowers can't move, bend, and touch to fulfill their reproductive needs. The pretty petals and fragrant perfumes are not to attract the opposite sex, but to attract bees.

Matchmaker, matchmaker

Like a matchmaker, bees direct the flower's sexual union, but it is quite by accident. As they go about their food gathering, collecting both nectar and pollen to feed themselves and their youngsters, ripe pollen grains stick to the stiff hairs on their legs. At the next flower, a few grains of pollen drop from the hairs and are captured by the sticky tip of the stigma that grows from the ovary. If that ovary is receptive, the pollen will grow down into the ovary, find the ripe ovum, and join with it. The fertilized ovum, which can now be called a seed, can get on with the business of reproducing cherry trees.

The petals have done their job of attracting bees. They dry up and drop off, along with the stamens. The seed, and the ovary surrounding it, grows, filling with sugars and starches intended to temporarily nourish the seed now and after it leaves the parent tree. Inside the seed grows a tiny germ — the baby plant itself. If you soak a dried lima bean and split it when it plumps up, you can see this tiny germ plant. It is the equivalent of an embryo in the process of growing into an infant. After the cherry has fallen from the tree, and when conditions of warmth, moisture, and soil are right, the germ germinates — sends out a single root, in search of water and nutrients, and a single sprout topped by two tiny leaves, in search of light.

In silence and in secret, without appearing to do anything at all, the cherry has sexually reproduced itself. A new tree is born.

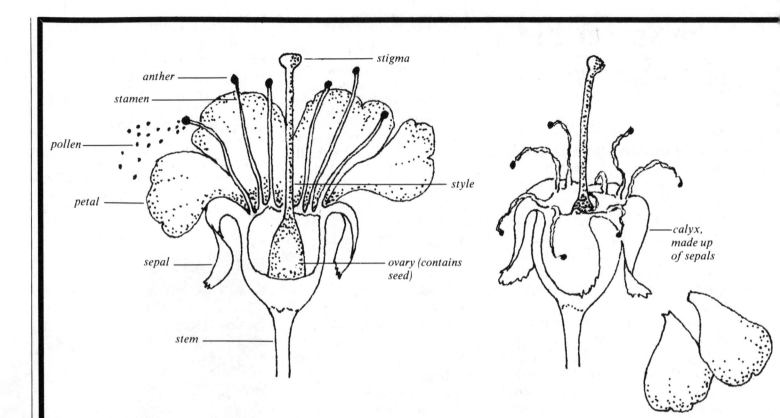

A cherry close up

1. *A cherry blossom sliced to show the inside. In the middle, the ovary, style, and stigma together are called the pistil — the female part of the flower. Stamens, with their pollen-bearing anthers, are the male parts.*

2. *The petals fall, pistil and stamens wither. But it is impossible yet to see if the seed inside the ovary has been fertilized by pollen. The band of sepals that covers the ovary is called the calyx.*

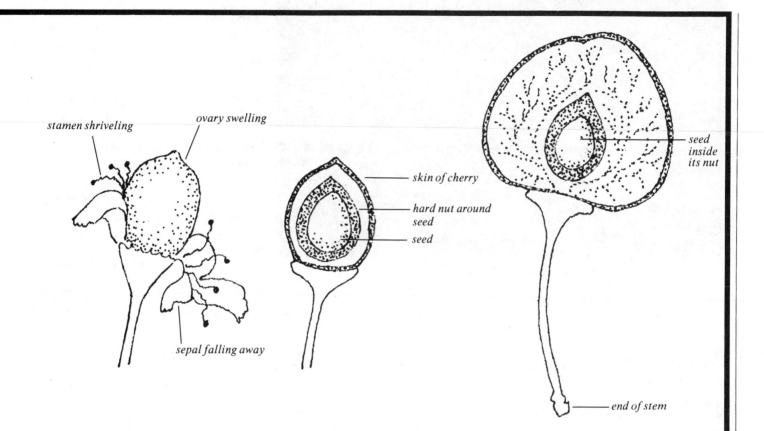

stamen shriveling

ovary swelling

sepal falling away

skin of cherry

hard nut around seed

seed

seed inside its nut

end of stem

3. The first sign that the seed has been fertilized is the swelling ovary. As it grows, it bursts the band of sepals and they too drop off the new cherry. On an apple, however, you can see the dried calyx at the tip of the fruit.

4. The unripe cherry, showing the inside. The seed is already protected by a hard nut, but there isn't much fruit to eat yet, and it would be hard, green, and sour.

5. The ripe cherry, showing the nut (or pit) with the seed inside and the network of veins which provide nutrition to the fruit as long as it is on the tree. The end of the cherry stem was also the end of the blossom stem, and is where the fruit finally detaches from the tree.

Because there are bees, flower bouquets come in all different colors.

How the bees made colored flowers

Once upon a time, 150 million years ago, there were no red, or yellow, or blue flowers. Flowers, then, were colored green with chlorophyll, like oak blossoms and birch flowers, or were white because they lacked chlorophyll, like magnolias and dogwoods. Most of them were pollinated, like corn and grass are today, by the wind.

As plants invented these first flowers, insects invented ways to use them for their own good. The early ancestors of flies, butterflies, and bees learned to eat their pollen and sip their nectar. Flying from meal to meal, getting pollen stuck to their hairy legs and dropping it off again at every stop, these insects fertilized the flowers from which they ate. Fertilization by insects is more reliable than fertilization by wind — a flower that can attract nectar- and pollen-eating insects is likely to produce more offspring than one that depends on the wind.

Busy bees

Bees, then and now, were the most numerous and greedy of insect pollinators. And bees have color vision. They can see blue, yellow, and even a color we can't see at all: ultraviolet, which looks the same as white to us. Every once in a while, those millions of years ago, a genetic mutation (an accidental change in cell instructions for producing a substance) would occur in a green or white flowering plant, and that plant would blossom out in color.

A mutation changes a single bit of instruction for making a substance. The process is something like the game in which you change one word into another by changing one letter at a time, with no nonsense words allowed. For instance, the instructions to make the word "sad" is the sequence of letters S-A-D. To make the word into "man", you must first substitute M for S in the instructions, creating the word "mad." Now you can change the last bit of information in the original instructions by substituting N for D, and you get "man." By puzzling out such substitutions — one bit of information at a time and with no change that results in a "nonsense" substance — scientists have figured out how the ancient pigments gradually became the colors we see in flowers now. For example, yellow pigments in buttercups and daffodils were created by small mistakes in instructions for carotene, a pigment still used by plants to help leaves make food.

Eye catchers

Bees found such colored blossoms more noticeable than green or white ones. They were more likely to visit those flowers than their less colorful relatives. Since the ova of colored flowers were, therefore, more likely to be fertilized than those of neighboring plants, such oddities flourished. As the ages passed, yellow flowers became more common; then, orange ones and orangy red; and finally, blue, pink, and violet flowers. Even today, most blossoms in the world are still green or white. Many are yellow. Fewer are orange. The rarest are blue.

Only pure red flowers cannot be credited to bees. Bees are color-blind to red — pure red looks to them as black does to us. An all-red flower, not purplish or orange, not streaked or flecked with other colors, is not pollinated by bees. There is probably a pollinating fly to thank.

The trees in your house

Along the grain of your floor, sap once flowed. At every knot, a branch once grew. Between each line of grain lies one year's thickening in the life of the tree from which your floors, tables, chairs, chests, salad bowls, and wooden spoons were made. What you are looking at, as you admire the pattern in a piece of wood, is something like a giant microscope slide — a slice cut across a tree trunk, or a slice cut lengthwise through it.

How wood is formed

Just beneath the bark of a tree is a layer of cells called the cambium layer. Only one cell thick, this layer is the source of all the wood and bark in the tree. This is true even if the trunk, like some redwoods in California, is broad enough to cut a car-sized tunnel through it.

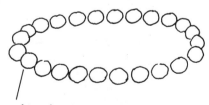

cambium layer

Brand-new cells made by the cambium along its inside surface are hollow, like tubes, and they are stacked atop one another. Their ends fuse together to form long vessels that reach all the way from root to branch tip. The sugar and oxygen supplied by the leaves travels downward through these youngest cells. As cambium cells divide to make more cells, those that are squeezed to the outside become bark — a tough protective covering for the tender cambium.

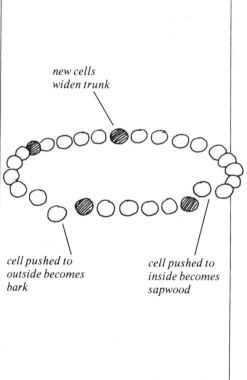

new cells widen trunk

cell pushed to outside becomes bark

cell pushed to inside becomes sapwood

Inside a tree

In the spring, a tree grows quickly and produces light-colored wood. During the summer, when the tree grows more slowly, the wood is darker. The dark areas form rings. Count the rings to find out how many summers old the tree is. This one is nine years old.

Trunk and branch split lengthwise.

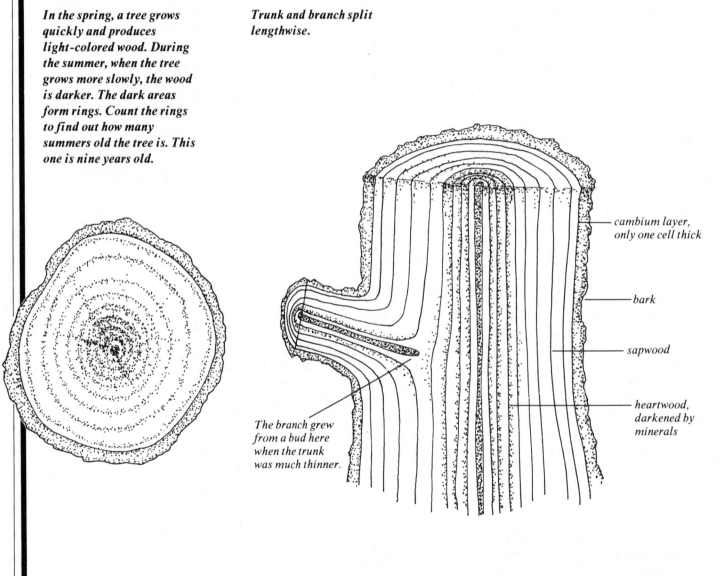

cambium layer, only one cell thick

bark

sapwood

heartwood, darkened by minerals

The branch grew from a bud here when the trunk was much thinner.

This might be a section of the same trunk, cut through the portion where the branch grew.

A slice through the outside of a log may have a wavy grain, because the saw has cut sometimes to the inside, sometimes to the outside, and sometimes right through a single ring.

The same log sawed through the center will have a much straighter grain.

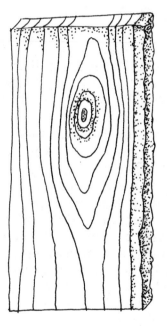

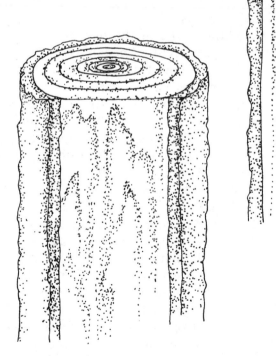

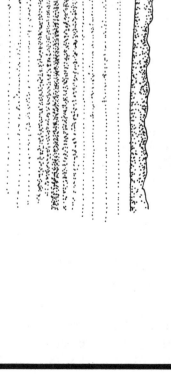

Those cells that are squeezed farther inside, as more cells are added change their function. They are still hollow vessels, but now they are called sapwood. They transport water, minerals, and stored sugars in the opposite direction, from the roots upward through the tree. Minerals absorbed by the sapwood cells gradually harden them or turn them into wood.

The cambium layer continues to expand its girth as it squeezes older cells farther outward and farther inward. The trunk or branch thereby gets thicker, and so does its bark. New sapwood cells take over the job of upward circulation as older ones accumulate more and more minerals. Eventually, the oldest sapwood cells, those in the center of the tree, become clogged and stiff with minerals. Once cambium, then young sapwood, these cells in their old age have become heartwood. Nothing circulates through heartwood and all its cells are dead.

Getting taller from the top

A tree grows in height or grows branches longer only at its tips. That's true of any houseplant, too. Measure a stem up to one of its leaves. No matter how much longer the branch grows, the measurement up to that leaf will stay the same. All the new growth comes at the branch tip, where new leaf buds form. Buds can form at many places along a stem, however, to add new side branches as well as tip growth. Looking at planks in furniture or split logs, you can see how big around a tree was at the time it sprouted a new bud along its trunk. The grain of the plank, made up of layers formed by the cambium, begin to be distorted just at the place where the bud first formed. The direction of the vessels of sapwood conform to the shape of the new branch so that circulation can serve it as well. The distorted shape of the grain is a knot.

When a very straight tree is also cut very straight, the grain is straight too. You can usually find such a straight grain in portions of oak flooring or oak furniture. Other trees, like maples, may have more uneven trunk shapes and wavier grains. Or they may have been cut at a slight slant, or the cut may have gone through an area of distortion close to where a branch emerged. Examine furniture and flooring, and try to imagine why the grain looks the way it does.

Plant surgeon

To become a surgeon, you must first understand the anatomy of your patient, how the various parts of the body depend on each other, and how the basic life processes are performed. Luckily, this is much easier with plants than with animals, and you can become a plant surgeon after only 10 minutes of higher education.

Inside view

The material from which a plant makes its food is gathered by the plant's roots. The large roots on plants anchor them in the ground; it is the tiny root hairs that grow from the smaller roots that do all the work of gathering. The root hairs' job is to absorb water from the soil, along with many chemicals that are dissolved in it (houseplant fertilizers contain nitrogen, phosphorus, and potassium, the three main soil nutrients plants need). This water-plus-chemicals circulates from the root hairs, along the rootlets up the roots, and into circulation tubes that run up the stem of the plant to the leaves.

Leaves are like laboratories in which chemicals are mixed

Plant works

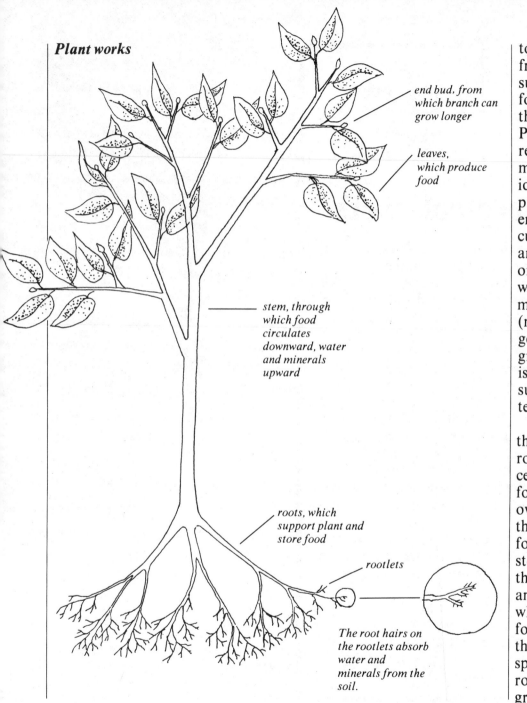

end bud, from which branch can grow longer

leaves, which produce food

stem, through which food circulates downward, water and minerals upward

roots, which support plant and store food

rootlets

The root hairs on the rootlets absorb water and minerals from the soil.

together, "cooked" with energy from light, and recombined into substances the plant can use as food. Leaves have holes in them through which they breathe air. Plant cells, like animal cells require oxygen, but unlike animals, plants use the carbon dioxide in air for manufacturing purposes. Light provides the energy to force the smaller molecules of carbon dioxide, water, and soil chemicals to attach to one another to make food. The waste product of the leaves' manufacturing process is oxygen (nearly 100 percent of the oxygen animals require is made by green plants). The resulting food is much the same as your food: sugars, starches, fats, and proteins.

Food circulates downward through leaves and stems and roots, nourishing all the plant's cells. The roots hold on to more food than they require for their own nourishment, storing it, in the form of starches and sugars, for future plant needs. When the stored food is needed, it enters the circulatory tubes and makes another round trip to help out where it is needed. Maple syrup, for instance, is boiled down from the sweet sap that rises, each spring, from the sugar maple's roots to provide food for the growing buds.

roots sprouting from a coleus stem kept in water

New plants from plant parts

Any body cell in any plant or animal contains, in its nucleus, a complete set of chemical instructions for making every single kind of cell in that plant or animal, and every single cell product, or even an entire new and identical individual. A skin cell has the instructions to make bone, blood, hair, and hormones as well as skin. A leaf cell has the instructions for making roots, stems, starch, and chlorophyll.

Where it is possible to cause a single cell from an individual to actually produce an identical individual, the process is called cloning. But cloning is seldom actually possible. For reasons not yet understood, adult cells of most living organisms — though they still contain a full set of instructions — can only be caused to make copies of their own type of cell.

Many plants, however, are able to replace missing portions of themselves. Cut a branch off a coleus, put it in water, moist sand, or a soil substitute such as vermiculite; certain stem cells will produce roots. Within a month, the cutting can be potted. A jade plant can produce a whole plant from a single leaf. Break a leaf off where it joins the stem. Lay it on potting soil. Keep the soil moist. Roots will sprout downward from the base of the leaf while tiny leaflets sprout upward. Heap a litttle soil around the plantlet and soon you will have another jade plant.

Both a jade plant grown from a leaf and a coleus plant grown from a stem are like clones — identical to the parent plant and produced without benefit of sex.

These jade leaves had dropped from the plant itself onto the soil below. Each leaf sprouted a plantlet within two weeks.

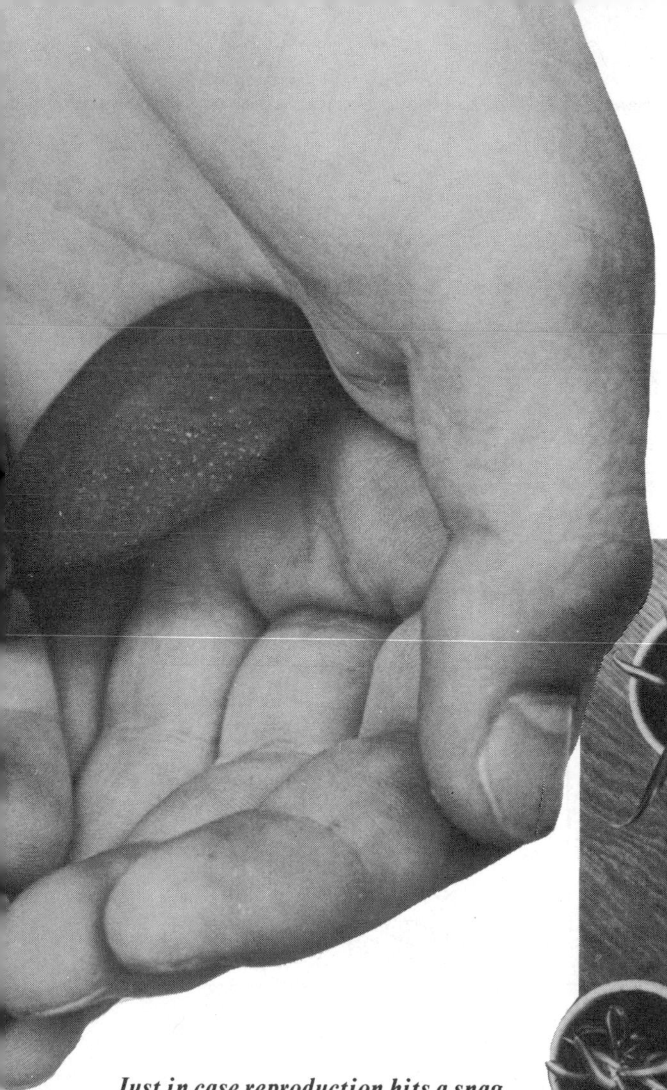

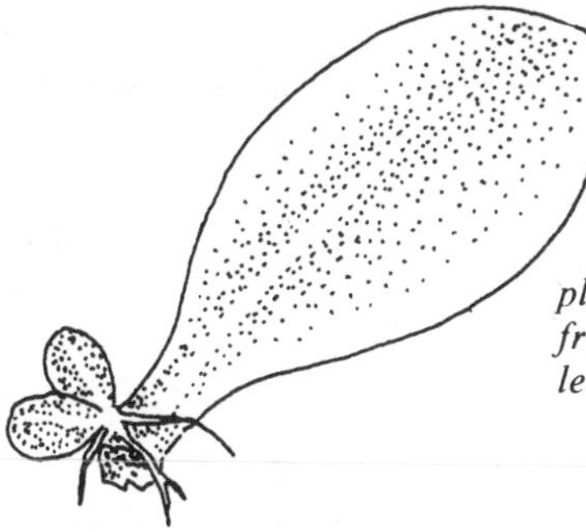

*plantlet sprouting
from a jade plant
leaf laid on soil.*

Just in case reproduction hits a snag,
some plants have devised nonsexual
ways to reproduce. A spider plant sends
out long arching stems that blossom at
their tips. But as the blossoms age, the
end of each stem produces leaves and
roots. Wherever they come into contact
with soil, a new plant grows. Eventually,
the "umbilical cord" stem between
parent and plantlet dries up and breaks
— the baby is on its own.

Casebook: Benjamina fig

The first patient treated was a Benjamina fig. This patient was admitted in terminal condition. A glance took in the fact that it had no leaves — they were on the floor beneath it. A closer look revealed aerial roots — roots that sprout above soil level and reach out in an attempt to find more soil for nutriments. Digging into the pot showed why: solid root, practically no soil, and no sign of healthy new white rootlets with their crucial root hairs.

Treatment had to be drastic: the surgeon prepared for surgery by sharpening a butcher knife, and laying out, in preparation, small pruning shears; a new, larger pot; a ten-pound bag of potting soil; a can of water; and a stack of newspapers. Surgery is a messy job; that's what the newspapers were for.

After paper was spread on the floor, the next step was to cut off aerial roots with the shears. Then the tree was removed from its pot to the paper, and four inches of old, discouraged root from beneath and all around the root ball was sliced away with the knife. The remaining roots, with their store of food, could then put their energy into the production of new, working

A bean maze

A lot of work will be saved if you start with a divided carton, that has a cover. Cut holes in the dividers to make the carton into a maze. The hole in the outside should face sunlight. Place the bean, planted in a small pot of soil, in a corner farthest from the outside hole.

Smart beans

Can a bean learn to get through a maze when light is its reward? Try it for yourself. Get a divided carton, with its top still attached, from the grocery or liquor store. Cut a two-inch hole in one side of the carton.

Plant three or four dried beans in a small pot and place it in a corner of the maze as far from the hole as you can. Over the next few weeks, keep the carton tightly covered so no light comes through the lid. You may have to seal it with freezer tape to keep light out. Put the box itself so that the hole faces a sunny window. Open the box every few days to water the beans. The illustration shows what will happen.

Plant stems always grow toward light; roots always grow toward the source of gravity. These are not the only things plants "know" how to do. If a carrot root hits against a stone, it will grow to one side until it is past the obstacle, and then continue downward. (Look for the crooked carrots that result; they are hard to find these days because farmers sift stones from the soil for carrot beds — but they miss a stone once in a while.) Some plant buds have heat sensors that test the air temperature, telling the plant when it is safe to open into leaf. A sensitive mimosa plant, sold as young plants and as seeds in plant stores, can feel even the slightest touch. If you brush your finger against a leaf, it folds up and pulls away from you.

To see if beans know which way is up, try this: crumple wet paper towels and stuff them in a jar. Place the dried beans between the paper and the glass. Keep the paper moist as the beans sprout and grow over the next week. When the roots and sprouts are over an inch long and the sprouts begin to show leaves on top, turn the jar upside down. Watch what happens over the next few days.

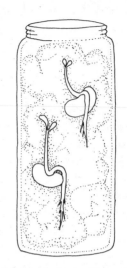

1. Sprout beans between jar wall and crumpled moist paper towels until roots are an inch or longer.

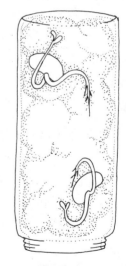

2. Turn jar upside down to see how both shoots and roots turn so they are still growing in the right directions.

rootlets. Before the roots could be harmed by drying out, the tree was replanted in the new pot, with nourishing new soil, and flooded with water.

But now the patient's life was endangered by this radical surgery. With stored food being used by the roots to grow new rootlets, there would not be enough food to feed the cells in the trunk and branches — and there were no leaves to manufacture more food either. To re-establish the balance between the two systems, the surgeon went to work on the rest of the tree. All small, crowded branches were pruned off with the shears. Then the ends of all remaining branches were cut back a full ten inches. Observers were close to tears. The patient in its mutilated state was given up for dead.

Within two weeks, the Benjamina fig was covered with tiny new leaves. Within a month, branch tips had grown several inches. The well-fed leaves, no longer crowding one another, could breathe freely, and bathe in sunlight. The patient was better than new.

Casebook: jade plant

The next patient was a jade plant, hospitalized for a malady

An adult will have to handle the job of trimming old roots off a plant with this large knife, as the roots are tough to cut through.

called "reaching." The symptoms were long, weak branches that drooped, and leaves that were widely spaced instead of thickly covering the plant. Like the appearance of aerial roots on the fig tree, reaching branches is a sign of a deficiency disease — with roots; a deficiency of soil; with branches; a deficiency of light. Just as roots may grow in an unusual manner in an attempt to find more soil, branches grow long and spindly in an attempt to reach more light. Meanwhile, without sufficient light, there is too little energy for food manufacture, a food shortage develops, and the plant can no longer support the growth of many leaves.

Long-term therapy was obvious: move the plant to stronger light, in this case from a north window to one facing southwest. Surgery was helpful, too. The long, weak branches were cut back considerably. Here the doctor used another fact of plant physiology: all along the stems and branches of most plants are small areas from which leaf buds can develop. But cells in the buds and youngest

Ginger pot

The ginger lying to the right in the pot has just been planted. The other one was planted several months earlier.

This is a ginger pot, from which succulent, fresh ginger root can be harvested. It is wonderful to use chopped up in Chinese and Indian dishes, and in barbecue sauce. To start a ginger pot, place a piece of fresh ginger root (sold in some supermarkets and any Oriental grocery store) flat and only half buried in a 12-inch pot of soil. Use any commercial potting soil. Keep the soil moist and the pot in good light, but not direct sun.

This flat portion of root will sprout thin roots on its buried, bottom surface, and green shoots on its exposed, top surface. The shoots will develop into five-foot high stems with ginger-fragrant, grasslike leaves. After a few months, the root will begin to grow new plump, bulbous portions, as well as thinner feeder roots. These plump portions are what you dig up and cut off for flavoring. Slice off the tender, pale new portions on the outside of the original section you planted. Wash them, chop them up and use them in any recipe that calls for ginger.

leaves at the tips of each branch produce a hormone that prevents the formation of leaf buds below the tip. Under normal conditions, this is helpful because the hormone encourages the plant to grow taller and wider, and thus spread itself to the light. In this case, however, cutting off the source of that hormone allowed bud areas all along the branches to develop. In two weeks, with the help of food stored in its roots, the patient had sprouted a numerous crop of young leaves along every branch. A daily dose of strong light and the hormone adjustment prevented permanent disfigurement, and restored the jade plant to luxuriant health.

How to plant a seed

To plant a seed, you need a container, soil, and seed. The container can be a can, jar, paper cup, or even an egg carton. The best soil to use is the kind you buy in hardware stores, plant stores, or in the supermarket. Lay newspaper out where you are working. Fill the container to the top with soil. Then mois-

Once this seed has been planted, the pot should be moved to a warm, sunny spot, and kept moist.

look nothing like the plant's typical leaves. From between these, the first true leaves will grow. When a seedling has grown several pairs of true leaves, it is old enough to be transplanted.

How to transplant a seedling

First, decide what containers to use for each plant to grow in permanently. Clay or plastic pots have a hole in the bottom so water can run through, preventing the soil from getting soggy, and the plant roots from rotting. Cover this bottom hole with a stone or piece of broken pottery so dirt won't come out along with the water. You will need a saucer under this kind of pot, too. If you want to use some other container, fill one or two inches of the bottom with gravel. This will help drain water away from the roots.

Prepare as many pots as you have seedlings to transplant. A container or pot four inches across the top and at least that high is a good starting size. When your plant grows too large for it, you can always move it to a larger container. Fill the container with soil, moisten the soil, and press it down somewhat. With your finger, push a deep hole into the soil in the middle of the pot.

ten the soil with water and press it down farther into the pot. To make a hole for the seed, just stick your finger into the soil.

How deep a seed should be planted has to do with the size of the seed. Tiny seeds like radishes, grass, and parsley don't need holes at all. You can place them on the surface of the soil, and then, scratch the surface to cover them just slightly. A large seed the size of an acorn can be planted three or four inches deep; medium-sized seeds like peas and beans can be planted about an inch deep.

You also have to figure out how close together to plant seeds. Grass seeds can be sprinkled close together, but most plants won't grow well if they are crowded. The best rule is to place seeds an inch apart from one another. This may still be too crowded, but at least you will be able to dig out each plant separately when they grow big enough to be moved to larger, individual containers.

Keep the container of planted seeds in a warm, sunny place, and keep the soil moist all the time. Some seeds, like beans and grass, may sprout in a few days. Others, like lemon and grapefruit seeds, may take weeks or even months to sprout. The sprouts will have two round or oval leaves at the top, which

Be sure you handle each seedling gently during the transplanting process.

When the pots are all ready, remove the seedlings from the container in which they have been growing. You'll hurt them if you try to pluck them out, and even handling their stems can crush them. If they are in a paper container, you can rip the sides and just let the soil fall away from the seedlings. If they are in a can or jar, loosen the soil around the edges with a knife. Then tap the rim of the container against the surface where you are working until the soil and seedlings fall out.

One by one, gently pick up each seedling, put it into the hole you have prepared, and push the surrounding soil against it snugly. If you have many seedlings to transplant, place them together in a plastic sandwich bag moistened inside with a few drops of water, or fold a wet paper towel around them, to be sure the roots don't dry out.

During the first day, the seedlings may droop. Add more water to the soil to help them along. By the next morning, they should look sprightly again. From now on, you have only to water them and keep them in a sunny place. Water them as the soil begins to dry out. You can fertilize them with houseplant fertilizer.

Growing very strange seeds

Besides corn kernels, there are dozens of seeds around your home that might (or might not) grow into interesting plants. Try grapefruit or lemon seeds, and apple pits. Try dill, caraway, whole mustard, and poppy seeds. Mustard, astonishingly, sprouts in 24 hours. Dried beans practically never fail. Don't neglect what the dog brings in: those burrs you hate removing are seeds too. The ends of timothy and other grasses are seed heads — plant them after they are dry and falling from the head. For a real mystery crop, gather woodland soil in the fall. Pour it in a pot, keep it watered and in a sunny window. Seeds you never knew were there will sprout — even maples and oak trees. (Use a field guide to identify your crop when the seedlings have grown a few leaves.) And if you get a Christmas wreath with pine cones on it, peek inside the cones' flaps — there might be more strange seeds to plant.

Popcorn kernels explode with enough force to send them several feet into the air. The mess you would have to clean up, however, makes this experiment not worth the effort, unless you're popping corn on a cookout.

Kernels to pop

Popcorn is not a modern novelty; it is, in fact, the original corn from which the sweet corn-on-the-cob you eat today was developed long ago. Once, all corn popped. Heat causes the starchy insides of the partially dried kernel to expand, pressing outward against the tough kernel wall. When the pressure is high enough, the wall splits, and the pressurized starch expands suddenly with a popping noise. Puffed breakfast cereals like wheat and rice are basically formed the same way.

Grow your own

You can plant kernels of popcorn yourself, grow them to mature plants, and harvest ears of genuine popcorn. Buy popcorn from a garden store or mail-order catalogue like Burpee. Popcorn kernels you buy in a grocery store won't produce good popcorn. Plant kernels of popcorn four inches deep in a 12-inch pottery pot. Keep the soil moist and fertilize with houseplant fertilizer once a week. You should have three corn plants in each pot, but plant more seeds than that in case some don't sprout. If you end up with too many plants, pull out the ones that are crowded so the remaining three are evenly spaced in the pot.

Keep the plants where they get sun for at least six hours a day. All day is better, but not possible unless it is summertime and you have a balcony or yard, or you live outside the city.

Within two or three months, the corn plants will be four or five feet high, and the tops of the plants will begin to grow tassels. The tassels of a corn plant are the male portion, and make pollen. Below the tassel, slim ears will be developing, each one topped with "silk." Each strand of corn silk is actually a tube

Growing popcorn

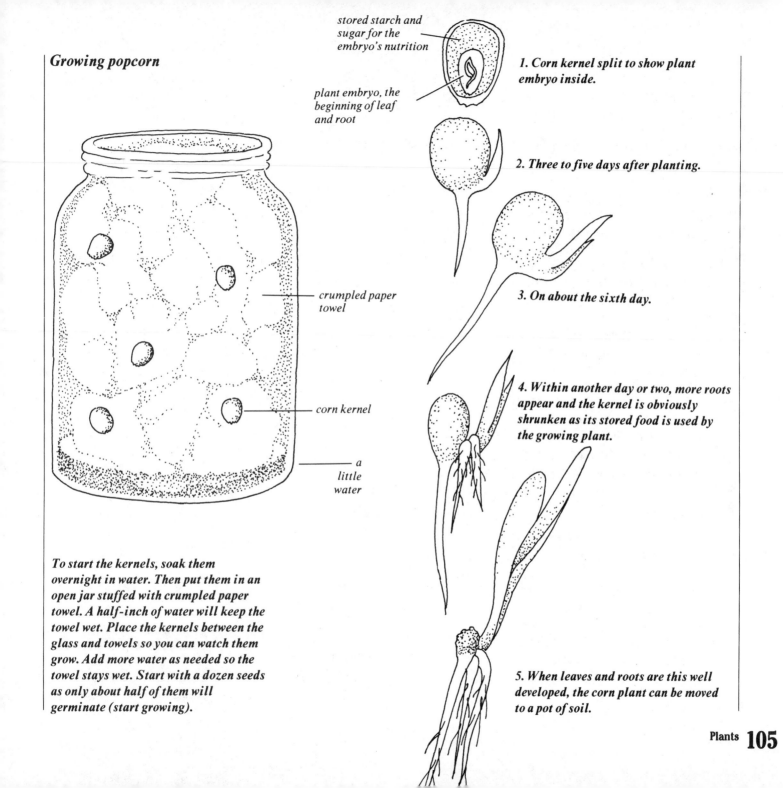

stored starch and sugar for the embryo's nutrition

plant embryo, the beginning of leaf and root

1. Corn kernel split to show plant embryo inside.

2. Three to five days after planting.

crumpled paper towel

corn kernel

a little water

3. On about the sixth day.

4. Within another day or two, more roots appear and the kernel is obviously shrunken as its stored food is used by the growing plant.

To start the kernels, soak them overnight in water. Then put them in an open jar stuffed with crumpled paper towel. A half-inch of water will keep the towel wet. Place the kernels between the glass and towels so you can watch them grow. Add more water as needed so the towel stays wet. Start with a dozen seeds as only about half of them will germinate (start growing).

5. When leaves and roots are this well developed, the corn plant can be moved to a pot of soil.

that leads down into the ear, ending at an ovum, or kernel.

The kernels won't grow unless each is fertilized by a grain of pollen. In a field of corn, wind blows the pollen into the air; it settles on the sticky, hairy corn silk, grows down through the tube and fertilizes the seed. But the pollen in a single plant's tassel usually ripens before the ova on that particular plant are ready to be fertilized, so the pollen from a plant ordinarily fertilizes the ova of a different plant.

This system creates problems for someone growing only a few plants in a pot. First of all, if there is wind, it would blow the pollen away; and second, all the pollen may be ripe before any of the kernels are ready for fertilization. You have to step in and see to the whole business yourself.

Fertilizing corn

Check the tassels for ripeness frequently. One morning, you will see that anthers have formed on the tassels; perhaps they are already beginning to produce a powdery crop of pollen which will fall when you tap an anther. Tie a plastic bag around the whole tassel, leave it on several hours, then shake the tassel inside its bag to harvest the pol-

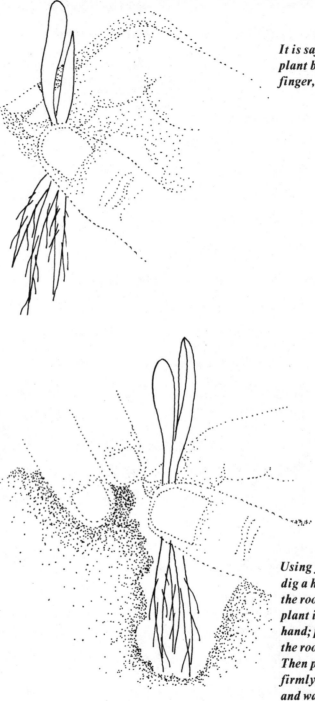

It is safe to hold the baby plant between the thumb and finger, like this.

Using your fingers dig a hole as deep as the roots are long. Hold the plant in the hole with one hand; push the soil around the roots with the other. Then press the soil down firmly all around the plant, and water it right away.

You can plant three plants in a 12-inch pot.

len. Remove the bag and spill the pollen carefully onto paper towels. Leave it to dry overnight, then put it into a jar, close the lid tightly, and store the pollen in the refrigerator.

Now, start checking the corn silk every day. When the kernels are ready to be fertilized, the silk will begin to droop at the top; if you look carefully, you will see that each strand has sprouted tiny hairs. These hairs trap the pollen.

Take the stored pollen from the refrigerator. Use a soft artists' brush to pick up pollen and brush it over the strands of silk. The kernel attached to any strand you miss will fail to develop. You have probably seen unfertilized kernels — small and pearly — among the fat, yellow, fertilized ones on ordinary cobs of sweet corn.

Harvesting time

Proof that your artificial fertilization has worked will be the swelling of the cobs over the next few weeks as the kernels inside them fill with starch. But even when the cobs feel quite plump, you must still wait before you harvest them. Continue to water and feed the plants. Eventually, they will begin to look sick, and finally turn to a tan color and begin to dry out. Stop watering, but wait some more. When the plant looks quite dead, partially husk (pull the covering leaves from) one cob to check the kernels. If the kernels are very hard and dry, strip the cobs from the stalk, husk them, and dispose of the rest of the corn plant.

Leave the cobs out to dry even more. In a few weeks, the kernels will begin to feel loose in their sockets. Then you can scrape them off the cob with a table knife.

Store the dry popcorn kernels in a tightly sealed jar until you want to pop them.

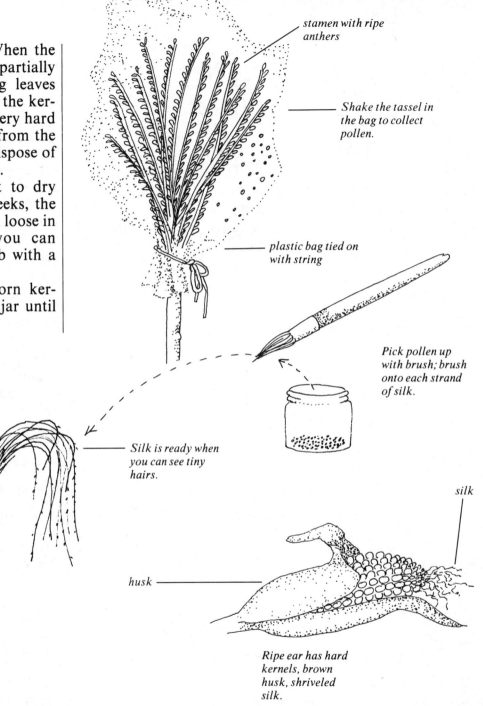

stamen with ripe anthers

Shake the tassel in the bag to collect pollen.

plastic bag tied on with string

Pick pollen up with brush; brush onto each strand of silk.

Silk is ready when you can see tiny hairs.

silk

husk

Ripe ear has hard kernels, brown husk, shriveled silk.

Animals

Muscle meat

The animals we are most intimately associated with are the animals we eat.

Most of the meat we eat is muscles. You can tell meat is muscle by picking at it with your fork to see that it is made of separate muscle fibers. Along with the muscle, you are likely to swallow some fat, and some connective tissue that holds one layer of muscle to another. When there is a thick layer of fat along the edge of a piece of meat — a steak or a chop for instance — you can bet that slice of muscle was taken from just below the skin. You can feel your own fat layer between skin and muscle by pinching yourself. (If the fold of skin between your pinching fingers is more than ¾ of an inch thick, you may have too much fat.)

Connective tissue is the gristle that is sometimes so tough you have to spit it out. Wherever you find connective tissue in a piece of meat, it marks the boundary between one muscle and another (and sometimes, like the gristle at the end of the meat on a chicken leg, the connection between muscle and bone). Look at the direction in which muscle fibers run to each side of a streak or layer of gristle. Usually they will run in somewhat different directions because the two muscles pull in different directions.

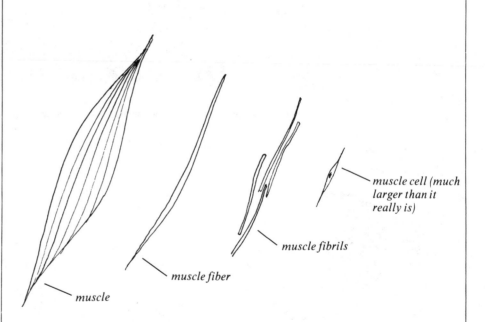

muscle

muscle fiber

muscle fibrils

muscle cell (much larger than it really is)

Each muscle is a bundle of muscle fibers. Each fiber is a group of smaller fibrils. And each fibril is formed from long, thin muscle cells. Muscle cells contract to shorten themselves, relax to lengthen themselves. When thousands of them shorten at the same time, the whole muscle contracts.

Butchering a lamb
This series of photos shows how a butcher views lamb. The whole lamb carcass arrives at the shop ready for butchering into familiar cuts.

The butcher first removes the kidneys from next to the backbone, then the diaphragm that separates abdomen from chest cavity. All the other organs were removed previously.

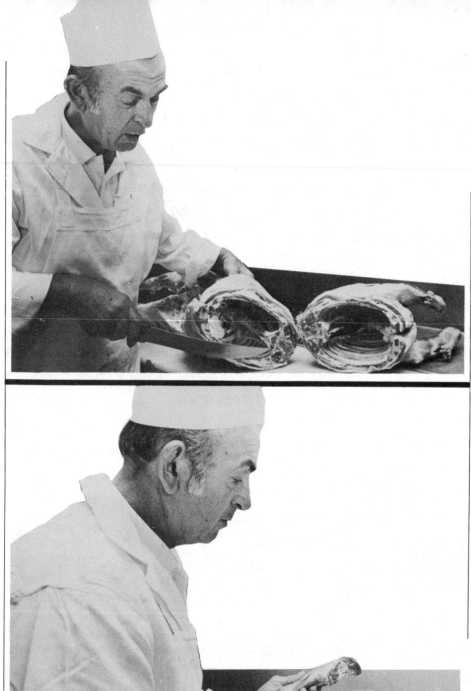

The lamb is separated into front and rear halves. The tip of the knife points here to the loin chops, to each side of the backbone. In the front portion, the same muscles will be rib chops, because each contains a rib.

A butcher's view of lamb

Cooks and butchers have given cuts of meat all sorts of fanciful names, sometimes after a recipe (London broil), sometimes after the way the cut looks (crown roast), and only rarely after the portion of the animal from which it came (neck). That makes it hard to learn much anatomy from a casual study of the meat case in the supermarket. The task is made harder by the way muscles are disguised by sawing through identifying bones, trimming telltale fat and gristle, chopping, rolling, and tying what was once a whole muscle specimen. These photographs show a whole lamb being cut into meats like chops, leg, and shank.

Before the chops are cut, however, the front legs are removed to be sold as lamb shanks...

. . . and the rear legs as leg of lamb.

The long ends of ribs are sawed from the front half. On a pig, these short rib ends are spare ribs.

These are the loin chops from the rear end after it has been split down the center of the backbone with a saw. Along the groove of the bone, you can see the white spinal cord itself. The spinal cord is a nerve. The flap of meat that curls over the loin chop — its "tail" — is belly muscle.

hind leg

foreleg or shank

rib ends

loin chops

rib chops

A butcher's view of you

This photograph shows where such meats as chops, spare-ribs, bacon, and ham would come from on you.

Your own anatomy is not so different from a lamb, cow or pig. Here you can see the same cuts of meat outlined and labelled.

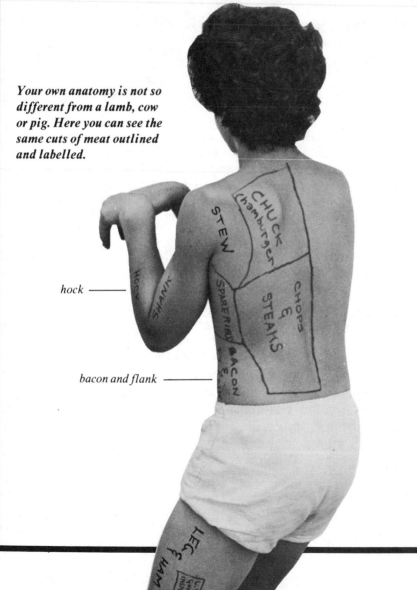

hock ——

bacon and flank ——————

What happened to the hamburger?

In a sense, it is fair to say that the hamburger you eat for dinner never really gets inside your body. You, like an earthworm, are basically a tube. Your body is everything that lies between the inside of the tube — the inside surface of your digestive system — and the outside, your skin. The earthworm ingests (takes in) dirt at the front end and expels dirt at the rear end. Your hamburger makes the same trip.

Unusable food

What has happened in between? There is almost nothing in a hamburger that your body can use without changing it drastically. The proteins in the meat may be just like our own, but they are much too large to go through the wall of your intestine, join your bloodstream, and slip inside your body cells. The fat molecules in the meat, the starch molecules in the roll, and most of the sugar molecules in the ketchup are just too large to squeeze through. The mole-

A hamburger on a roll with ketchup is a good choice for a meal before a test. The sugars in the roll and ketchup are instant energy foods because your body can use them either whole or, by a simple cut, as smaller sugars. Your brain needs more sugar than any other part of your body. The starches in the roll last longer — they can be broken down into sugars as required. And if your cells suffer damage as a result of thinking hard, the hamburger has the proteins they need for self-repair.

cules you eat have to be cut up into tiny pieces — small enough to slip through the wall of your intestines into your bloodstream. That is what digestion is: molecule cutting.

By the time you have chomped your way through a hamburger, you feel you have finished eating. But not a single body cell has yet been fed. Chewing, swallowing, and filling up your stomach is only the beginning of a process that takes about four hours from the time you eat your dinner until your cells get their food (they get their sugar sooner — about two hours; and their fats even later, up to eight hours after your meal.)

Digestion begins

Digestion begins in your mouth. The smell of hamburger makes your mouth water. The saliva you produce is the first of the chemicals (called enzymes) that will cut apart molecules. Saliva cuts up starch molecules in the hamburger roll. When you chew that first bite, you are exposing more surface area to the action of saliva. When you swallow, the contents of your mouth are pushed down to your stomach, where strong muscles mash the food even smaller. Lots of water is added, too, and acid, and more enzymes that specialize in cutting apart the protein molecules in the meat.

By the time you have finished your meal, the hamburger is sloshing around, being mixed with water, acid, and enzymes. This liquid mixture is spurted bit by bit from the stomach into the small intestine: your stomach isn't completely emptied of sugars, starches, and proteins for hours; fats may stay in your stomach for over six hours before they are emptied into the intestine. All sorts of enzymes are poured into the small intestine each doing its own different slicing job on fat or sugar or protein or starch molecules. And now, for the first time, what your cells recognize as food — no longer a hamburger at all — is actually beginning to enter your body.

Lots of guts

The small intestine is about 12 feet long, but its length is nothing compared to its surface area. The surface is made of zillions of small bumps; if you were able to spread it out smoothly, it would cover an area 10 times the area of your skin. All along this surface are the tiny ends of blood vessels. Whenever a molecule is cut up small enough, it is able to slip between the cells that line the intestine, and into a blood vessel. The bloodstream delivers the small molecules to cells all through your body, even inside your bones.

But now what? These tiny molecules are not the proteins of which our cells are made, or human fat, or bone, or muscle, or nerve. Just as enzymes first cut your meal into pieces small enough to slip between your cells and into your bloodstream, now other enzymes reassemble the pieces into the bigger molecules

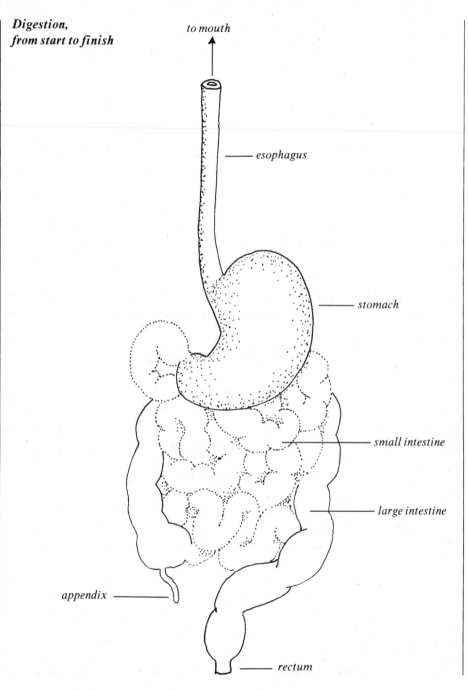

Digestion, from start to finish

to mouth

esophagus

stomach

small intestine

large intestine

appendix

rectum

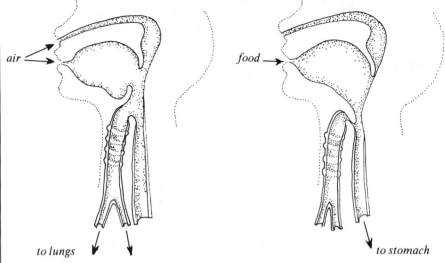

When you breathe, flaps at the back of your mouth and in your throat are open so air can go through your nose and mouth, and into your lungs.

When you swallow, both flaps are forced shut so food doesn't get up your nose or down your windpipe.

Tracking the asparagus

Eat some asparagus for dinner one night. Then sniff your urine the following morning. You'll smell dinner all over again. The molecules responsible for the smell of asparagus are absorbed through the walls of the small intestine, but they are not used by your body's cells. They simply circulate along with the blood until they pass through the kidneys, where they are filtered out and concentrated in urine. The length of time between eating asparagus and smelling the molecules all over again gives you some idea of how speedy the system is. (Remember to subtract the six hours it may have taken to finish digesting the asparagus.)

You can speed up the system even more by drinking cola, tea, or coffee. All three contain caffeine, a stimulant that speeds up body processes. Two cups of strong coffee in the morning may cause kidneys to secrete enough urine to make your bladder uncomfortable within an hour.

of which human cells are made. In many cases, the components of the original hamburger may be reassembled into exactly the same molecules they were when you swallowed them.

Eating the leftovers

But there is plenty of hamburger that enzymes can't cut apart, or don't have time enough to cut apart. Those molecules that remain too large to slip through the intestinal walls continue on down into your large intestine, or bowel. There, they become dinner for a host of bacteria who make their home inside of humans. They, like you, secrete enzymes that cut up molecules, absorb them as they become small enough, and leave the leftovers which we call feces. Feces are portions of hamburger that neither human being nor bacteria have digested — plus a lot of bacterial corpses. Ten to 50 percent of feces is dead bacteria (some live bacteria as well). There are more bacteria in your body than there are people on earth. The next time your parents accuse you of eating enough to feed an army, you can agree with them — an army of bacteria, anyway.

The costliest urine in the world

Unless you subsist entirely on ice cream and potato chips, it is very doubtful that you need any extra vitamins or minerals. Grains, fruits, vegetables, meat, and dairy products have in them everything your body needs. And they don't have to be "balanced" for every meal — you could eat beans on Friday, hamburger Saturday, cheese Sunday, and salad Monday without depriving yourself.

There are only three groups of people who need vitamin and mineral supplements: those whom a doctor has diagnosed as deficient in some nutrient; young children who live in areas where drinking water is not supplied with fluoride; and infants whose only food is breast milk (which lacks vitamin D). Most extra vitamins and minerals, the ones you pay for at the drugstore and don't really need, have only one place to go: through the kidneys and out. Vitamin-conscious Americans are estimated to produce the most expensive urine in the world.

Tooth cast

You can make a cast of your teeth, similar to those made by orthodontists (dentists who specialize in straightening teeth with braces), by first making a mold of them with grease clay (plasticene or plastilene), then casting the mold in plaster. If you have braces, however, don't do this experiment. The clay would stick to your wires.

Making the mold

An artist's-quality clay, such as the pale pink kind made by Caran D'Ache, is easiest to use. Knead it between your fingers to soften it before beginning. Then, shape a piece of clay that fits inside your mouth and is about ¾ of an inch thick. Put it into your mouth only as far back as

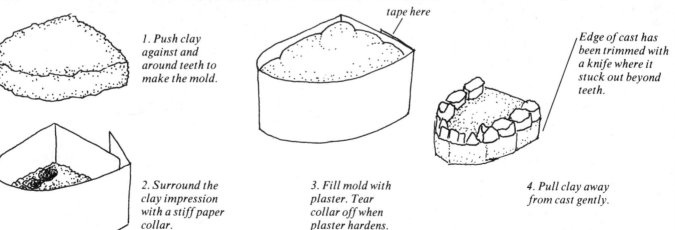

tape here

1. Push clay against and around teeth to make the mold.

2. Surround the clay impression with a stiff paper collar.

3. Fill mold with plaster. Tear collar off when plaster hardens.

4. Pull clay away from cast gently.

Edge of cast has been trimmed with a knife where it stuck out beyond teeth.

feels comfortable — you don't have to get all your molars (rear grinding teeth) in. Press the clay up against the roof of your mouth and against the inner and bottom surfaces of your upper teeth. Then work the clay up the sides of your teeth to above where they meet the gum all around. Let the mold drop down and put it aside while you mold your bottom teeth. Hold your tongue as much out of the way as you can while you mold the bottom. If any clay sticks to your teeth after the mold is removed, brush them.

To cast the two molds, each has to have a paper collar fitted around it to hold the wet plaster. With a paring or pocket knife, trim the molds to the shape shown here. Ask an adult for help with this. Cut strips of paper two inches high and warp one around each mold. Tape the collar together, and also wrap tape from side to side along the bottom of the molds so plaster won't leak out.

Pouring the plaster

Mix a cup of plaster with a half cup of water according to package directions. Put the molds on a meat tray or foil in case they do leak. With a small brush, paint plaster into the tooth impressions, and then blow on this layer to be sure plaster gets into all the points and crevices. (If you just dump plaster into the mold, the cast will have missing portions, as though you had a mouthful of broken teeth.) Fill the mold with plaster now, about 1 ½ inches deep. Bump the casts up and down a couple of times to dislodge any bubbles. Wash the container you mixed the plaster in right away.

Let the casts sit now for at least six hours so the plaster can harden. Take off the collars and pull the clay away gently. You may want to neaten up the finished cast by paring away uneven plaster edges.

The finished cast will show you have several kinds of teeth. Front teeth, called incisors, are shaped like chisel blades. Four top and four bottom incisors overlap, like a pair of scissors, when you bite. To each side of them are pointed teeth called canines, the same pointed teeth that are dangerously longer in dogs. Behind the canines are bicuspeds — two-pointed teeth. Put the top and bottom casts together to see how the points of the top bicuspids fit into the valleys of those below. Even farther back are flatter teeth called molars.

As you eat a dinner, try to be aware of how you use your

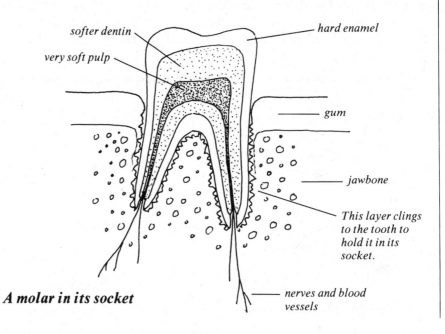

softer dentin

hard enamel

very soft pulp

gum

jawbone

This layer clings to the tooth to hold it in its socket.

nerves and blood vessels

A molar in its socket

A finished tooth cast of the upper jaw.

various teeth. You snip off a bite of carrot stick with your incisors, but then move it to the molars to grind it small enough to swallow. When you yank meat off a chicken leg, you're more likely to sink a canine tooth in to tear the flesh plus a couple of bicuspids to get a firm grip.

Because teeth are specialized for eating different foods, scientists can tell what an animal eats by examining its teeth. Dogs have huge canines for tearing meat. Look in your dog's mouth to see if you can find any flat, grinding molars. If you don't find any, you can bet dogs don't live on grains. Cows, on the other hand, have no need for pointed fangs. Their flat teeth are made for grinding grass.

More potatoes, please

If you were trying to lose weight, and you had your choice of eating a five-ounce potato or a five-ounce steak for dinner, which would you choose? The steak, of course. But you would be acting out of prejudice, and you would be wrong. A five-ounce potato contains 110 calories; a five-ounce steak contains 500. In our country, where the average person eats twice as much protein as his body needs, and starchy foods are mistakenly accused of being "empty calories," the potato is sadly misunderstood.

For an adult, a baked potato, eaten skin and all, is nearly a sufficient diet all by itself. A potato is loaded with vitamins and minerals: among others, it offers iron, thiamin, niacin, phosphorus, and a full 20 percent of your daily need of vitamin C. The particular starches potatoes contain can be used quickly and completely by your body for its energy needs; potatoes contain necessary proteins, too.

If you can resist sour cream or butter, your kidneys won't be troubled with poisonous waste products from fat digestion. (Fat really is empty calories — we can't use it efficiently at all.) Your intestines will appreciate the fiber in the potato skin, and your stomach will appreciate the bulk of the potato flesh. So next time, don't hesitate — eat all the plain potatoes you want.

The gelatin myth

Guitar teachers often ask their students to drink gelatin to strengthen their fingernails. Hairdressers claim it makes hair glossy. It's pure protein, such people argue, so it must be good for you.

The gelatin you buy in the supermarket, and that is used to gel everything from gumdrops to jellied soups, is made from an animal substance called collagen. You have come across collagen in the form of translucent gristle in meat. Collagen is what makes bone and cartilage tough and somewhat elastic.

Gelatin is definitely a protein and humans definitely require protein to strengthen their hair and nails. But because the collagen in gelatin is designed to give strength to tissues, it is also made of exceptionally long protein molecules. Remember, any form of protein you eat is unusable as is. The molecules must be cut apart and reassembled to form usable proteins.

Theoretically, there is nothing about this particular protein that our various enzymes could not cut apart into smaller pieces and reassemble into hair and nail protein. The problem is time. Food only remains in our small intestine for, at most, eight hours, usually half that time. Molecules that are easy to take apart are going to be disposed of quickly. But very large molecules, like those in gelatin, take time — more time than we have. Gelatin, protein though it is, is not a very useful human nutrient.

Altogether, your body needs 20 different, shorter protein pieces called amino acids to reassemble into every sort of human protein. We can make 12 of these shorter pieces from the essential eight; so, we could get along on food that contains only those eight absolutely necessary amino acids. We don't need nearly the amount of animal protein we eat, but a diet of vegetables alone won't do either. Plants contain insufficient quantities of amino acids. Vegetarians must get the missing ones from animal foods like eggs, milk, and cheese.

News from the bowels

Vomiting is your digestive system's way of getting rid of food, so it can stop work and rest, when it is irritated. The irritation may be caused by toxic substances excreted by bacteria in spoiled foods, but is more frequently a short-lived virus infection.

Next time you throw up, you will no doubt be fascinated to realize exactly what has happened. Here goes: you have just emptied your digestive tract all the way from the beginning of your large bowel, up 12 feet of intestine into your stomach. It's quite a feat. The awful sensation you have experienced does not come from your stomach. Your stomach's only part in vomiting is to remain absolutely relaxed. It's your intestine that is very active. Instead of squeezing downward, the muscles have reversed direction, and are squeezing everything inside, from the bottom up, back into your stomach. Meanwhile, your belly muscles and your diaphragm give a mighty heave in unison, expelling the mush from your stomach upward — and out.

The unpleasant flavor is the taste of the chemicals your body has added to your dinner. It sure doesn't taste like hamburger anymore.

More bad news

When undigested dinner arrives at the large bowel, it is still a liquid mush. The walls of the bowel are not designed to take in any more molecules; they are designed to remove water molecules. It's an important job. Quarts of water have been added to your dinner to ensure that enzymes mixed well with it. Your body can't afford to lose all that liquid, so the bowel now reabsorbs it, leaving the mush a solid mass of feces.

Knowing this, you can understand what happens when things go wrong in the bowel. If food remains there too long, too much water is removed: feces are dry and hard; you are constipated. When the walls of the bowel are irritated — by a virus, toxins in spoiled food, sharp or rough foods, even by your own nervousness before a test — they don't absorb water well enough. The result is diarrhea.

Intestines can make the silliest noises as they go about their serious work.

Rumblings

The next time someone says their stomach is growling, put your ear to their belly and listen. What you hear is not the stomach at all, but the intestines. Squishy sounds are liquid food being pushed through the intestines by waves of muscular contraction. The action is similar to swallowing — or to pushing toothpaste through the tube. Rumblings are gas, mostly methane, bubbling through the food tube. Some of the gas is swallowed air, but a lot of it is produced by your bacteria. You may notice that certain foods — beans, cabbage, cauliflower, and broccoli — cause more gas than other foods. This is because you don't digest those foods particularly well, so there are more leftovers for your bacteria. The more they get to eat, the more they multiply; and the more bacteria there are, the more gas they produce. If beans are musical fruit, bacteria blow the horn.

Organ meat

Some people think they're yucky, some people love them: organ meats. Whether you eat them or not, these often nutritious foods also give you an idea at how you look inside. Some can be cut apart to show you a little of how they work. This list will tell you what organ meats really are; what you can notice without buying them, by peering into the package or display in the meat department; and what you can see for yourself by cutting into them.

Tongue: just what it says it is — a tongue. The calves' tongue sold in stores is quite large and has bones embedded in the muscle at the base. The muscles in a tongue run in many different directions to allow the tongue enormous flexibility, so the meat appears to have little grain. You can get an idea of how thick tongue skin is by looking at a slice. The paler, slightly rubbery, outside layer is tongue skin; it ends in little projections which give roughness that's helpful for grooming and for moving grass toward the rear of the cow's mouth.

Gizzards: one of the two stomachs of a bird. Digestion takes place in the other stomach. The gizzard is nearly solid muscle, and is used for grinding up hard foods, like grain. You will find a gizzard packaged along with the neck, heart, and liver in a whole chicken. Cut into it to see the muscle fibers.

Tripe: a cow's stomach. The stomachs of grazing animals, like cows, are divided into four compartments. Tripe is a compartment designed as a storage chamber to hold unchewed grass while the cow is grazing. Tripe is white because it is not muscular, like our churning stomach, and doesn't need the enormous blood supply that hard-working muscles require. The folds that give tripe a rippled surface open out as the stomach is stuffed with grass. When the cow has finished grazing, it regurgitates (vomits) the grass, bit by bit, into its mouth to chew it up (that's what cows are doing when they "chew their cud"). Cuds are re-swallowed, and passed along to other stomach compartments and on into the rest of the cow's digestive system.

Natural Casings: the outside membrane of pig or lamb intestines. The very best sausages are stuffed into natural casings rather than synthetic substitutes.

Butterflies

There you are, waiting for the dentist's drill, or dreading the test you didn't study for. And there they are: those butterflies in your stomach. What is that awful feeling? It is the feeling of more or less bloodless guts.

When you are frightened, whether it's because your dentist is about to attack or your wits are about to be tested, your body prepares to think fast, fight back, or run away. A hormone (chemical message) called adrenalin pours into your bloodstream. The message tells your circulatory system to rush blood, laden with its oxygen fuel and nourishing sugars, to your outer muscles so you can hit harder, run faster; and to your brain so that you can react quicker, think better. But the blood has to come from somewhere. A lot of it comes from your intestines. As the blood drains away, the muscles of the gut relax, digestion stops, the production of enzymes — including the saliva in your mouth — halts, and you are left with a dry mouth, a fluttery, sick, empty feeling in your belly.

The reaction isn't going to help you out with the dentist, but it is going to help you out in that test. Mild fear increases your ability to run in a race, act in a play, and use your head in a test. But fear that is more than mild messes you up instead of helping you. If you feel there is no way you can face the drill or get through the test, try this: run, jump, or do any exercise vigorous enough to leave you sweating, panting, and physically worn. You can sometimes trick your body into thinking that you have already taken care of the emergency through that burst of action, and it can now stop flooding you with the adrenalin that summoned the butterflies.

This transparent intestinal membrane is thin, stretchy, strong, and makes a pleasant crackly sound as your teeth pierce it. The size of the sausage gives you a good idea of how thick an actual intestine is. Small sausages are cased in lamb intestinal membrane, larger ones in pig casings. The membrane is peeled off the intestine as a sock is peeled off a foot — all in one long tube. Meat is stuffed into one end until the tube is filled; links are made between sausages by twisting. You can peel the casing off a sausage to get a look at the membrane.

Brains (sometimes called *cervelle,* the French word for brain): the brain of a calf. On the surface, you can see the typical pale coloring and the convoluted texture of the outer layer of the brain. This texture gives the brain much more surface — and therefore many more cells — than would be possible if it were smooth. Dissection will show you nothing of how the brain works. Even your most complicated thinking, imagining, dreaming, feeling, and remembering is done by microscopic cells which give and receive chemical messenger molecules and electrical signals. How chemicals and electrical signals become thoughts and images and feelings, and how these are stored, is almost a total mystery. But here's one clue that is both wonderful and awful to think about: if you teach a planaria (a simple, quarter-inch long worm with only a few "brain" cells) how to run a maze to find its food, then grind it up and feed it to another planaria, the other planaria suddenly knows how to run that maze. Planaria, at least, can eat knowledge.

Kidneys: meat departments sell lamb and veal kidneys. Kidneys are organs that clean poisonous substances from the blood, cut and reshape them into safer chemicals, add water, and dump the mixture through tubes into the bladder. The mixture is called urine, and it is excreted through the urethra when the bladder feels full.

Many people assume that since urine and feces come out of the body close to one another, they are both leftovers from what you eat and drink. Actually urine has nothing to do with digestion. There is no physical connection between the stomach or the intestines and the kidneys and bladder. The substances kidneys have to deal with are waste products that all sorts of body cells accumulate as they work. These are dumped into the bloodstream. The blood circulates through the kidneys, where the smaller waste molecules and some water molecules slip through the holes of a sort of strainer and down tubes that lead toward the bladder. The larger blood molecules can't get

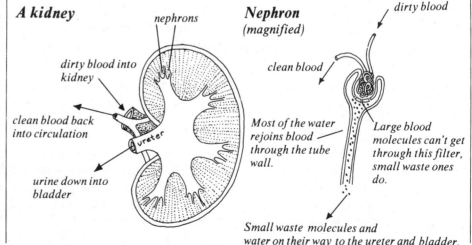

A kidney

nephrons

dirty blood into kidney

clean blood back into circulation

ureter

urine down into bladder

Nephron (magnified)

dirty blood

clean blood

Most of the water rejoins blood through the tube wall.

Large blood molecules can't get through this filter, small waste ones do.

Small waste molecules and water on their way to the ureter and bladder.

through the holes, and simply continue on back into the bloodstream.

The filtering is done in microscopic structures, but if you slice a kidney, as shown in the illustration, you can see the pattern of tubes through which the urine made in the kidney flows into the ureter (the tube which leads from a kidney to the bladder) on its way to the bladder.

Night urine is stronger than day urine. You can see that for yourself: your first urine in the morning is a deeper yellow than the almost colorless urine you excrete during the day. Your muscles, not your kidneys, cause the difference. During the day, muscles are working hard; waste products begin to pile up inside the muscle cells. By evening, you can feel the results: muscles loaded with waste products feel weak, slow, heavy, even achy. As you sleep, your muscles get a chance to stop their other work and expel their wastes into the bloodstream. Kidneys have much more work at night than during the day, and their effort shows up in the higher concentrations of yellow urea (a nontoxic chemical made by cutting apart toxic ammonia that cells have expelled as wastes) the next morning. The amount of urine

You can't hear a heart beat

The noise you hear when you listen to someone's heart is not a heartbeat. It is the sound of heart valves slapping shut. You can't hear the beat itself, which is a silent contraction of the heart muscles.

You can hear the heart's noise best on the left side of a person's chest. But the heart is not on the left side. It is in the middle of your chest. The heart is tilted so that the top leans over backward and to the right, while the bottom is tilted forward and to the left. The bottom tip actually touches the chest wall; where it touches — to the left of center — is where you can hear the sound best.

you excrete depends mostly on how much liquid you drink. Your body is about 70 percent water, and that's the way it tries to keep itself. The more you drink, the more water is absorbed by the intestine, and the more diluted (thinned with water) your blood becomes. Your kidneys remove this excess water along with wastes.

Livers: chicken livers, calves' and cow's (beef) liver are all sold as meat. The shape, color, and texture is about the same as a human liver. The liver is a chemical factory which works mostly to cut apart or reshape harmful chemicals (such as alcohol) into harmless ones. The liver also stores fat. You may find some chicken livers that are paler and

yellower than others. The color comes from pale yellow fat cells stored between the other cells of the liver. Cutting into a liver won't tell you anything about how it works, because the cells work through chemistry, not through a physical structure, like the heart.

Sweetbreads: the pancreas of a cow (only occasionally available in supermarkets). This wildly expensive delicacy is an endocrine gland, responsible for manufacturing insulin as well as other enzymes that control chemical reactions, including digestion, in your body. Like other glands, it is the cells that do the work (they secrete the enzymes), so cutting into it will not reveal anything.

Hearts: chicken hearts come with whole chickens, in the same package that contains the neck, gizzard, and liver. You can slice a raw chicken heart in half lengthwise to see that it is divided into chambers, connected to large blood vessels toward the top, and has flaps that control the flow of blood. But a bird's heart does not have the four chambers that a mammal's heart has. Unfortunately, beef hearts, which used to be the closest thing to a human heart in meat markets, are now sold only to pet food companies. But a squirrel, mouse, or any mammal has a heart similar to the one in the drawings here.

The way a heart works is very hard to understand. The problem is that the lub-dub sound you hear when you put your ear to someone's chest is four things happening almost at the same time. Blood, filled with oxygen in the lungs, is being delivered into one chamber. Then, it is being pushed back into the body through another chamber. Meanwhile, blood from the rest of the body, where oxygen has been used up, is being delivered to a third chamber. And this blood is being pushed out of the heart back toward the lungs to get more oxygen. The complicated system of chambers and valves is what prevents the oxygen-filled blood from mixing with the oxygen-emptied blood.

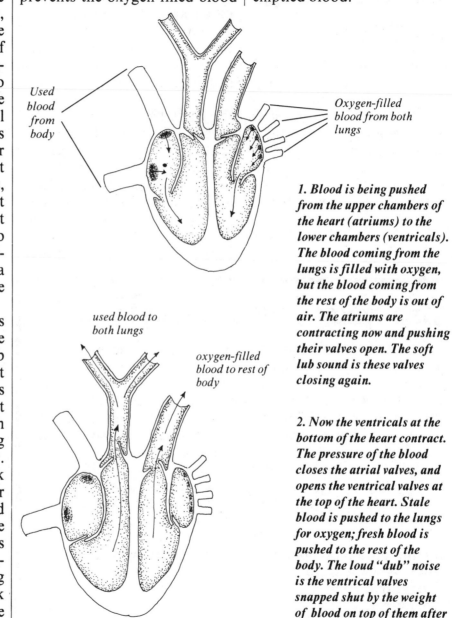

Used blood from body

Oxygen-filled blood from both lungs

used blood to both lungs

oxygen-filled blood to rest of body

1. Blood is being pushed from the upper chambers of the heart (atriums) to the lower chambers (ventricals). The blood coming from the lungs is filled with oxygen, but the blood coming from the rest of the body is out of air. The atriums are contracting now and pushing their valves open. The soft lub sound is these valves closing again.

2. Now the ventricals at the bottom of the heart contract. The pressure of the blood closes the atrial valves, and opens the ventrical valves at the top of the heart. Stale blood is pushed to the lungs for oxygen; fresh blood is pushed to the rest of the body. The loud "dub" noise is the ventrical valves snapped shut by the weight of blood on top of them after the contraction is over.

Animals **125**

The breathing machine

Breathing is so automatic it's difficult to even feel what is happening as lungs inflate and deflate. Lungs have no muscles, and so are not capable of filling themselves. Your trachea, or windpipe, that connects your mouth and nose to your lungs, acts only as a passageway for air. The work of getting air in and out is done by a large muscle called the diaphragm. The diaphragm separates your belly from your chest, and is connected all around its edges to your rib cage. As it contracts and relaxes, it changes the amount of space there is within your chest, sucking air in as the chest expands, and pushing air out as the chest becomes smaller. Try breathing without letting your chest move and you'll see it's impossible. You can really feel your diaphragm contracting when you have hiccups. Hiccups are spasms (jerks) of the diaphragm muscle. Holding your breath often gets rid of hiccups because it forces the diaphragm to remain inactive.

The lung machine on the next page is a model of how your own lungs work. Use a clear plastic bottle, such as the kind Windex and similar housecleaning aids come in. (Round bottles are harder to get the balloon diaphragm onto.) With a pointed knife (and perhaps with help — this isn't easy), cut out the bottom of the bottle. Don't cut away the bottom edge — you'll need it for strength. Cut off the top part of a large balloon and throw it away. Tie the stem end in a knot and slip the open portion over the bottom of the bottle. Pull it up snugly around the bottle.

Attach a small balloon to a plastic straw with a rubber band. Stick the straw into the bottle as shown, sealing the top with grease clay (plastilene). When you pull the balloon diaphragm

Cut large balloon here; tie nozzle in knot.

See your blood vessels

You can see the blood vessels in your own eyes with your own eyes. Get a flashlight and go into a dark room. Cover one eye with your hand. Hold the flashlight below the other eye with its beam pointed upward and slightly toward the open eye. Look straight ahead. The pattern you see is the shadows of blood vessels. These shadows are always there, but you are too used to them to notice. Because light is now entering your eye from beneath, the shadows are falling in a place you are not accustomed to — now you notice them.

There's a way to see how blood pumped through arteries makes them swell in and out, too. Stick the end of a toothpick into a small lump of clay. Hold your hand palm up, and sit the toothpick upright on your wrist, toward the outer edge. When it sits on the artery that comes close to the surface at that point, it will sway back and forth at each beat of your heart.

Lung model

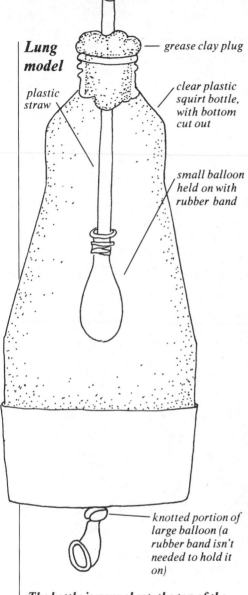

- plastic straw
- grease clay plug
- clear plastic squirt bottle, with bottom cut out
- small balloon held on with rubber band
- knotted portion of large balloon (a rubber band isn't needed to hold it on)

The bottle is your chest, the top of the straw your nose, the small balloon a lung, and the stretched rubber at the bottom a diaphragm. When you push the diaphragm upward, the balloon-lung shrivels. When you pull it downward, the balloon-lung inflates.

down, the little lung will inflate. When you push it up, the lung will deflate.

The second lung machine shown is a device for finding out how much air your lungs can hold. Fill the jug and the kitchen sink with water, then lower the jug into the sink and turn it upside down. Slip the plastic tube into the opening, and hold the jug in place. Take a deep breath, and blow all the air in your lungs through the tube into the gallon jug of water. The bubbles pushed through the tube and into the jug will push water out. The amount of air in the jug when you've exhaled all you can is the amount your lungs can hold. If you like, you can mark the jug into pint measures by filling it with one pint (two cups) of water at a time before you begin, and marking each new level with a glass pencil or freezer tape. The marks will give you a good way of comparing the lung capacities of various members of your family.

Lung capacity tester

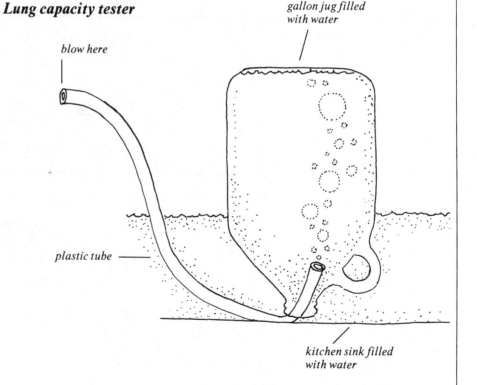

- blow here
- gallon jug filled with water
- plastic tube
- kitchen sink filled with water

Inside a squirrel

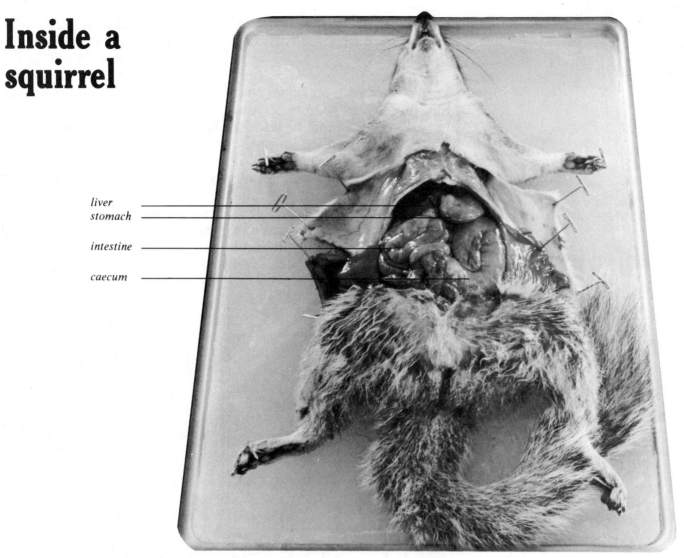

liver
stomach
intestine
caecum

What you see inside the body of any small mammal, like this squirrel, is similar to what is inside your own body. The liver is a dark, reddish-brown, floppy mass. The stomach is not, as many think, down in the belly, but right beneath the ribs, next to the liver. Most of the belly is filled with intestine. In the squirrel, the very enlarged section of intestine is the caecum, an area in which bacteria are used to aid digestion. (Your appendix is what remains of a human caecum). The large intestine, or bowel, begins just past the caecum.

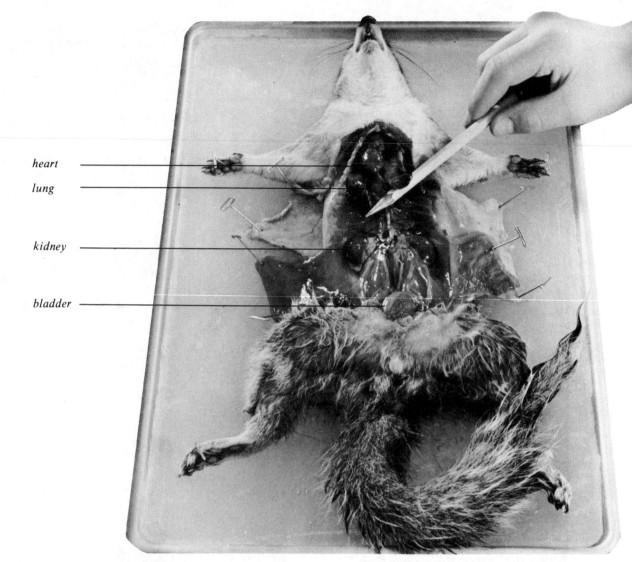

heart

lung

kidney

bladder

Here the digestive system is removed to show the kidneys. They are two dark, bean-shaped organs neatly tucked into the ribs along the back. They were originally connected by tubes called ureters to the bladder which lies just within the hips. With the rib cage open and the diaphragm — the muscle you use for breathing — removed, you can see the lungs and heart. The heart is a small, dark-red, oval organ. The lungs fill the rest of the chest. Lungs have no single, hollow space inside — the whole spongy-feeling organ is filled with small air sacs.

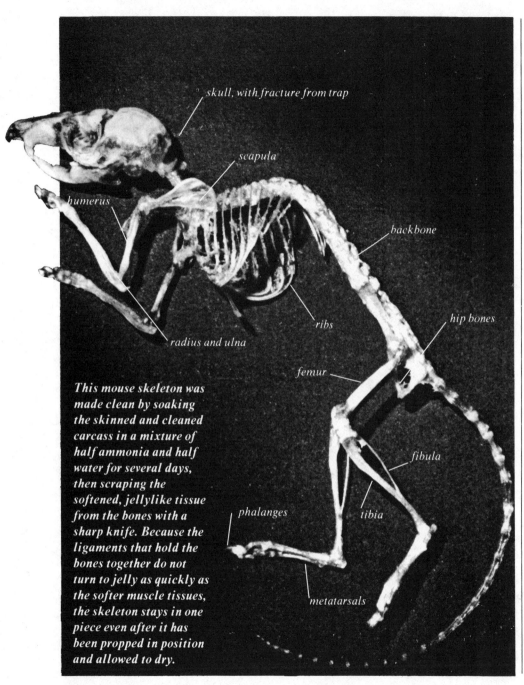

skull, with fracture from trap

scapula

humerus

backbone

ribs

radius and ulna

hip bones

femur

This mouse skeleton was made clean by soaking the skinned and cleaned carcass in a mixture of half ammonia and half water for several days, then scraping the softened, jellylike tissue from the bones with a sharp knife. Because the ligaments that hold the bones together do not turn to jelly as quickly as the softer muscle tissues, the skeleton stays in one piece even after it has been propped in position and allowed to dry.

fibula

phalanges

tibia

metatarsals

Self repair

The very moment that you cut yourself, your body goes to work repairing the damage. By an incredibly complicated process that requires 13 different chemicals, tiny fibers (threadlike shapes) form in blood when tissue (skin muscle or any other kind) is damaged. Blood cells are trapped between the fibers, forming a sort of mat called a clot. The clot plugs up the wound, preventing any more blood from leaking out. Over broad injuries, like scrapes, more material is added over the next few hours to begin to form the hard, thick substance called a scab.

Now, beneath the scab or in the clotted cut, skin cells get to work making more skin cells to fill in the gap. Cells on the outer edges of the damaged area contract (pull themselves smaller) to close the wound, add new cells by splitting themselves in two, and gradually moving inward. Scab pickers know this from experience: each time you remove a scab, the injured area is smaller, and it is surrounded by new skin (which is pink because it has not had time to produce much pigment in its

About bones

A piece of bone cut lengthwise

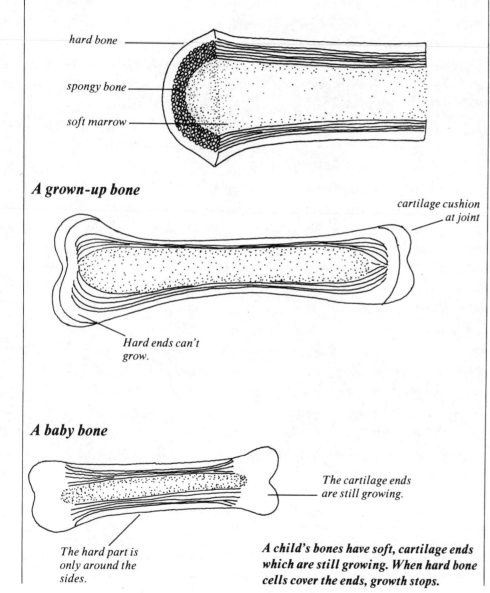

hard bone

spongy bone

soft marrow

A grown-up bone

cartilage cushion at joint

Hard ends can't grow.

A baby bone

The cartilage ends are still growing.

The hard part is only around the sides.

A child's bones have soft, cartilage ends which are still growing. When hard bone cells cover the ends, growth stops.

cells; thin and tender because it is not yet covered by a thick layer of dead cells). When the damaged area is covered by new skin cells, the wound is healed.

Broken bones

The body's first step in repairing broken bones is the same as in repairing broken skin: to form a clot at the injury. The clot acts as a glue to hold the ends of the bone temporarily together. During the next two weeks, cartilage cells gradually replace the clotted area. New bone cells now grow over both the inside and outside surfaces of the cartilage. After two or three months, there is a lump of new bone going right through the shaft where the bone was broken. It is not yet the right shape — cells called osteoclasts must remove bones cells from the lump to shape that portion of the bone properly. You can see why putting a cast on a broken arm or leg is helpful: the cast itself doesn't repair the break, but keeping the broken ends still and in the right place certainly helps your cells keep things straight.

Scars are the body's emergency repairs, used only when the normal method of healing would be too slow to plug a wound right away. The cells most responsible for making scars are called fibroblasts. Fibroblasts not only reproduce themselves faster than skin cells, they also move quickly to wherever they are needed in your body. They produce collagen — the same substance that gives gristle and cartilage their strength and rubbery quality. Scar tissue, white like cartilage and tough like gristle, is mostly collagen. Your body can form scar tissue to repair breaks not only in skin, but in muscles, nerves, or organs like the intestines and stomach.

When bacteria do manage to invade your body before an opening can be plugged, you have still another defense. Varieties of white blood cells called macrophages (the word means "big eater") travel to the injury and gobble up bacteria. Many of the macrophages die in the process, but so do many bacteria. When the fight is over, the battlefield is strewn with the corpses of bacteria, macrophages, and other dead cells — a collection you know as pus. When the pus has either drained out or been disposed of by fresh troops of macrophages, the remaining live cells around the battlefield get on with filling in the gap.

White meat on a chicken is light because it is supplied with less of a blood supply than dark meat. More blood is required by muscles used for prolonged effort, like running around the chicken yard all day. Less blood is needed by muscles used for only brief effort, like fluttering out of the farmer's way. The breast and wing meat of ducks is dark; they use those muscles to fly long distances.

The chicken bones you can easily identify are labeled here. The skull and the foot from the ankle down are missing. The scapula, or shoulder blade, is hidden behind the humerus in the wing. Separate verbetrae are clearly visible in neck and tail, but they are fused together in the hip area.

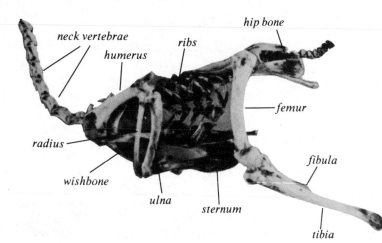

neck vertebrae

humerus

ribs

hip bone

femur

radius

fibula

wishbone

ulna

sternum

tibia

See if you can identify any of these chicken bones.

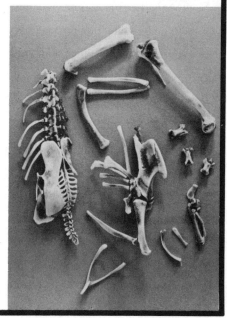

A scientific way to eat a chicken

You can study anatomy as you eat a chicken — so long as you do it unobtrusively. The bones from this barbecued chicken are shown here neatly gnawed, scraped, dried and stuck back together with white glue where joints had come apart. Some of them are labeled so you can compare them to bones on your own body, page 134, or to the mouse skeleton, page 130. As you eat a chicken, notice how the joints work. In the wings and legs, the shape of the cartilage that forms the joint can only move against one another in a certain way. Once the chicken carcass is cleaned, you can also see how the big ball joint at the top of the thigh bone rotates in its socket at the hip, and the wing rotates at the shoulder.

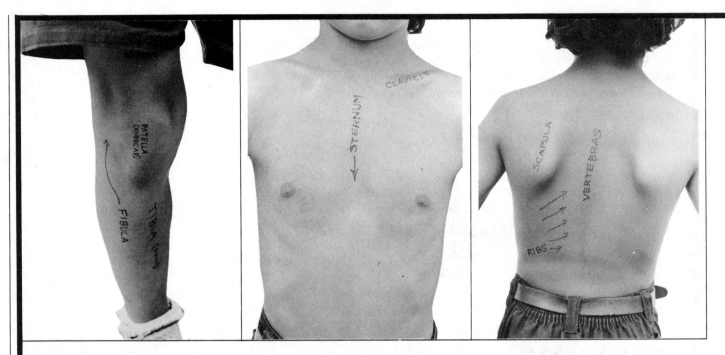

From the bottom up, here are some of the bones you can locate in your own body. The kneecap, or patella, is easy to find. The lump to the outside of your leg is the end of your fibula. Your shin is the flat surface of your tibia.

Where your ribs join in front is called the sternum. Running from the middle of your chest to each shoulder is your collar bone, or clavicle. Your clavicles and scapulas are bones that hold your arms in place.

The vertebrae that make up your backbone start with a bump called the coccyx — all that's left of your tailbones. They continue up to your skull. Ribs are attached to both sides of your backbone — 11 on each side. The wing-like bone on each side of your back is your shoulder blade, or scapula.

Skinny bones

The photographs here show you the bones you can feel for yourself on your own body. Many of the same bones are labeled on the mouse skeleton on page 130, and on the chicken skeleton on page 133, so you can see how a man resembles a mouse and a bird.

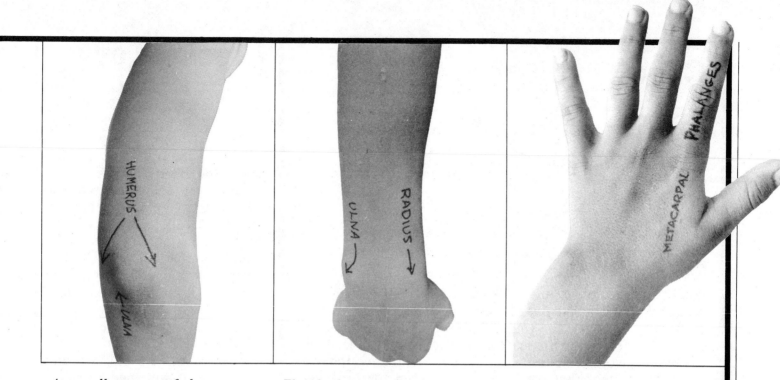

At your elbow, you can feel two bumps to either side. They are the end of the humerus, the big bone in your upper arm. The bump in the middle is the top end of your ulna, one of two bones in your lower arm.

The other lower arm bone is the radius. Feel for the two bumps in your wrist. The outer one is the end of the ulna, the inner one the end of your radius.

Wrist bones, not bumpy enough to feel, are called carpals. Hand bones are metacarpals and finger bones phalanges. Toe bones are called phalanges too, but ankle bones are tarsals, foot bones metatarsals. Your heel bone is the end of one metatarsal.

Goose bumps

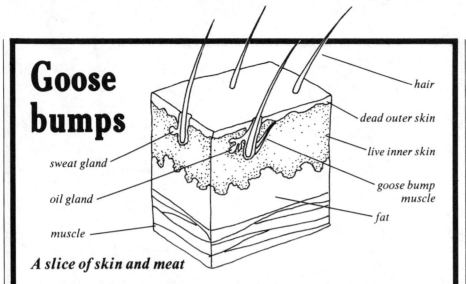

hair

dead outer skin

live inner skin

goose bump muscle

fat

sweat gland

oil gland

muscle

A slice of skin and meat

Goose, chicken, and turkey skins are covered with goose bumps. If you examine one of these birds carefully before it is cooked, you can see for yourself what each goose bump is: the pocket from which a feather used to grow. Look along the rear edge of a wing or tail to find a pin feather — the soft root of a feather that didn't come out when the bird was plucked. You may also find hairlike feathers at the foot end of the drumstick, and the tip of the wing.

Are your goose bumps the same thing? Take a look the next time you're shivery cold. Each goose bump has a hair growing from it, just as each bump on a bird has a feather growing from it.

But why do your hair pockets stand up when you're cold? For no good reason, actually. In humans, goose bumps are leftovers from a time when we, like other animals, were furry.

In feathery birds and furry mammals, a tiny muscle is attached to the side of each pocket that holds a hair or feather. When the animal becomes cold, the muscles contract, and the hair or feather is pulled more upright. Air trapped between a bird's "ruffled" feathers or an animal's fluffed-up hairs forms an insulating layer that keeps out the cold. We still have the muscles, and they can still pull the skin into little bumps, but we've lost our long fur.

Chicken ova

When you eat an egg for breakfast, you are eating a single cell. The tiny patch of white that floats to the top of the yolk of a raw egg when you break it into a dish is the ovum itself.

Before the ovum leaves the ovary on its way to being laid, an enormous yolk forms to one side of it. Some of it seems to be made by the ovum itself but, amazingly, most of it is made in the hen's liver, from which it is carried in blood vessels to the ovary. The yolk, however, is part of the cell — a food storage compartment held into a round shape by a thin membrane — when you break the membrane, the yolk spills all over. This single cell, made up of the ovum, its yolk, and surrounding membrane, is among the largest ova in the world.

Traveling ovum

The ovum, with its yolk, travels down a tube called the oviduct that leads, eventually, into the bird's cloaca, from which it will be laid. (Cloaca means "sewer," a name chosen because bird feces and urine leave by the same opening.) As it travels down the oviduct, layers of raw egg white, made by cells

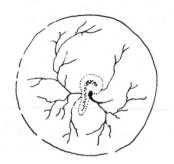

At three days, the embryo looks like a backward question mark. It has already grown blood vessels over the yolk.

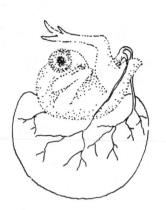

At 11 days, you can recognize the embryo is a bird. The yolk stalk, attached to its belly, carries nourishment from the yolk. The yolk is being used up.

The chick hatches after three weeks in the egg. It is feathered, but wet; and it is too tired to stand.

in the oviduct, are wound around it. There are two kinds of white: one is translucent (you can see light through it); the other looks like two twisted, thicker white strings. The thicker strings are like ropes that hold the slippery yolk more or less in the center of the slippery white. Around the egg white, another membrane is formed, again by special cells in the oviduct — followed by three layers of shell, made mostly of calcium. You can prove that there are at least two shell layers in the most obvious way: a brown egg is brown on the outside only. The inside of a brown eggshell is white. The eggshell is covered with small holes, called pores, through which air enters and waste gases leave.

When the shell is complete, the hen pushes the egg out. At this point, the egg is gathered and put into a box, ready for your breakfast.

Destined for breakfast

The egg we are describing here will never be a chicken. To become a chicken, the hen's ovum has to be fertilized. And for that you need a rooster. Sperm come out of the rooster the same way eggs come out of a hen: through the cloaca. Mating in chickens is called cloacal approximation, which simply means getting the two cloacae together. That would seem rather tricky, but it works every time. The rooster shown on page 50 mates with each of his hens every evening, starting with the oldest, ending with the "spring chickens." Each hen lays a fertilized egg or two the following morning. The ovum is joined by a sperm while it is in the oviduct, before egg white or shell have been wound around it. Commercial egg farmers go to great lengths to be sure no roosters are among their hens.

Occasional slip-up

Occasionally, you see an egg with small spots of blood in the yolk or white. Because the first sign that an egg has been fertilized is the beginning of a red network of blood vessels (they will eventually reach around the yolk to absorb food for the growing embryo, the still developing, unhatched chicken), people have assumed a blood spot means a careless farmer has allowed a rooster in the henhouse. Blood spots, however, are the hen's own blood. As her ovary gets ready to expell a ripe egg, tiny blood vessels may break, leaking a few drops of blood around the ovum. "Organic" eggs, the latest fad at health food stores, are fertilized eggs; a blood spot on the yolk of such an egg could probably be the embryo's own.

Because even a fertilized egg that gets in with the others by accident is kept refrigerated, the fertilized ovum (by now it would be called an embryo) is dead. Were it alive, blood vessels would soon grow from the embryo, out into the surrounding yolk to absorb nourishment for the growing chick. The egg white, beside acting as a shock absorber protecting both the embryo and its yolk from getting bumped, provides additional food for the embryo. The embryo itself now looks like a backward question mark. It next grows a tube, called a yolk stalk, into the yolk. Blood vessels in the yolk stalk absorb nourishment from the yolk. Within a few weeks, the yolk and white are nearly used up, and the chicken is almost ready to hatch. What is left of the yolk is taken into the chick's belly, through where the yolk stalk is connect-

To one side of the yolk is one of the ropy strands that hold the yolk in place inside the white.

ed. A tiny scar remains, much like your own belly button. Now, the chick begins to breathe air from the air space at one end of the shell. You can see the air space between the shell membrane and the shell itself at the broad end of an egg. Finally, the chicken gets out of the shell, in an orderly manner, by pecking a circular hole in one side.

And how do humans do it?

A female baby is born with all the cells that will become her eggs — including those that may be fertilized and become her babies. These cells are stored all through her life in two ovaries, which are low in her belly, one on each side. From the beginning, a girl also has all the other equipment she will need to bear children. Her uterus — the walnut-sized, very muscular container that will hold the developing baby — is in the center of her belly, very low, and is protected by the bony front portion of her hips. At the top, two tubes lead out from the uterus; each ends in an open funnel next to, but not attached to, an ovary. These are called fallopian tubes, and their job is to carry eggs to the uterus. The vagina is a much thicker tube that leads, from the bottom of the uterus, to the outside of a girl's body. This is the tube through which a baby is born. Though the vagina lies between the rectum, through which feces exit, and the urethra, through which urine leaves the bladder, it is not connected to either. During childhood, the vagina is partly closed by a very thin bit of skin, so the opening may not be obvious.

Female puberty

Beginning about the age of 12, and continuing for the next 35 years or so, a female's body prepares, once each month, for the ripening, and possible fertilization, of one egg. Each egg in its ovary develops inside a tiny sac called a follicle. As the egg matures, the follicle wall softens, then breaks. The egg escapes from the ovary. It is now free in the body, and has no way of its own to find where it should go. Cells in the funnel portion of the nearby fallopian tubes wave tiny hairs, to guide the tiny egg into the nearby fallopian tubes.

Meanwhile, the uterus has been preparing for the arrival of a fertilized egg. (It has no way of knowing yet whether or not this particular egg will be fertilized.) A cushiony surface forms within the uterus, filled with a rich supply of microscopic blood vessels. This is the blood supply that a developing embryo will put to use both for nutrition and oxygen during the first days of its life.

Menstruation

But let's first see what happens if an egg is not fertilized. Whether it is fertilized, or not, an egg travels down the fallopian tube and into the uterus. An unfertilized egg is not capable of producing the chemicals that an embryo uses to give further instructions to the uterus; the result is that the cushiony surface, with the extra blood it carries, detaches from the uterus and flows down the vagina and out. The fluid carries the egg with it. This process is called menstruation and occurs every month, except when a woman is pregnant or producing milk. The amount of blood is quite small, the process is normally comfortable, and the period of bleeding

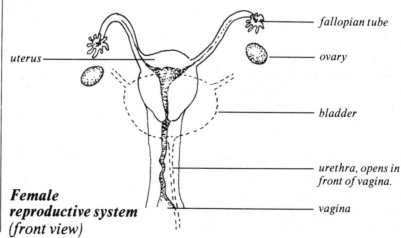

Female reproductive system *(front view)*

uterus — fallopian tube — ovary — bladder — urethra, opens in front of vagina. — vagina

usually lasts less than a week. Unfortunately, much is made of this normal and easy period by people who are rather upset by the thought of blood and fear that bleeding must mean something is injured. Such nervousness may explain why people are reluctant to talk about menstruation.

Menstruation does not occur if an egg is fertilized because a fertilized egg produces chemicals that inform the uterus to keep its nutritious lining. To become fertilized, a woman's egg must unite with a man's sperm.

Male puberty

The anatomy of a male human is designed specifically to safeguard his sperm cells, and to transport them safely to a mature egg. A boy baby, unlike a girl, does not have with him at birth all the sexual cells he will produce in his lifetime. Instead, from the time a boy is about 14 years old, the cells that are to become sperm begin to divide at a very rapid rate. All during his adulthood, a male can produce as many as 350 million sperm each day.

Sperm are produced and stored in a male's testicles (made up of two glands called testes held in a sac called a scrotum). A male's two testes are suspended outside his body, instead of remaining inside like female ovaries. Male sexual cells are delicate; they must be kept at a steady temperature. The scrotum contracts and expands as the surrounding temperature changes. When the scrotum is cold, it contracts tightly, pulling the testes up close to the body for warmth. When the scrotum is warm, the skin relaxes, allowing more air to circulate and cool the testes.

Sperm are tadpole-shaped cells which can move through fluid on their own by a swimming motion of their tails. As they leave the testes through a

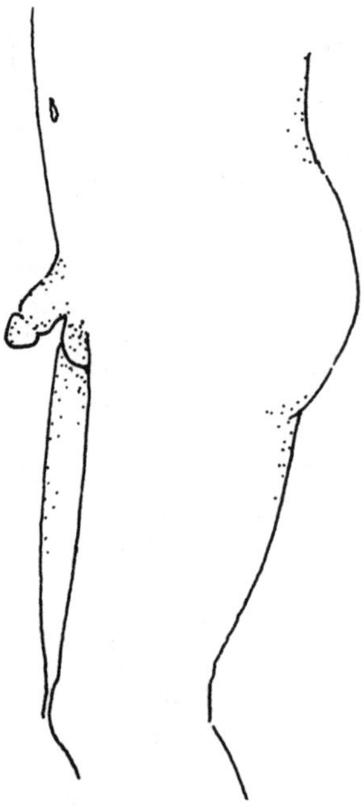

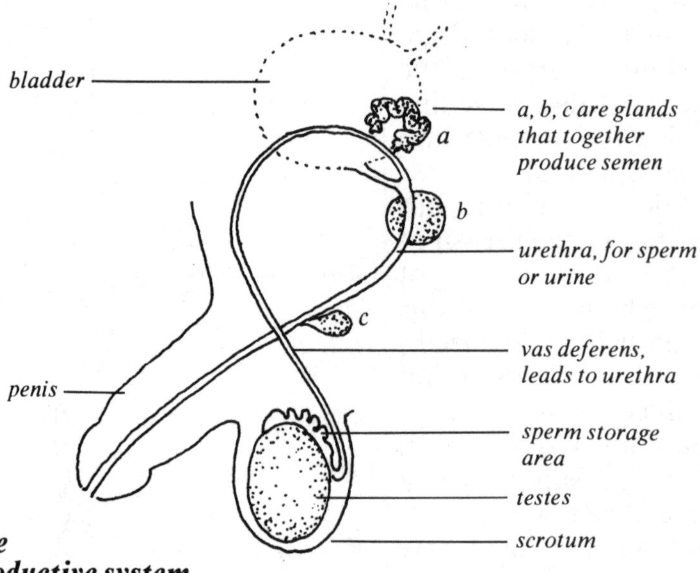

Male reproductive system (side view)

bladder

penis

a, b, c are glands that together produce semen

urethra, for sperm or urine

vas deferens, leads to urethra

sperm storage area

testes

scrotum

tube called the vas deferens, several glands pour fluid semen over them. Semen is a milky colored, slightly salty liquid that protects the sperm and provides the liquid environment they need for swimming.

Sperm mixed with semen continue through the vas deferens, up over the bladder, and into the male's urethra where it enters the penis. From there, it takes the same route urine would, through the end of the penis, to the outside. A man's semen and urine, however, can never use the urethra at the same time because a muscle shuts off the flow of urine when semen is passing through the tube.

Fertilizing an egg

To fertilize a female's egg, sperm must make a long and hazardous journey through the woman's vagina, up into her uterus, and beyond, into a fallopian tube. All through the journey, the energetically swimming sperm are endangered by the somewhat acidic mucus (slippery substance) in the woman's vagina, and the sheer length and difficulty of the trip itself. Of the millions of sperm that start the trip, only a few hundred may survive long enough to approach the egg. And of these, only a single sperm enters the

What little boys are made of

Boys may not like to hear this, but their scrotum, testes, and penis all developed, before they were born, from basic female anatomy. You might say with fairness that female structures are the "original" which, with some changes, serve the male as well.

Testes, for instance, start out indistinguishable from ovaries. Just before birth, or even some days later, the testes descend from inside the baby boy's body into his scrotum. The male scrotum starts out as the same two lobes of flesh girls have to either side of the genital area. As a boy baby develops, these two lobes move back somewhat and become hollow so the testes will fit inside. Girls have a small piece of flesh between the two lobes called a clitoris. From this a penis forms in the male, as the flesh grows to enclose the urethra. A girl's clitoris is in front of her urethra, and has no part in urinating, but it is as much involved in physical sexual feelings as a male's penis.

These changes that make an embryo develop as a male are guided by male hormones (messenger chemicals) whose instructions come from a particular chromosome carried only by males. Without these additional instructions, an embryo continues to develop as a female.

egg; the instant a sperm penetrates, a coating that is impassable to all other sperm forms around the egg.

Sexual intercourse

Sperm are given a head start, so to speak, by the way they are put into a woman's vagina. The method relies, as it does in other animals, on sexual feelings that are both emotional and physical. A man and woman, moved by affection toward one another, kiss and caress. As they touch, the man's penis and the area around the woman's vagina both begin to swell with blood. This swelling is pleasurable and, at the same time, creates feelings of longing for more closeness and more touching. The man's penis gets larger and quite stiff (this is called an erection); the woman's vagina, at the same time, produces a slippery mucus. When the man's penis is fully erect and the woman's vagina slippery enough, the man can push his penis into the woman's vagina. This closeness, in which man and woman are joined as deeply as they can be, feels almost as though they were one body. They now move together, comfortably and pleasantly, until sperm enter the woman's vagina. Sometimes together, sometimes at different times, both the man and the woman experience a vigorous muscular spasm (a rhythmic tightening and relaxing of penis and vagina) called orgasm. At this point, the semen and sperm are spurted forcibly from the penis, so they are already headed at high speed in the direction of the uterus.

Nature's reasons

Human mating is called intercourse, which really means an exchange or intimate connec-tion between people. There are some animals that only mate when fertilization is possible, but there are others who mate, not only to breed, but to renew bonds of devotion with their mates. Humans use intercourse that way.

In our species, males and females have mild sexual feelings even in childhood, and quite strong feelings from adolescence on. Adults can and do enjoy intercourse whether there is a mature egg ready for fertiliza-tion or not. Scientists think that the evolution of such constant sexuality (female, in particular, since this is unknown among other animals) is basic to the human behavior called mar-riage, in which one male and one female remain tied to one anoth-er emotionally throughout adult life. Allowing a part of someone to enter your body, or entrusting a part of your body to another person during intercourse requires trust, gentleness, and love. Intercourse strengthens those feelings, creates a sense of unity between male and female.

If human sexuality serves to tie a couple to one another for long periods of time, it has cer-tainly been a good evolutionary strategy. The bond keeps mother and father together to care for offspring which have unusually long childhoods.

Until this century, nature's wisdom in bonding couples, and society's wisdom in insisting that the bond be permanent, has assured a two-parent sharing in child rearing. Now, many people feel that intercourse is "merely" sexual, and is not a bond with one loved person. Whether or not separating sexuality from devotion is wise remains to be seen.

How babies are born

When you see the very large bel-ly of a pregnant woman, it seems impossible that so huge an object as a human infant can get out through a hole as small as the vagina. After all, the vagina is just about the right size to be filled by a man's penis, and that is not nearly so large as a baby. And how, anyway, can the uter-us, normally the size of a walnut, expand to hold a baby and still have the strength to push it out?

Both uterus and vagina are extraordinary organs. The uter-us, even when stretched to baby size, is the strongest muscle in the human body. When it begins to contract during labor — first

Hard work for embryos

Nice as it might be to think a baby's mother provides it with the nourishing placenta, the life-line umbilical cord, and the protecting amniotic sac in which the embryo safely floats, the embryo does most of the work. It is the embryo that grows the sac, produces the cord, and supplies much of the placenta. The mother's uterus cooperates by adding to the placenta so that, eventually, there is no way to tell which part is mother's, which child's. But, even though blood vessels and tissues in the placenta are so intertwined, there is actually no physical connection between mother and baby. Oxygen and nutrients from the mother's blood, and waste products from the baby's blood, can pass back and forth between the mother's and the embryo's capillaries (the tiny ends of blood vessels, so thin only blood cells in a single file can squeeze through) where they lie next to one another in the placenta. The two systems interlock without actually connecting.

at longish intervals; gradually, at intervals of a minute or less — it presses so hard against the baby that there is nowhere for it to go but out. Nature has seen to it that most babies turn upside down a week or so before they are born. (Don't bother to ask how they "know" to do so — no one has the answer yet.)

Labor day

A baby's skull is the the largest part of the baby (because a human brain is enormous compared to that of other animals), but it is specially constructed to take the pressure it must now undergo. Skull bones, which in you are fused together in zig-zag joints, are not yet connected. Because there is space between the skull bones, a infant's skull can be compressed without damage during birth. So, head first, the strong skull taking most of the pressure, the baby is pushed from the uterus into the vagina. The vagina, always somewhat elastic, becomes much more so toward the end of pregnancy. It really can stretch wide enough for the baby to slip through and be born.

Not that this job is an easy one, either for the mother or for the baby. The first part of labor is somewhat uncomfortable as the uterus contracts, becoming hard to the touch like any contracted muscle. Toward the end of labor, the contractions are stronger than any muscular activity the mother has ever undergone, and each contraction feels rather like a muscle cramp that lasts for less than a minute. Then the uterus relaxes comfortably until the next contraction. During the last few minutes of labor, the mother feels an irresitible urge to push, as one would in the middle of a bowel movement. This urge begins as the baby's head emerges from the uterus into the vagina.

Pushing a baby out is like any terribly hard work. It makes the mother sweat, hold her breath, and grunt.

Some women find that labor hurts, many women don't. Over the last 20 or so years, more and more women are taking special breathing and relaxing classes to help them learn to control the discomfort they may experience in labor. This controlled breathing, although taught to human females, is instinctual in other female mammals. In the case of childbirth, if discomfort is experienced, it can be a joyful feeling because now the mother knows the baby is nearly born. That's hard to imagine because, until a woman gives birth, any discomfort always meant that something was wrong. But this discomfort which she knows is right, and is going to produce a baby son or daughter, seems quite different.

Pushing out the baby

The rest of birth usually goes very quickly. A dozen pushes — or perhaps only a couple — sends the baby popping into the world.

The baby is soaking wet and very slippery when it is born; it is still attached to its mother by its thick, twisted umbilical cord, and is bluish in color because it has not yet breathed oxygen into its own lungs. The baby usually breathes its first breath without help — babies are no longer spanked at birth and there never was much reason to do that. Now the cord can be clamped shut so blood no longer circulates through it, and in a few minutes, cut with scissors some inches from the baby's belly. The cord end dries up and falls off during the next few weeks, leaving the mark we call a belly but-

Find the button

Since dogs, cats, and every other mammal are nourished before birth through an umbilical cord, they, like humans, have belly buttons. Look for a belly button on a pet cat or dog. It won't be big, but it is there.

ton. There is no pain at all from cutting the cord; umbilical cords have no nerves to transmit pain. Within a half hour, the mother's uterus contracts again to expell the placenta, which plops out with a warm and pleasant feeling that marks the end of labor.

Both mother and baby, the one tired from pushing, the other tired from being pushed, now are able to fall deeply and peacefully asleep until their next meeting.

Cell reproduction

The nucleus of every ordinary cell is filled with pairs of microscopic threads called chromosomes. Strung along each chromosome are many thousands of beadlike bits called genes. Each gene contains chemical instructions for how to make various parts of you.

Some genes carry instructions for making the very long protein molecules of hair; others, the instructions for the shape of a nose; others, the chemicals your cells produce to digest food, capture oxygen, or control emotions. Human cells have 23 pairs of chromosomes. The number of genes on each chromosome hasn't been figured out yet, but it is between five and 10 thousand. Since each gene carries a book-length set of instructions, your chromosomes are like a vast library of information on how to make and maintain a human being.

Cell division

But let's make up a less-complicated, one-celled creature that looks something like a ball to see what happens to its genes when it reproduces. The cell contains a single pair of chromosomes. Each chromosome is strung with three genes: the first for color; the second for size; and the third for bounciness. Each member of the chromosome pair has all three genes. The instructions on these genes, however, are not identical. In this cell, one color gene on one chromosome has instructions for red. The other color gene, on the other chromosome, has instructions for blue. The red gene is "stronger" (or dominant); the cell will only follow its instructions. The blue gene is still there inside the cell, but its message is "weaker" (recessive), and hence ignored.

The size of the cell is controlled by its size genes. In this cell, one size gene has instructions for large; the other, for small. But in this case neither gene is dominant or recessive. The cell blends the two sets of instructions; it is medium-sized.

Of the two different bounciness genes carried on the cell's chromosomes, one is for unbouncy, the other for bouncy. The unbouncy gene is dominant over the recessive bouncy gene. Therefore, this cell is red, medium-sized, and doesn't bounce much.

Asexual reproduction

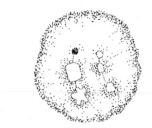

Red, medium-sized, unbouncy female ball.

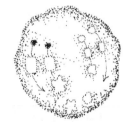

The ball gets ready to divide by making another set of genes, which are joining together into an identical pair of chromosomes.

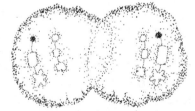

The two daughter balls will be just like their mother.

◉	*red color*
○	*blue color*
▯	*big size*
▢	*small size*
✾	*bouncy*
◌	*unbouncy*

Sexual reproduction

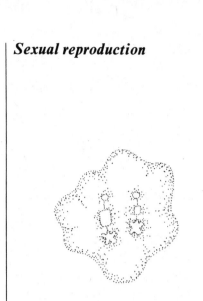

Blue, medium-sized, bouncy male ball.

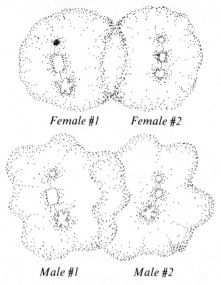

Female #1   Female #2

Male #1   Male #2

Female ball and male ball prepare for sexual reproduction by dividing. Each new cell now has only one chromosome.

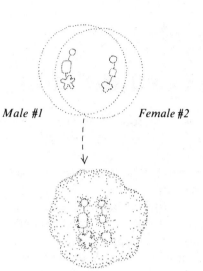

Male #1   Female #2

Child is blue, medium-sized, and unbouncy.

Like mother, like daughter

Let the cell reproduce asexually now, by splitting into two cells like most of the cells in your body do. The "mother" cell gets ready to divide into two "daughter" cells by duplicating its single pair of chromosomes. Each chromosome chooses from around itself the chemicals of which its genes are made; it then builds them into an identical set of genes. The cell now has not two, but four chromosomes; each of the original ones has produced an identical copy of itself.

The chromosomes now move to opposite sides of the ball, in pairs. To one side of the cell is a chromosome with genes for red color, large size and bounciness, paired with a chromosome with genes for blue color, small size and unbounciness. On the other side of the cell is a duplicate pair of chromosomes, also carrying those genes. The ball can now split into two cells; each of which has exactly the same pair of chromosomes and the same genes the mother had. These two daughters are red, medium-sized and unbouncy. (Notice there is no longer a mother cell: she has divided herself into two daughters.)

Cell meets cell

Asexual reproduction is the way all body cells such as skin and bones reproduce. But sex cells — sperm and eggs — do it differently. Let's say the female ball — an egg — is joined by a male ball—a sperm. He also has two chromosomes, with three genes on each. His size genes, like the female cell's, are one for large, the other for small, so he too is medium-sized. His two color-genes happen to both be for blue, so he is blue. And he is bouncy, since both of his third genes are for bounciness.

He and the female cell pre-

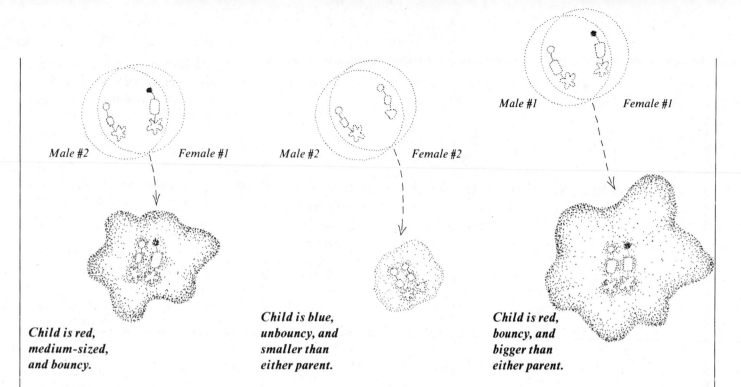

Male #2   *Female #1*

Male #2   *Female #2*

Male #1   *Female #1*

**Child is red,
medium-sized,
and bouncy.**

**Child is blue,
unbouncy, and
smaller than
either parent.**

**Child is red,
bouncy, and
bigger than
either parent.**

pare for sexual reproduction. You would think that as the mother cell split in two to become two daughters, male and female cells could simply join to become a single offspring. But an offspring that results from such a joining is an impossibility: it would have double the normal number of chromosomes — four altogether — and the instructions carried by so many genes would be too confusing to follow.

Because each creature must always have the same number of chromosomes each parent had individually, these two cells have to undergo a change before they

can join. Each parent divides into two. This time, however, instead of duplicating, the chromosomes within each cell simply move off from one another and the cells split. There are now four cells, each with only one chromosome, and a single set of instructions on its three genes. Such cells, with only half the usual number of chromosomes, are sexual cells such as a sperm or an egg. Now the two cells created from the female, and the two cells created from the male can join with one another as eggs do with sperm, to create new individuals with a pair of chromosomes each. One chro-

mosome will be from the female cell, the other from the male. You can see from the drawings that there are four different ways the two male and two female sexual cells might join with one another. Each different combination will result in a different combination of genes in the offspring, and therefore different messages as to what each new cell will be like.

Every child who gets two blue genes (one from mother; one from father) is blue like daddy. Every child who gets a red gene from its mother will be red because the red gene is dominant over the blue gene it got

X and Y

A single pair of chromosomes determined whether you became a boy or a girl. The gender (sex) chromosome that carries instructions for being female is called an X chromosome. The one that carries instructions for being male is called a Y chromosome. Every cell in a female's body, including those cells that will become egg cells, has a pair of X chromosomes. In a male's body, the same pair is made up of an X and a Y chromosome. As you can see, when sperm cells make their last sexual division to become ready to fertilize an egg, one of the two sperm cells that results has an X chromosome, the other a Y. All the woman's egg cells will end up with a single X. If the sperm that fertilizes the egg also carries an X, the baby with two X chromosomes will be a girl. If the sperm cell carries a Y, the baby with one X and one Y chromosome will be a boy. Since half of all sperm are Y and half X, there's an equal chance that a baby will be a boy or a girl.

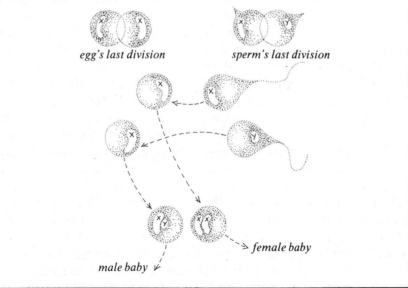

egg's last division   *sperm's last division*

→ *female baby*

male baby ↙

from its father. Children who get a bouncy gene from both parents will turn out bouncy, but ones who get a bouncy and an unbouncy will be, like their mother, unbouncy. There can be all kinds of sizes, even though both parents were medium-sized. Some children will get two bigness genes and be big. Some will get two smallness genes and be small. Only those that got one of each kind will be the same size as the parent cells.

Although the cells in human bodies have 23 chromosome pairs, they divide to make more skin cells or more bone cells much the way this single cell divided asexually. Daughter skin cells are exactly like their mother skin cell.

Ready to reproduce

Our reproductive cells, before they are grown up, have exactly the same kind and number of genes and chromosomes that our skin cells have. Like the ball when it was ready to repro-

In real life, when the egg makes its last division, one part gets all the cell material. The other part, with one X chromosome, dies. That's why there is usually one, not two, eggs to fertilize. Both halves of the sperm cell, one with an X, the other with a Y chromosome, survive.

duce sexually, egg cells and sperm cells do not duplicate their pairs of chromosomes in their final division. So each egg cell and each sperm cell has only one gene of a kind. As with the ball cell's genes, some may be dominant, some recessive, and others able to blend their instructions with another gene.

What happens, of course, is that you are, in some ways, like one parent, in some ways, like the other; and you have features that are blends of both. You may, if you received two of the same recessive genes, have some feature that seems nothing like your parents at all. When you think of all the possible combinations of genes you might have gotten from the mixing between your parents, you can see why it is that no two people are ever quite alike.

For some features, you can trace back and make a guess at whose eggs and whose sperms carried which genes. This, for instance, is a guess at how two out of three children in one family turned out blue-eyed and the other child brown-eyed. Blue eyes are recessive; brown eyes are dominant. The eye colors of relatives back to grandparents on both sides are shown, and the nature of their eye color genes are guessed at.

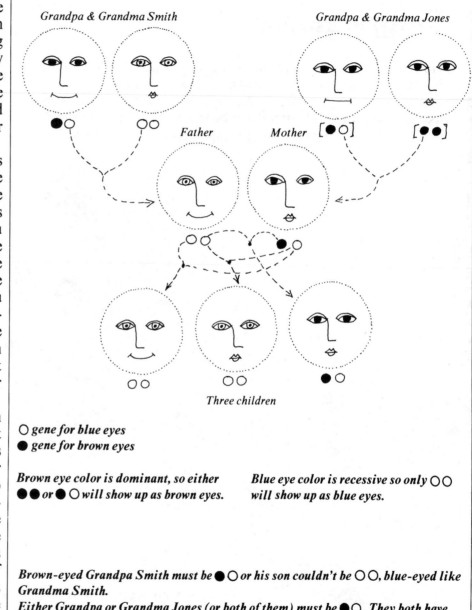

Grandpa & Grandma Smith

Grandpa & Grandma Jones

Father *Mother*

Three children

○ *gene for blue eyes*
● *gene for brown eyes*

Brown eye color is dominant, so either ● ● *or* ● ○ *will show up as brown eyes.*

Blue eye color is recessive so only ○ ○ *will show up as blue eyes.*

Brown-eyed Grandpa Smith must be ● ○ *or his son couldn't be* ○ ○, *blue-eyed like Grandma Smith.*
Either Grandpa or Grandma Jones (or both of them) must be ● ○. *They both have brown eyes and so does their daughter, but since two grandchildren are blue-eyed, Mother must be* ● ○. *One blue gene came from a Jones grandparent.*

Funny genes

Genes don't necessarily carry only serious or important instructions. The abilities shown here don't, as far as anyone knows, offer any special advantages — except to kids who like showing them off. Each can be traced back in your family to guess whose eggs or sperms most likely carried them.

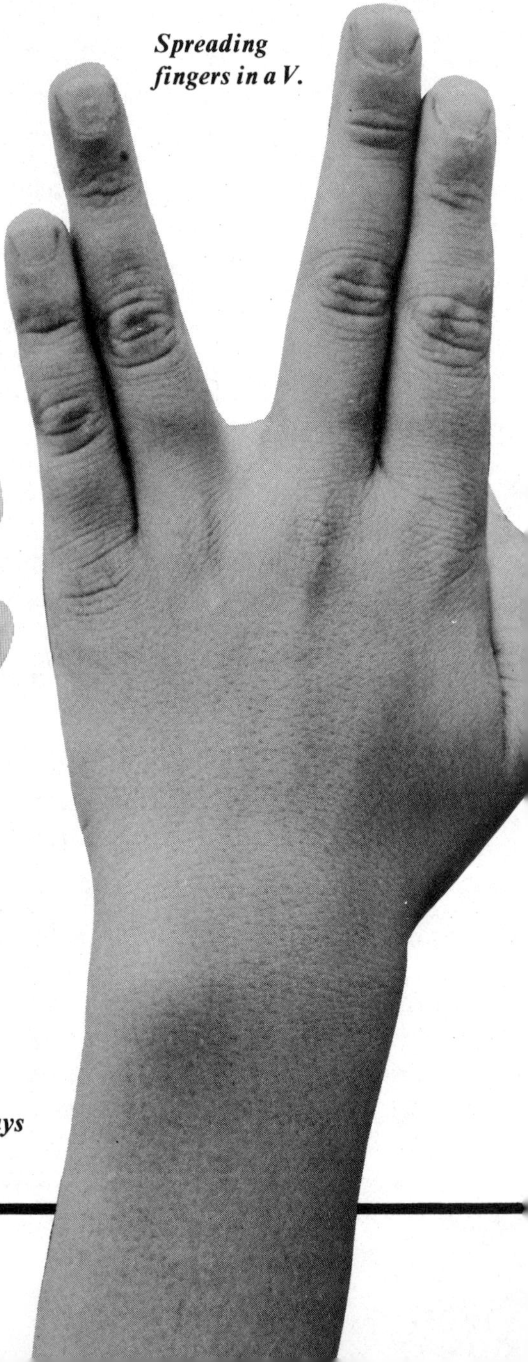

Spreading fingers in a V.

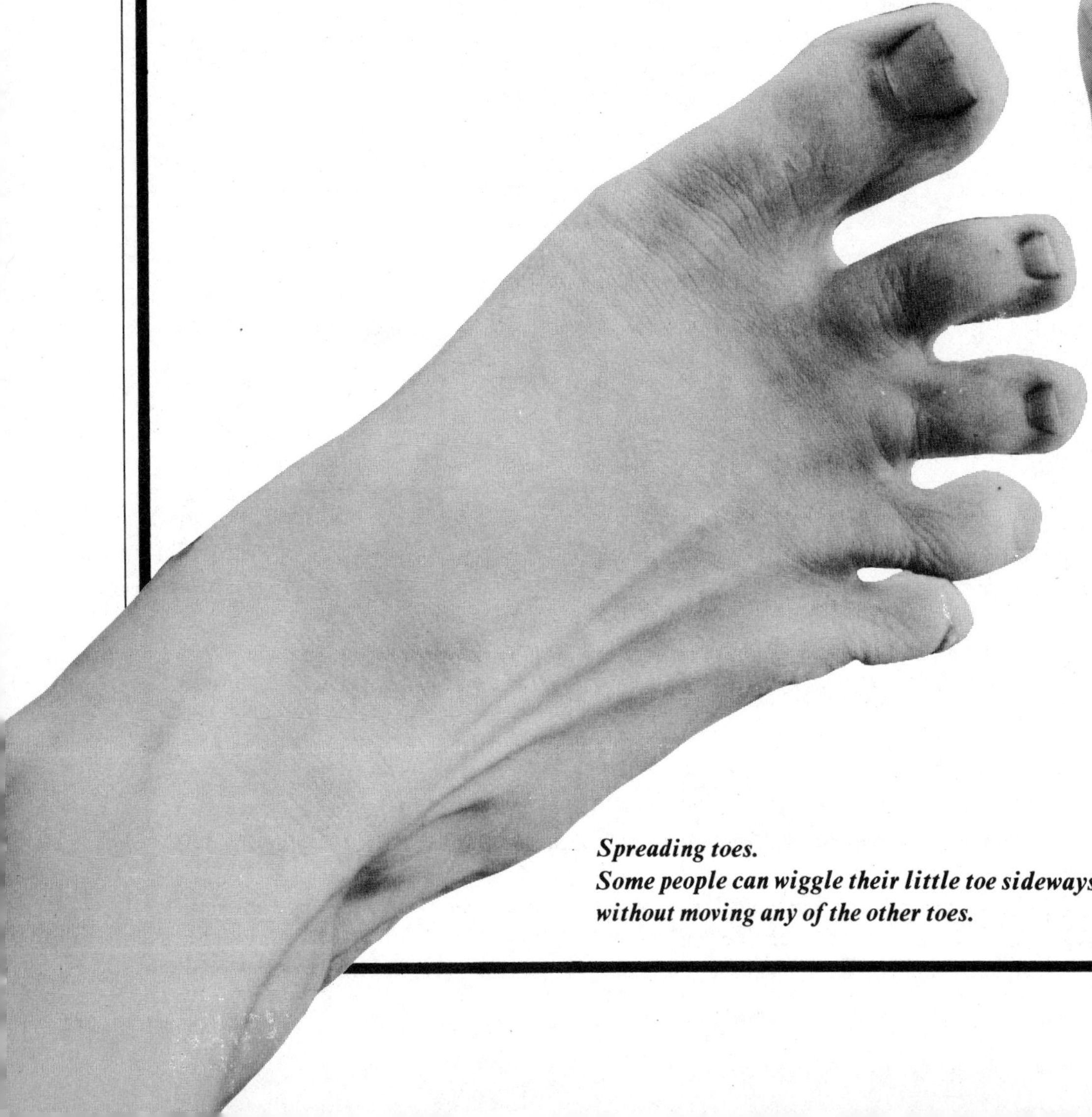

Spreading toes.
Some people can wiggle their little toe sideways without moving any of the other toes.

Tongue rolling.

A "double jointed" thumb bends backward as well as forward.

Bending first joint of fingers without bending the other joints.

Mamma

Mamma is a Latin word. It means mother. It means breast, too. And it probably came about from the lip-smacking motion that also forms the words yum-yum. Not only is "ma ma" the first word most babies learn to say in America, but also in China, France, Nigeria, Russia, and probably almost any other place. Breasts are mamma-ry glands. Animals that have mammary glands are called mamma-ls. Mammas, both the people and the glands, are obviously very important to humans; we have named all our furry friends after them.

Mammas — the glands — always come in pairs; two in humans and apes, up to eleven pairs in some other mammals. The origin of mammary glands is humble: they have evolved from oil glands in ordinary skin. Both males and females have the glands, and in male human babies they may even produce a pre-milk compound called colostrum for a few days after birth. But after that, the male gland remains small and useless.

Baby's first food

Female mammals come with two types of openings from their milk glands: the kind in which milk empties into a hollow tube, called a teat or dug, with a single hole in its end; and the kind called a nipple, in which milk is emptied through narrow tubes and out many holes. Humans have nipples. When you squirt milk from a cow's dug, it jets out in a single stream, like a water pistol. When you squirt milk from a human breast, it shoots in many directions like a sprinkler.

Milk from any mammal contains every nutriment the infant of that species normally needs. In whales, which put on large amounts of fat to keep warm in the cold ocean water, the milk is enormously fatty. Cow's milk is about equally balanced between fats, proteins, and carbohydrates (both starches and sugars). Human milk has less fat than cow's milk, but much more sugar. It tastes something like skim milk left over from a bowl of sugar-coated corn flakes.

Milk also contains most of the vitamins an infant needs. In the case of humans, it lacks vitamin D, which points to the probability that humans originated in sunny climates where infants could manufacture their own vitamin D with the help of ultraviolet rays from sunlight. In northern countries, where

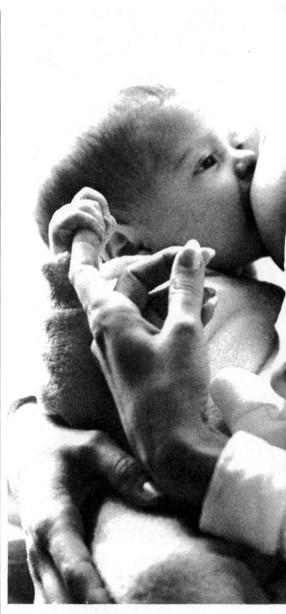

During intimate moments such as this one, a baby gets to know his mother.

infants and children may not get enough sunshine on their skins, they can get rickets (a disease in which bones are not hard enough) unless another source of the vitamin — vitamin D fortified cow's milk, vitamin pills, or cod-liver oil — is added to their diet. Along with vitamins and basic nutrients, milk also contains whatever immunity (disease fighting) chemicals the mother's body contains. For instance, puppies from a dog that has been immunized from distemper don't need distemper shots until they have been weaned. Some drugs, including alcohol and nicotine from cigarettes, also slip into milk in small amounts.

Milk from one species may not be usable by another species. Many humans have trouble digesting cow's milk. The result is a bellyache — from mild to really uncomfortable. With the wisdom our own bodies often have, the brain makes a connection between the food and the discomfort it causes. You yourself aren't let in on the "thinking" behind it; but children who have trouble digesting cow's milk are often the ones who insist they hate milk.

Getting to know each other

Humans nurse their babies every few hours, day and night, for a large portion of a newborn infant's waking hours. These hours are not only spent in filling the baby's belly. Babies at the breast suck in a pattern: bursts of enthusiastic sucking, interrupted by a holding action in which they mouth the nipple, but aren't really drinking from it. Invariably, during holding actions, the baby looks up into his mamma's face. And, of course, she looks down at his. Their eyes make contact. The mother, without thinking, talks to her baby. As he gets older, his lips slacken, the nipple slips from between them, and the baby coos back. A dialogue ensues — the baby's introduction to human conversation.

Within the first weeks of life, a human breast-fed baby can tell the difference between his mother's smell and any other human. Offered the fragrance of his own mother's milk and that of another woman, he turns to the familiar smell. Obviously, this is a sensitivity we lose later, but that's all right — short-lived as it is, the baby's acute sense of smell has served to tie him to his mother from the first days of his life. The tie quickly results in an early suggestion of logical thinking. A mother who is breast feeding may wish to give her baby a bottle once in a while. But she finds the baby fussy and uncooperative when she attempts it; he acts as though he is annoyed and frustrated. If she lets someone else offer the bottle instead, the feeding may proceed quite smoothly. The other person doesn't smell of his mother's breast anyway, so, the baby appears to reason, there's no alternative worth struggling for.

A baby at the breast is clearly taking more than breakfast. He is taking in distinctions between one thing or person and another thing or person, drawing intelligent conclusions, entering into a delicious social life with others of his species. With humans, and with all life, the mechanics of how our bodies work to nourish and maintain us are so intertwined with how we behave that it is impossible to untangle them. We eat with love as much as hunger; and when we are much older, we will still feel empty when we are lonely, beg reassuring cookies from our mammas, and give sweets to our valentines.

Invisibles

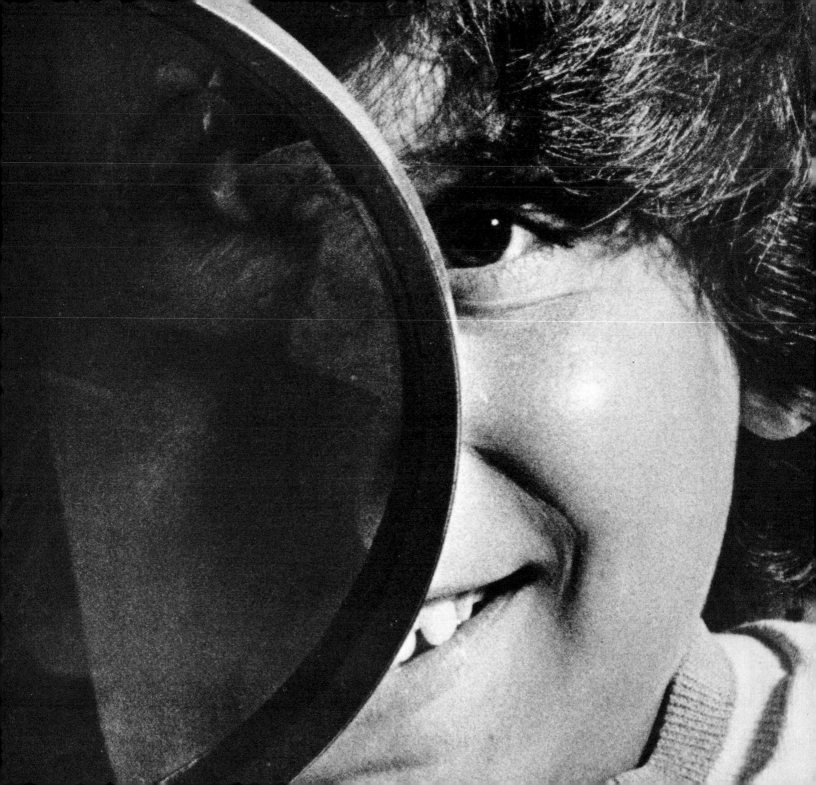

Invisibles:

The sun's first high-energy photons strike at seven o'clock. They send the cockroaches scurrying for cover. The cat's eyes narrow; too many photons are painful. The geranium begins to use them right away to attach together 6 carbon, 12 hydrogen, and 6 oxygen atoms exactly — a breakfast of sugar molecules. Similar plant sugar molecules stand waiting, in the shape of cubes, near the coffee pot which is now bubbling as it absorbs energy from electrons drifting through its wires.

The humans too can feel the first photons. Energetic photons collide with molecules in human eyes, snapping the molecules into different shapes, sending electrical charges along nearby nerves. Less energetic ones are accepted into skin, speeding up its vibrating molecules, spreading warmth.

Soon the air is filled with other messages. Bunched molecules, spreading outward from wildly vibrating vocal cords, beat familiar patterns onto human eardrums. Huge, wonderfully shaped molecules collide their way through the air bumping inside noses. And human brains, busy as always with the task of sending electrical charges here and there, making hearts thump, lungs expand, stomachs move in hunger, turns from dreaming to processing these latest messages: morning again, a sunny morning. A familiar voice, calling out familiar words: "Breakfast's ready." The smell of bacon, coffee, rolls, and sizzling butter — zing go the charges to feet and hands, legs, arms, back, and belly. Time to get up.

Strange as all this sounds, these messages of charge and photon, these substances of atom and molecule, these are all we know after our brain has finished decoding them. Love and laughter, dreams and insights, blue and red, sharp and hot, morning, fried eggs, even toasters, magnetic refrigerator doors, eyeglasses, and light bulbs only exist because of bits of energy called photons, and bits of stuff called atoms. They are the world as we know it.

Morning as usual

Touches

Molecule to molecule

When you wake up in the morning feeling full of energy, the feeling is actually quite correct. You *are* full of energy, even if you are lying in bed, doing nothing at all. With the slightest movement, you can transfer some of your energy to something else. Turn your head and the pillow moves: the energy of your movement has been transferred to the pillow which, in turn, moves. Rub your finger back and forth against the bedpost. The wood is not free to move away like the pillow, but energy is still being transferred from your moving finger to the wood. Feel the area you rubbed: it is warm. The warmth is energy. Say "Good morning," and your vocal cords transfer the energy of their movement to air; the air in turn hands off that energy to the walls, back to your own ears, and to the ears of the person to whom you spoke. Each object hit with sound energy vibrates as the energy is absorbed.

Transferring energy

You are not the only thing that has energy. The breakfast you are about to eat and the air you are breathing will release energy to your body when they are combined. The sunlight that gets in your eyes is transferring energy. So is the radiator you warm your hands over and the dog that jumps on you to say hello.

Every substance there is, whether it is living or nonliving, on our Earth or at the farthest reaches of the universe, has energy which can be transferred as noise, movement, heat, light, as well as other forms. Energy transfer is, in fact, the only way substances can have dealings with one another. Nothing can touch you and you can't touch anything without a transfer of energy. You can't take a nap without warming your bed, or a hot shower without absorbing heat. You can neither hear nor see without energy leaving one substance and being absorbed by another.

In fact, you know nothing, actually, about stuff itself since the only way you can know of it is through the energy it and you absorb and release. You know how things look because of the light energy coming from them; how they feel because of the energy of your push against them; how they sound because of the energy of their vibrations; how they taste or smell because of the energy released in chemical reactions with your own cells. Yet, though you can't know anything about matter without dealing with its energy, you can't know anything about energy without dealing with its matter; because, until energy is transferred from stuff to you or from you to stuff, you cannot detect its presence.

Understanding us

Almost all the stuff you know is made up of molecules. Molecules, like cats, dogs, cockroaches, and humans, have structure and behavior. What they are like and how they behave explains why clapped hands make noise, flowers smell, breezes blow, silver tarnishes, dresses are red, rocks are hard.

All we have with which to know these things are our sense organs and our brains, which in turn are made of molecules. All our understanding is communicated from molecule to molecule.

Molecules are clumps of atoms held together by an attractive force between them. They can be very large (made of as many as 15,000 atoms), very complicated in shape, and rather loosely packed like most of the thousands of kinds of molecules that are you. They can be medium-sized and crammed tightly together, like the molecules that are rock. Or they can be small and quite spread out from one another, like the molecules that are air.

Let's say you are holding an empty quart jar. Empty as it looks to you, the air inside that jar is about 4,920,000,000,000,-000,000,000 (4.9 sextillion) oxygen molecules, 7,740,000,-000,000,000,000 (7.7 quintillion) carbon dioxide molecules, 18,300,000,000,000,000,000,000 (18 sextillion) nitrogen molecules, plus similarly astronomical numbers of water and other molecules. All this stuff actually fills only about 1/2000 (0.05 percent) of the jar, or approximately the volume of a pinhead. The rest is really empty space — absolutely nothing at all.

The shape of molecules

Molecules come in all sorts of sizes and shapes. Some are small and neat; they fit well against one another. Others may be large and clumsily shaped; they don't mesh well at all.

You can see that shapes can make a difference in how molecules stack together by doing the following wonderfully simple, but strange experiment. Set out a two-cup measuring pitcher. Pour into it one cup of water exactly, and one cup of rubbing alcohol. Now take a look at how much liquid is in the pitcher; it should be two cups, but it is less than that.

Neither alcohol molecules nor water molecules mesh well with their own kind. But when you combine them, the alcohol molecules can fill the niches between water molecules. The whole volume of mixed molecules scrunches together — the space it fills is less than the original spaces they occupied.

Constant activity

For all this emptiness, what is going on inside that jar (and in all the air surrounding you) is absolutely wild. At room temperature, the molecules are racing about at the rate of about 1,500 feet per second, or as fast as rifle bullets. Each separate molecule collides with another or with the sides of the jar several thousand million times each second. The effect of all these collisions exerts pressure against a surface and is what, for instance, holds out the sides of a blown-up balloon. Air molecules also are pulled toward the earth by the force of gravity. The air about you presses on each square inch of you with a weight of 15 pounds. Your own molecules inside you are pressing outward against the air, like molecules in a balloon. (If they weren't, you would be crushed — by nothing but air; and if the air weren't pressing back against you, you would explode from your own internal pressure).

Wave your hand through the air. The slight pressure you feel is air molecules hitting your skin as your hand moves among them. Breathe against your hand. The warmth you feel is fast-moving molecules hitting harder than the ones at room temperature and transferring their extra energy to your skin.

Molecules in motion

Heat is a measurement of molecular motion. Temperature tells you how fast air molecules (and all other molecules, too) are moving. The faster they move, the higher their temperature. Fast-moving molecules, like speeding trains, carry more energy than slow-moving ones. When they collide with one another, the impact sends both molecules hurtling away from one another. The energetic molecules become more spread out from one another as they collide and bounce apart.

When heat is lost, the opposite happens. The molecules slow down; now when they hit, their low-energy collisions don't bounce them so far from one another. Cool molecules are more tightly packed than hot ones. When you take your temperature or even when you just hold the thermometer in your hand, the molecules of the liquid in the thermometer spread out as the motion of your own molecules is transferred to them. The liquid expands and rises in the

Holes in water

Drop some vegetable coloring into a glass of water. The dye molecules stay together at first, sinking in a swirl toward the bottom. But if you leave the glass undisturbed for a day or so, the color will gradually spread until it is evenly distributed throughout the water. It can do that because water is full of holes.

The situation looks something like this: bunches of molecules surround gaps between them. Each time a molecule moves into a gap, it leaves a gap where it was originally. Now another molecule can move into that gap, in turn, leaving a gap behind it. So, for each moving molecule, there is also a moving hole. Hole by hole, new molecules entering the water can find their way to anywhere within the liquid.

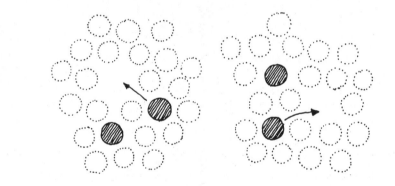

The dark dye molecules move through the water molecules from hole to hole, each time creating a new hole behind them.

thermometer.

A moment after you breath on your hand, the spot on which you breathed will feel cooler than the surrounding skin. Tiny clumps of water molecules from your moist breath are stealing that extra energy — and using still more radiating from your skin — to break apart, leave your surface, and join the air as water vapor. The coolness you feel is the missing heat. Minute and delicate as these movements and changes are, you have no trouble feeling them.

Molecules don't always attract

Other encounters with molecules may be much more violent. You stub your toe against a rock. The pain is severe. The same force that binds molecules together is working in the opposite direction to push others away. This repulsion between your foot and the rock is strong enough to rip open the tough skin on your toe. If this weren't so, your toe would simply sink through the rock without feeling a thing.

In fact, if every kind of molecule held to its companions and repelled strangers as strongly as a rock, your skin would not get dirty: nothing would stick to it. But you can stick your toe into clay and come out with a dirty toe. Clay molecules are only loosely bound to one another, and can bind to your skin molecules as well. The very slight pulling between your skin and strawberry jam molecules is what lets you know to wipe your face. When you get jam between your fingers, you can feel just how much strength is needed to pull the jam molecules apart. When you hammer on a rock to break it, you need much more

Hard, flexible, and slippery

Iron feels hard, clay slippery, and plastic flexible. The reason they feel different from one another is because the molecules of which they are made hold together in different ways.

The molecules of some hard materials hold to one another on all sides. Picture the structure of such a molecule as a cube which has magnets on all six of its sides. Each side holds to the side of another molecule. The result is a rigid structure, like rock or metal, that doesn't give in any direction when you push against it, Fig. a.

If the cubes had two less magnets, they would hold to one another on four sides, but not on top and bottom. The result would be layers. Each layer would be firm, but it would slip easily over the layer below. This is more like the structure of clay or graphite, in which sheets of molecules slide over one another, feeling slippery to our fingers, Fig. b.

Remove two more magnets and your cubes will fit together as long rods. Now they slip along one another at their tops and bottoms and also along their sides. This sort of connection is what gives many plastics their flexibility, Fig. c.

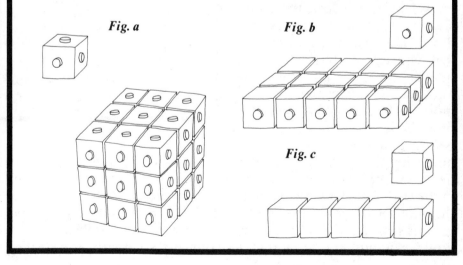

Fig. a

Fig. b

Fig. c

strength to force those molecular bonds.

All this — the movement of molecules, their giving and taking of energy, their repulsions and attachments — you can feel with your skin. Yet your skin, too, is only made of molecules.

A good look at muddy clay molecules binding to skin molecules.

What makes a spring springy?

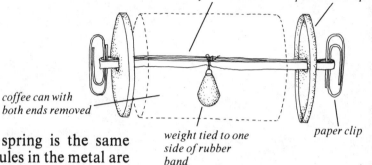

Boomerang can

heavy rubber band

plastic can top

coffee can with both ends removed

weight tied to one side of rubber band

paper clip

The strength it takes you to stretch a spring is the same amount of strength with which the molecules in the metal are pulling one another back together again. All you are doing when you stretch a spring is forcing molecules farther from one another; the minute you relax your pulling, they scrunch right back together again, and the spring returns to its original position.

The same is true of any elastic substance, whether it is a rubber band or your own skin. Stretching increases the distances between molecules; when released, they pull back together again. Only when you stretch a rubber band so hard that it breaks are you pulling molecules far enough from one another that the force between them is too weak to pull them back together. If you stretch a rubber band until it breaks, you'll know just how strong the force between rubber molecules is.

Twisting a rubber band also stretches bonds between rubber molecules. Even if a rubber band remains twisted for a period of time, the force is still there, still pulling. This simple toy, made of a coffee can, two plastic lids, a rubber band, and a lead sinker or other weight, uses the stored energy of that force. Roll the toy along the floor. As it rolls, the rubber band inside twists more and more. When the molecules exert so much pull on one another that the rolling movement is not powerful enough to separate them any farther, they begin to pull back together. If you release the can, the rubber band untwists and the toy comes rolling back to you.

Remove both ends of a coffee can. On a breadboard, cut a small hole in the center of two plastic can lids using a pointed knife. Tie a heavy weight, such as a lead sinker or a bolt with as many nuts on it as possible, with string to one side of a heavy rubber band, right in the center. Push one end of the rubber band through the hole in one lid from the inside and secure it by pulling a paper clip through the loop. Put that lid on the can. You'll need help to pull the rubber band through the can and then through the second lid. Ask someone to hold the can down until you have secured the band to the second lid with a paper clip. Put the second lid on the can, and your toy is ready to roll.

Air and water toys

All these toys work because molecules are always on the move. The parachute descends slowly because it has to push air molecules out of the way as it goes.

Parachute

To cut a circle, fold an opened out plastic trash bag in quarters and cut a curve with scissors through all four layers.

1 foot

1 foot

30 inches

To get strings equal lengths, loop eight 6-foot pieces of string around a pencil. Slide them close together, then cut them straight across, about 30 inches long.

2-foot circle cut from large plastic trash bag

self-adhesive label

string looped through hole

label with a hole punched

Bend self-adhesive labels around the edge of the circle at eight evenly-spaced places. Punch each folded label with a hole-puncher. Loop the strings through the holes, making sure the ends are even.

strings from parachute loops, gathered together

curtain ring

Tie toy or other object here.

Hold the ends of the strings even with one another after they are all attached to the parachute, and tie them to a curtain ring or large paper clip. Then tie any small object you want to weight the parachute.

The ping-pong ball in the ball raiser stays within the stream of air coming from the straw because molecules around it are moving faster, pressing harder.

Ball raiser

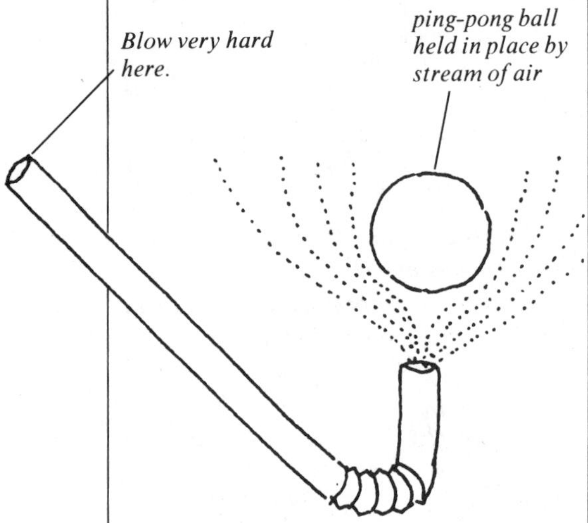

Blow very hard here.

ping-pong ball held in place by stream of air

Bend a bendable plastic straw so the short spout sticks straight up when you blow. Place the ping-pong ball on the spout and blow very hard into the other end to raise the ball and trap it in the stream of air. If you blow hard, the ball will stay suspended several inches above the straw for as long as your breath holds out. You can keep it up longer if you blow less hard, but the ball will hover only ⅛ inch above the straw.

The warm air balloon rises because colder, heavier air, pulled by the force of gravity, falls below it, hoisting the lighter balloon up.

Warm air balloon

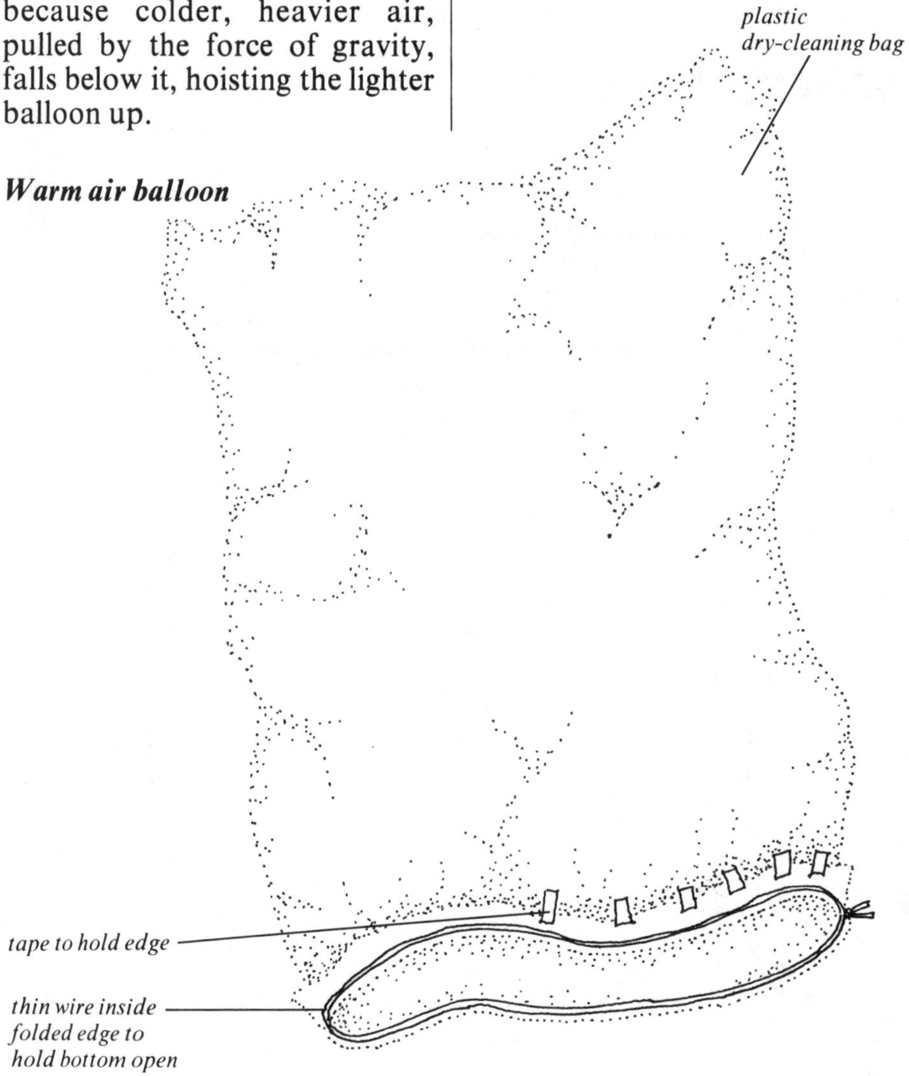

plastic dry-cleaning bag

tape to hold edge

thin wire inside folded edge to hold bottom open

Tape the opening at the top of the bag shut. Turn the bottom edge up several inches over a thin piece of wire or string, and tape it in place. Gently pull the two ends of the wire to make the opening only a little larger than the end of a vacuum hose, and twist the wire ends together or tie the string. Let a vacuum cleaner run a few minutes to warm it up. Using the exhaust end, fill the balloon with warm air, and let it rise.

The diver rises as you press the air molecules down harder against the water. The pressure doesn't affect the diver; it is now more buoyant than the water, and floats to the top. When you pull the rubber upward, the pressure on the water decreases. Now the diver sinks.

Gravity plays a part in the waterspout toy, as well. Water spouts toward the bottom of the can have more molecules being pulled down on them by gravity than spouts toward the top of the can, so the bottom spouts strongly, while the top spout merely dribbles.

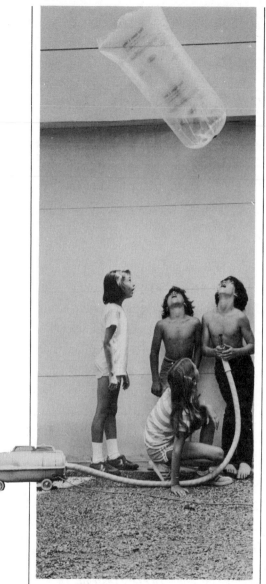

A cleaning bag balloon works best in cool weather. The one in the photo didn't go too high because the temperature was nearly 80 degrees that day — not much cooler than the air in the balloon.

Diver

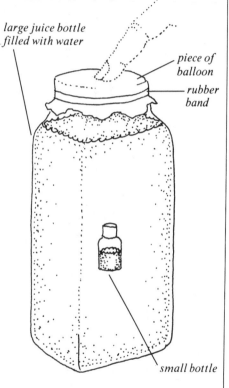

large juice bottle filled with water

piece of balloon

rubber band

small bottle

The diver is a small, tightly capped bottle filled with enough water to let it float in the middle of the large bottle. Use an eyedropper to add a little water or to remove some until the bottle floats correctly.

Water spout

Large can with holes punched using a hammer and thin nail. Make the holes about 1 inch apart.

The draft detector is lifted up by warm air, pushed down by cold air.

Draft detector

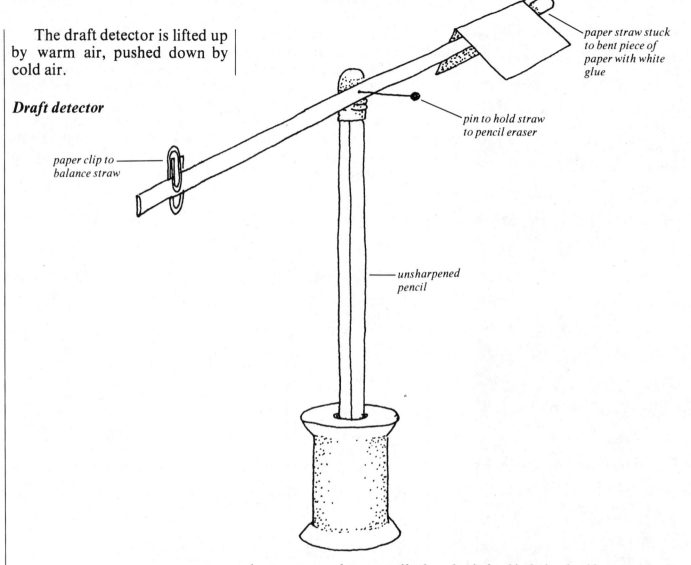

paper straw stuck to bent piece of paper with white glue

pin to hold straw to pencil eraser

paper clip to balance straw

unsharpened pencil

A paper straw works more easily than plastic for this device, but if you use plastic, jiggle the pin through the straw to enlarge the holes until the straw moves very easily. Also, white glue won't stick to plastic; tape the paper in place instead. An ordinary pencil fits snugly in a regular thread spool. Balance the straw exactly by moving the paper clip or adding another. Try the finished draft detector over a radiator or warm stove, near windows in winter, below the opened refrigerator, or even over a lighted lamp. A warm draft will lift the paper end; a cool draft will push it down.

The loop of thread in the soap circle toy opens out to a perfect circle because the molecules of the soap film around it are all pulling on the thread equally.

Soap circle

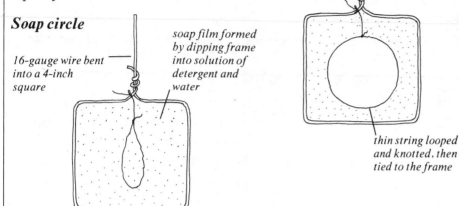

16-gauge wire bent into a 4-inch square

soap film formed by dipping frame into solution of detergent and water

thin string looped and knotted, then tied to the frame

Mix ½ cup of dish detergent and 8 cups of water to make a soap solution. If it isn't soapy enough, add more detergent. Put the soap solution into a container large enough to dip the wire frame into. The soap film forms easily. Pop the film inside the thread loop with a pencil point to see the perfect circle form instantly.

The balloon rocket is harder to understand. Usually, all the molecules in a balloon are zinging every which way — no more in one direction than another. The balloon stays put because each push by a colliding molecule is cancelled out by the push of some other molecule colliding on the other side of the balloon. When there is a hole in the balloon — say, the open nozzle — molecules that would ordinarily hit at that point escape instead. The push of molecules hitting opposite the hole — toward the front — is no longer balanced by an equal push from the nozzle end. In this unbalanced situation, the balloon itself is pushed forward. This little toy would work as well in outer space as it does here because it doesn't need any air to push against.

Balloon rocket

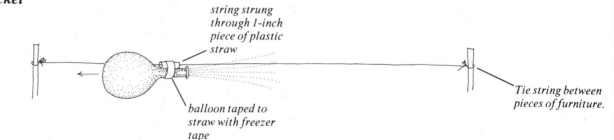

string strung through 1-inch piece of plastic straw

balloon taped to straw with freezer tape

Tie string between pieces of furniture.

String a 4-foot piece of thin string through the piece of straw. Tie each end of the string to the back of a chair or some other pieces of furniture you can move to a distance of about 4 feet apart. Lightly tape a deflated balloon to the section of straw. Slide it close to one end of the string, blow it up then let it go. The rocket will shoot to the other end of the string.

How to keep cool in a hot bed

Your skin is full of holes through which sweat oozes when your body becomes too warm. Sweat is mostly water molecules. When water is a liquid, as it is when it is sweat, the molecules are bonded, rather loosely, to one another. As heat energy is added to them, however, they move more and more quickly, and their motion breaks these loose bonds. Now the molecules separate from one another and, small and light as they are, take off into the air. They are still water, but now in the form of a vapor (or gas) instead of a liquid. That's called evaporation. By absorbing heat energy from your skin, sweat drops become energized enough to evaporate. Since the heat has come from you, you are now cooler.

When sweating doesn't keep you comfortable enough (and it often doesn't when you're trying to sleep in a broiling hot bedroom), you can use the same principle to cool a whole area around you. Dampen a couple of bath towels with a laundry sprinkler. Drape the damp towels both over your sheet and over your body.

So large an area of water molecules, all stealing heat from you and your bed, works much better than sweat alone.

Messages from the surface

Skin is made of two layers. On the surface is a layer of dead cells, thick enough to protect the living skin beneath, thin enough so you can still feel through it. You can see the dead layer very easily as the raised skin of a blister. The layer is thick on places like fingers that have to take a lot of wear, quite thin on places like your back, where sunburn peels it off. The living skin layer underneath is much thicker and packed full — a single square inch contains several yards of blood vessels, three times that length of nerves, perhaps hundreds of sweat glands, several oil glands, and a few dozen hairs.

Embedded in all this are sensors that react to changes in their local environment. One type senses the addition of heat, another the loss of heat, a third senses motion slight enough to be called pressure, a fourth detects disturbances violent enough to be called pain, and still another senses disturbances we call a tickle or an itch. Each sensor lies at a nerve ending. When a nerve ending is excit-

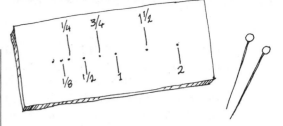

ed (given energy) by a sensor, the extra energy triggers the firing of a tiny electrical impulse along the nerve to the brain. The nerve endings all look about the same, and the impulse each carries to the brain is also the same. But the type of excitement needed to make the nerve fire differs according to the type of sensor that triggers it; the part of the brain that receives the message is different, too. Since the location of each nerve ending is mapped in the brain, a two-part message is sent: the type of sensation and the area that is feeling it. Messages are made "louder" (more painful, colder) when more nerves fire or a nerve fires more frequently.

Locating sensors

The sensors aren't scattered evenly over your skin. For instance, the ones that register pressure are more closely spaced around your lips and in your fingertips than along arms or legs. You can find out just how far apart they are this way: cut a piece of stiff cardboard an inch wide and two inches long. Leave a half-inch at each end so you can hold the strip, then using a thin needle pierce the middle portion with holes spaced as shown. Stick two larger sharp needles through the first two holes. Ask a friend to close his eyes (or you can do it to yourself, if you concentrate) and

press the needles lightly to his skin. If he can feel both points, he has pressure sensors in that area no more than ⅛ inch apart. If he feels only one point, the sensors in that spot are farther apart than the needles. Try this on various parts of the body until you know which areas have the most closely spaced pressure sensors. Then move one needle to the next hole and do the test again.

Sensor tests

To see how pressure, pain, heat, and cold sensors are distributed unevenly in skin, try this: on the back of your hand, using a very fine ballpoint pen, draw a ¼ inch square. Divide it into a checkerboard of four squares to a side. Draw a larger checkerboard on a piece of paper, so you can keep track of what you find out. These are the testing tools you'll need: for testing cold, a paper clip with one end straightened and cooled by an

Different skin sensitivities can be tested within an area that's only ¼ inch square.

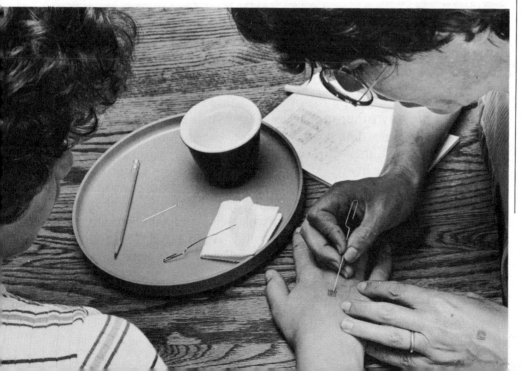

ice cube; for testing heat, an opened out paper clip heated in a cup of very hot water; for testing pressure, a pencil with a dull point; for testing pain, a sharp needle. Use one tool at a time in each square, then repeat using another tool. Each time you feel a sensation, mark that box in the paper chart with a letter (H for hot, C for cold, P for pressure, and X for pain). There will be squares in which you can't feel all four sensations.

Brainwork

It's easy for you to recognize something you feel as hard and rough, or soft and squishy, or shaped like a key, or made of cloth, but it's difficult to realize what a job of analysis the brain really has to do to recognize such simple things. Try to force yourself to be aware of what the sensations actually are as you identify materials by touch. When you touch metal, your skin molecules are robbed of heat. A message of cold is sent to the brain. Pressure sensors are stimulated, too, but as you run your fingers along the metal the sensors are all stimulated about the same amount. Your brain analyzes the messages to mean smooth as well as cool. Wood might send the same message of

Trick the itch

About 70 percent of our population is allergic to poison ivy. The oil in the leaves and stems is recognized as foreign protein molecules by skin cells. In their work to destroy the intruders, they produce chemicals called histamines, and histamines make you itch.

There is a way to trick your skin cells into releasing all the histamines they are capable of producing at once so that, for the next few hours, they can't make any more of the itchy stuff. The trick is to speed the cells' ability to bond molecules by adding heat energy — that is, raising the temperature of your skin. Stick your itchy hand, foot, or any part of your body under the hottest water you can stand; hold it there for about ten seconds, so plenty of heat can be transferred to your cells. At first, your skin will feel as though it were being scratched, and you would expect this to make the itching even fiercer. But when you withdraw your itchy skin, it will feel entirely normal. Even if you rub or scratch the area, the itch will not return for hours — or even the whole night.

Bigfoot

Since skin is made of cells that are made of molecules, you have to expect that it must obey the same rules as other molecules. Like any other molecules, those inside you are in motion all the time. The cooler they are, the slower they move, and the more tightly they can bunch together without shoving one another away. The warmer they are, the faster they move, and the harder they jostle against one another, pushing farther apart. Does that mean you expand and contract? It sure does. Shoes that fit you well when your feet are cold may feel tight when your feet get hot. A ring that fits snugly when your hands are warm may fall right off your finger when your hands are cold.

smoothness, but lack the message of coolness.

As you run your hand along a sheet of sandpaper, pressure sensors are stimulated unevenly — more in one spot than another, and at intervals, as any single sensor is moved from one grain to the next. Your brain can interpret not only that the material is rough, but can form an image of how rough (try it with different grades of sandpaper). If you try to identify materials with other parts of your body — your forearm, for instance — you'll find it very difficult.

The fact that more than one kind of sensor is involved in most encounters with the world explains why you can tell a kiss from a tap and a cut from a bump. A tap is only pressure, but a kiss may add heat, and then convey coolness as the bit of moisture it leaves behind evaporates. The proportions of all three sensations are quite different from having a warm, damp sponge thrown at you. A cut sends a message of pain, but only a little pressure. A bump sends pain and lots of pressure.

Unless you move your hand around, even a bullfrog is hard to identify by touch.

A skin illusion

Among the things we are all convinced we have learned is the difference between hot and cold. An experiment bound to confuse you, however, is this: fill one cup with water that feels neither warm nor cold to your hand — skin-temperature, in other words. Fill another with ice and water and a third with hot tap water. Soak one finger on one hand in the ice water until it is quite cold and a finger on the other hand in the hot tap water until it is quite warm. Now dip both fingers into the skin-temperature water. To the cold finger, the water will feel warm; to the hot finger, the same water will feel cool.

Your skin can't gauge temperatures; it can only detect changes in temperature. A change from icy cold to room temperature will be registered as warm, even though it isn't warm in our usual sense of the word. That explains why the sunbather sticks his toe in the water and complains of how cold it is, while those who have been swimming for a while argue that the water is perfectly warm.

A sixth sense

Your sense of touch works closely with another sense. It is a sixth sense, the kinesthetic (movement) sense. It tells you where the various parts of your body are at any moment, what position they are in, whether they are moving, in what direction they are moving, and how much speed and effort is in the action. The nerve endings that convey these messages to the brain are embedded in the muscles and the tendons, to which they are attached. Try identifying things by touch alone — that is, without moving your hands. You can do this by closing your eyes and having a friend place your hand on one object after another.

Without movement, your brain is deprived of several kinds of information. For instance, it doesn't get the sequence by which nerves in the skin are stimulated. (A bumpy leather wallet might feel the same as a smooth one because the bumps can only be felt as a sequence of pressure sensations.) Clues such as hardness or resilience may be missing, too. You might not be able to tell a piece of paper from a piece of wood. You can't feel how hard the wood is unless you push against it; hardness is a message of effort, not touch. You would be missing any clues as to shape. The movements of your hand over the contours of a surface are needed for your brain to form an image of shape. Touch alone won't do.

Although all the nerve endings that bring you messages of pain, pressure, heat, cold, position, motion, speed, and effort are all in working order when a person is born, babies have to learn how to interpret the messages. Test this out with a child who is only two or three years old. Choose a few small objects the child is familiar with, like a sock, a small stuffed toy, and a washcloth. Check that he can identify each one by name. Then put them into a paper bag. Ask him to reach in and find, say, the sock — without looking. To you, this would seem easy, but you may find you have to make the objects far more different from one another for a toddler to identify. He can feel as well as you, but still has trouble forming accurate images.

Noises

What strikes the ear

When a noise is loud enough — like a terrible clap of thunder or a sonic boom — you can feel it against your skin. But there is one bit of skin in particular that is fashioned to detect sound more accurately: the little piece of skin called an eardrum.

When you hear that boom, what is it exactly that strikes your eardrum? The same thing that strikes your skin: molecules.

Molecules as sound

Sound waves are a series of compressions (bunched-together places) and expansions (thinned-out places) in molecules. These waves go out in every direction so that if you could see them, they would look like concentric (one outside the other) rounded shapes spreading out from the source of the noise. The source is motion — the rhythmic kind of motion called vibration.

Take a thin ruler — wood or metal — and hold it with one hand tight against the edge of a table so that about eight inches stick out. Twang the free end to make the ruler vibrate up and down. You will hear a humming sound. This is what is happening: as the ruler first moves quickly upward, it sweeps air molecules tightly together above it and thins out those beneath it. Then as it moves down again, it compresses the air molecules below it, this time, and thins out those above. Meanwhile, the first compressed group of molecules, which occurred when the ruler first moved up, is now expanding; as it does this, it pushes other molecules into compression beyond it.

So long as the ruler continues to vibrate and push the air into a pattern of compression and expansion, you can hear the disturbance as a humming noise. The air molecules themselves are not racing around the room. Their only role is to push against other molecules nearby, transferring the force of the disturbance across the air. The disturbance — the sound — moves through the air 1,120 feet each second. Although the molecules themselves are not the sound, without them there is silence. No shout or bang can be heard in outer space because although there are molecules, the distances between them are too great to transfer vibrations.

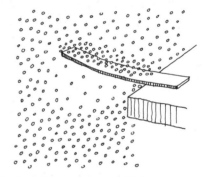

As the ruler moves upward, it sweeps molecules together above it, thinning them out below.

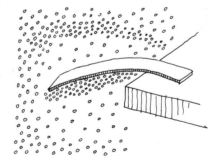

As it moves down, it sweeps another bunch together beneath it, thinning those above. The first compression is already moving outward.

173

What does it look like?

Since it is difficult to draw sound as it would really look like if we could see the compressed and expanded pattern of molecules, people draw it as waves instead. The crest of the wave corresponds to the compression; the trough corresponds to the expansion. The more compressed the molecules, the taller the wave is drawn, and the louder the sound our ear would hear.

This wave represents a loud, low sound.

The same low sound, but softer now.

A sound almost as loud as the first, but at a higher pitch.

The same high pitch, but not as loud.

The height of a sound wave is called its amplitude (loudness). When an object vibrates quickly, the compressions of molecules are close together. As it vibrates more slowly, the compressions are farther apart. The distance formed between the compressions (wavelengths) is shown in waves by how far apart each crest is from the next. When compressions hit our ear at longer intervals, we hear the sound as low (low frequency). The more frequently they hit, the higher the pitch we hear (high frequency).

You can picture this business of frequency by thinking of an adult and a toddler walking at the same speed down the street, just as two sound waves in air move at the same speed. But the short-legged toddler — like short wavelengths — must take more steps (higher frequency) to keep up with the long-legged adult.

Wave collectors

Your ear is shaped like a shell to collect sound waves. As each compression wave "breaks" against the shore of your eardrum, its force is transferred, pushing the drum into motion. The eardrum, in turn, pushes against three tiny bones. The first of the bones is attached to the drum; the third in the arrangement is attached to a coiled tube filled with liquid. The three bones are arranged in such a way that, like a dog's wagging tail, the slight motion at the drum end is exaggerated at the tube end. The pumping movement of the last bone against the liquid inside the tube

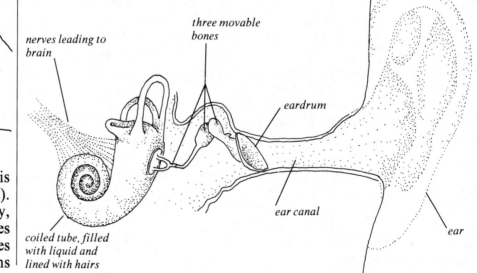

nerves leading to brain

three movable bones

eardrum

ear canal

ear

coiled tube, filled with liquid and lined with hairs

sets the fluid in motion. The fluid, in turn, pushes against the tiny hairs that line the tube. These hairs are connected to nerves that transmit the entire pattern of movement — its rhythm, speed, and strength — to the brain. But how the brain, which has not "heard" the sound at all, translates the message into noise, is not understood. In fact, it is perfectly reasonable to assume that the quality of sound is something which we invent in our heads after we have been hit by waves of molecular disturbance to which our ears are sensitive.

Two ears are better than one

If you doubt you really need both ears, stuff one with cotton. Then ask someone to hide a loudly ticking alarm clock somewhere in the room. Close your eyes, and try to find it by hearing alone. You'll have more trouble than you think trying to find it. With both ears open, it's quite easy — the ticking sound hits the ear nearest to the clock a fraction of a second before hitting the farther ear, giving your brain a clue to direction. Another hint given your brain is that the sound in the ear facing the noise is louder. Your head gets in the way of sound waves approaching the other ear.

Earwax and eardrums

Roll a small cone from paper and tape it in place. Cut the tip off so there is no sharp end. You can use this cone as an otoscope (the instrument a doctor uses to examine your ears) to see a friend's eardrum. Try it in a dark room, using the light from a bright penlight. Lay the cone gently in your friend's ear, and ask him to pull on his earlobe this way and that to straighten out his ear canal. If all you see is wax, he'll have to clean it out. (Wax is normal, however; it is the ear's way of catching dust and moving it out of the ear.) Some people's ear canals are quite curvy; you may not be able to straighten it out enough to see to its end. The eardrum, when you do see it, looks pearly gray, smooth, and flat. When a doctor examines you to see if you have an ear infection, the sign he is looking for is a reddish color to the drum, and an outwardly curved surface, evidence of pressure from pus behind the drum.

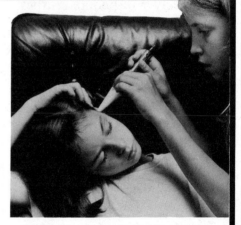

Place the otoscope gently at the edge of a friend's ear when looking for the eardrum. Never poke or push it in too far.

The short life of a sound

If each noise were to linger long in the air, you would hear chaos. Luckily, sound neither lasts long nor carries far because it has to compete with the random motion of air molecules.

Picture a huge crowd of people gathered in an open space, just sort of milling about, bumping and pushing, but not moving in any particular direction. Suddenly, at one end of the crowd, there is a huge push forward. The first layer of people crushes into the next, those into the next, and so on. There is a wave of compression moving through the crowd. But the people, even as the compression pushes them, are still milling around in random directions. The wave that started out crisply becomes more and more disorganized. By the time it reaches the opposite edge of the crowd, the pattern will be quite a mess.

The same thing happens to a sound wave. Close to the source of sound, the compressions are crisp patterns of tightly packed molecules. But the molecules have no goal in mind. They simply mill about, bumping and

The energy of just one small push to the first domino in this set-up will be transferred in a wave from domino to domino...

pushing in any direction. The compressions become less tight as the wave travels — and the sound hits more softly on our ears. When the pattern is totally messed up by the milling crowd, we hear nothing at all.

Making waves

A wave is a disturbance that has a shape. But a wave is not made out of stuff. Take a ripple in the bathtub, for instance. If you float a cork or a ping-pong ball on the surface and then create ripples by dropping something into the water, you'll notice the ripples form in repeated circles around the point of impact. Each circular ripple spreads, hits the sides of the tub, and rebounds from it. The floating cork moves up with the crest of a ripple, down with the trough between ripples; but it isn't carried along with any ripple to the edge of the tub and back. That's because the water itself isn't going anywhere — the ripple isn't made out of water. The ripple is a disturbance: it can lift the cork and drop it down again as it passes. And it has a shape — in this case, a series of circular

... all the way to the end of the chain. But when they have all fallen, the dominoes will not have traveled anywhere.

crests between which are troughs. The only reason you can see it is that it disturbs the surface of the water as it passes.

The sense that a wave is a moving disturbance, rather than a moving substance, is even more convincing when you "jump" a wave at the beach. You are lifted up and set down again, but you are not carried along with the wave. The energy of the disturbance, however, shows up when it can no longer be carried along the surface of the water and plunges itself out with enormous strength against the shore.

Going nowhere

Here are ways to make waves. The first is the familiar domino topple. Set dominoes up on end so that as the first is knocked over, it starts a chain reaction until all the dominoes topple. The dominoes don't move out of position at all, but the wave of disturbance continues for the length of the set-up. The set-up shown here branches the wave in two separate directions, sends it up steps, and transfers it to a whole new chain.

A Slinky toy can be used to produce a compression wave that may help you visualize what happens to molecules when they are squeezed. Lay the Slinky flat along the floor. Stretch it to about two feet long, and hold it that way with your two hands. Jerk one hand toward the other and back again quickly. The compression wave will travel along the coil to the other hand, hit it, and bounce back again. The bouncing continues until so much energy is lost that the wave peters out. Yet the Slinky itself hasn't traveled anywhere.

Here a Slinky wave is traveling from right to left. It will bounce back and forth several times between the two people's hands.

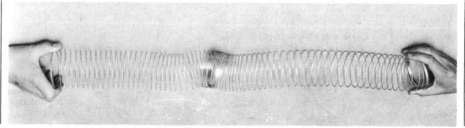

Trap the molecules

You can see what it takes to compress molecules by trying to make clapping noises with your hands in these ways: press your hands together very, very hard. That's plenty of pressure, but no noise. Now open your fingers and clap with only your fingers as quickly and hard as you can. You may get a small noise, but the only molecules you have been able to compress are those trapped in the small spaces between fingers. Now clap both closed hands together. The sound can be remarkably loud. There is plenty of air between your hands, and you have brought them together so suddenly that the molecules have not been able to slip through your fingers in time to avoid compression. If you try to clap slowly, they will all escape you.

Emptiness sounds loud

You can trap molecules not only to produce noise, but to get rid of it. If you've ever lingered in a home for a few minutes after

More old blankets will have to be hung in this basement corner to absorb the amplified sound of a rock group!

moving men have taken everything away, you may have remarked that the house sounds empty. The sound of emptiness is louder than the sound of a furnished home. Picture the compression wave from your clapped hands traveling in all directions through an empty room. The disturbance hits the bare walls and floors and bounces back. Even though a clap may not seem to linger long in the air, the compression wave travels back and forth at the rate of 1,120 feet per second, hitting your ear not once, but many times. The clap seems louder (you are hearing it both as you clap and as the wave almost at the same time bounces back) and it sounds hollow (some of the bounces are coming back to you fractions of a second later, like quick echos).

But let's say the walls were covered with felt and the floor with carpet. The compression wave again leaves your clapped hands and hits the wall and floors. There, the force of the wave penetrates into all the spaces between the felt and carpet fibers. As bouncing occurs in these tiny spaces, however, the pattern is disrupted. Instead of the wave re-emerging unchanged and noisy, the pattern is messed up to the point of silence.

Where's the fire?

If you think of the sound waves produced by a siren as a series of dome-shaped waves originating from an ambulance or fire engine, you can see why you know whether the siren is coming toward your home or speeding away from it. As the engine moves at a steady speed, each new throb of sound is sent out a little farther forward than the last one. Since each throb of compression spreads equally in all directions like a sphere, but each successive one's center is a bit farther forward than the preceeding one, the throbs are farther apart behind the vehicle and closer together in front of it. Your ear judges pitch by how frequently it is hit by a compression, so the siren sounds high-pitched as it approaches (since there is less space between each compression and so more of them hit per second) and then low-pitched as it passes and speeds away from you. To the fireman, the siren doesn't change at all.

The sound of a scream as a person plunges from a skyscraper roof doesn't change in that person's ears either, but when you pretend to fall a long distance, you automatically wail in an evenly decreasing pitch to convince your audience you are falling away from them at faster and faster speed. From the ground, the long scream would sound higher and higher as the person fell faster and faster toward you.

Soundscope

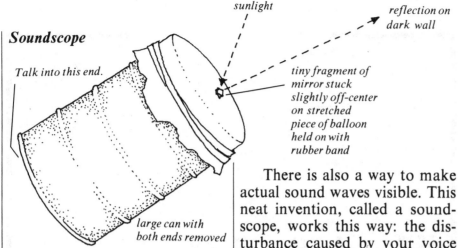

Talk into this end.

sunlight

reflection on dark wall

tiny fragment of mirror stuck slightly off-center on stretched piece of balloon held on with rubber band

large can with both ends removed

Before you start making a soundscope, blow up a large balloon, tie the end, and leave it for several hours to stretch the rubber.

Remove both ends of a coffee can. Deflate the balloon by pricking it at the stem end, and cut out a large, circular piece of rubber. Get someone to stretch the rubber over one end of the can while you put the rubber band on to hold it.

Glue the tiny piece of broken mirror to the stretched rubber slightly off-center with white glue. Be careful not to cut yourself.

When the sun is shining through the window, move the soundscope around until you catch sunlight on the mirror and see its reflected spot of light on a shaded wall. Try to prop the soundscope in this position on a chair, with books or pillows. Then shout, sing, groan, or whatever, into the open end of the can to see how the spot of light moves. The rate at which it quivers is the frequency or pitch of the noise you're making. The distance it moves shows the loudness.

There is also a way to make actual sound waves visible. This neat invention, called a soundscope, works this way: the disturbance caused by your voice when you talk into one end of the can hits the stretched rubber on the other end, setting it in motion. Like your eardrum, the motion mimics the frequency and amplitude of the sound wave. It vibrates farther in and out for loud sounds than for soft ones; vibrates more quickly for high sounds than for low ones. The bit of mirror must move accordingly, and so, when light is reflected from the mirror onto the wall, you can see the characteristics of the wave. Experiment with sound — loud, high, and low sounds. Compare the jiggling reflection with the waves drawn on page 174.

Thunder time

The noise of thunder and the light of lightning in a thunderstorm are produced at the same moment. But the light moves through the air much faster than the noise. Light travels at 186,000 miles each second, so when you see lightning, even if it is several miles away, you are seeing it almost exactly when it happens. Sound, however, takes a full five seconds to travel a single mile. So unless a thunderstorm is directly overhead, the sound of thunder will reach you later than the flash of lightning. You can use this lag to find out how far away a storm is, and whether it is approaching you or moving away from you. You'll need a watch with a second hand. Count the number of seconds between a flash of lightning and the crash of thunder that follows it. Divide the number of seconds by five. For instance, if you counted 20 seconds between flash and crash, the storm is four miles away. If you do it several times and find that the distance is getting shorter, the storm is headed your way. If the distance grows longer, the storm is passing you by or going away from you.

A humming skull and other ways to hear better

Bang the tines of a fork hard against the floor, and then touch the handle end of the fork to the wall. Listen. You can hear the wall vibrating the rhythm (resonating) to the fork's vibrations, even though the fork seemed to make no noise at all.

The bones in your own skull and jaw resonate to the vibrations of your voice. Hold your fingers in your ears and hum softly. The sound is actually louder than when you take your fingers from your ears. If you've ever wondered why your recorded voice sounds unfamiliar to you, but not to anyone else, that's the explanation. Only you are used to hearing your voice from the inside as well as the outside. When you put a seashell to your ear, the sound you hear is a very private one: the "tide" of blood rushing through your own ear, amplified by the shell.

Hearing helper

If your skull acts as a resona-tor, vibrating in the same rhythm as your vocal cords and, thereby, adding to the loudness of the sound, your ears act as sound focusers. Both methods amplify sound, or make it louder. The original hearing aid or earphone was a cone-shaped object that collected more sound waves from the air than the small shell of your outer ear can collect. Roll a large sheet of heavy paper into a cone, put the small end to your ear, and see how much it helps you hear slight sounds.

Because the molecules in the air are free to move about randomly, air is not the best conductor of sound. Solids, in which molecules are packed more tightly, carry organized compression waves much farther. Indians used to put an ear to the ground to hear the pounding of hooves at distances too great for the air to carry. And, nowadays, anyone who really wants to hear what is said behind closed doors knows the best way is to put an ear to the door itself.

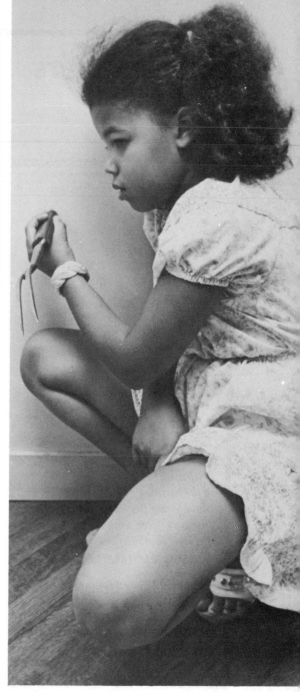

This kitchen fork, with a steel shaft going all the way through its handle, made a louder noise when banged and held against the wall than a table fork.

Noisemakers

Pig grunter

large can with hole punched in closed end for string to go through

string held inside can by tying to paper clip

Twanger

Stretch a thick rubber band around a book, and slip a pencil between it and the book at each end. Twang the rubber band. The tone it produces is the only one possible with a rubber band of that thickness, held at that tension, and at the length determined by the placement of the pencils. If you shorten the length by holding your finger down exactly halfway between the pencils and twanging, the tone you hear will be exactly an octave higher than the first tone. The rubber is vibrating exactly twice as fast as it did when it was twice as long. Why our ears recognize the underlying math of doubling, tripling, or quadrupling the number of vibrations per second as the same note remains a mystery, but all the sounds of music that strike us as pleasing prove to have a mathematical basis.

With a nail and hammer, pierce a hole in the bottom of an empty coffee can. Cut a 3-foot length of string (nylon "mason's" line works very well) and thread it through the hole. Tie the inside of the string to a paper clip to hold it in place.

Wet the string. Hold the can by the bottom rim and pull along the string to make noise. You can get loud grunting sounds by holding the string tightly between your index finger and your thumbnail as you pull along it.

Noisemakers from left to right: a comb and tissue paper kazoo, a pig grunter, and a vacuum cleaner hose.

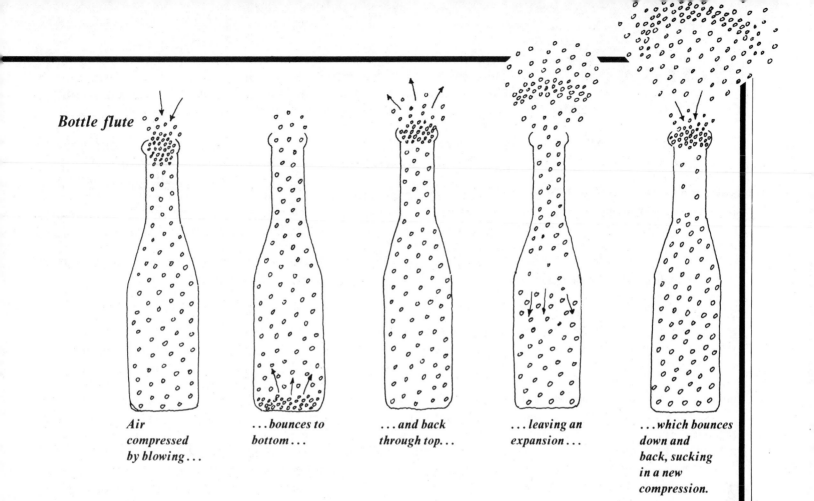

Bottle flute

Air
compressed
by blowing...

...bounces to
bottom...

...and back
through top...

...leaving an
expansion...

...which bounces
down and
back, sucking
in a new
compression.

The container that holds vibrating air in a wind instrument determines the sound it makes. Get together an assortment of empty bottles and, one at a time, rest your bottom lip on the edge of the opening and blow. The larger bottles will make a low hooting sound, and the smaller ones will hoot at a higher pitch. What is happening is that you are compressing bunches of air molecules as you blow across the mouth of the bottle. Each compression bounces to the bottom of the bottle and back again. The length of the bounce from top to bottom determines the length of the sound wave from the bottle, so the shorter the bottle, the closer together the compressions, and the higher the pitch. You can tune a series of identical bottles by partially filling some of them with water.

Harrumph!

Vocal cords work something like a reed instrument: air from your lungs is pushed past the two cords to set them vibrating. Close your throat to cut off air and you can't make a peep. Make the humming noise that seems to require the least effort and then the highest-pitched noise you can manage. The strain you feel when you make a high noise is the pull of muscles stretching your vocal cords tighter. These muscles control the pitch of your voice by thinning, thickening, lengthening, shortening, stretching, and relaxing the vibrating cords. When people get angry, all their muscles tense, including those attached to their vocal cords. Voices rise in anger. You can tell when someone is nervous making a speech to the class, too, by the higher pitch of his voice.

Thick and thin

The difference between men's and women's voices lies in the thickness of their vocal cords. Men's vocal cords are thicker, so they vibrate more slowly to produce a deeper sound. Children, although their vocal cords are thin like women's, don't sound like women. Here the difference is largely in the sinus spaces inside our heads. Like the hollow box of a guitar, sinuses add resonance to our voices. Children's sinuses are hardly developed. Their voices have a thinner, less rich quality than a grown person's.

The individual design of each person's vocal cords, sinus spaces, mouth, tongue, and teeth so affect the sound of our speech that no two people sound exactly alike.

What goes into talking

When you talk, only half your time is actually spent producing noises. The other half of speech is silence. And much of the noise you do produce is not made by your vocal cords. You may be surprised to discover that the letters "th" stand for two quite different sounds, depending on whether you use your vocal cords or not. With your hand on your throat so you can feel when your vocal cords vibrate, say the words "thin" and "then." The "th" in "thin" is unvoiced; the "th" in "then" is voiced. Your tongue is in a slightly different position, too.

Speak aloud slowly with one hand in front of your mouth and the other on your throat. Keep your mind on what is going on with your tongue, lips, and throat. Some sounds come out with a puff of air, while others can be made with your lips closed (the air comes out your nose). The hard sound of "g" requires a carefully timed closing at the back of your mouth. To make the sound of "v," you have to let air out between your teeth and lower lip; if you stop your voice, the sound will come out as "f."

You can form all the vowel sounds merely by moving your tongue to change the inside shape of your mouth, though the sounds will not be as clear as if you moved your lips to shape the space more completely. The amount of practice it takes to get all these movements to work together explains the babbling of babies; but it doesn't explain why, as they grow, they practice throat clearing, coughing, sneezing, crying, barking, howling, whining, and shooting and siren noises.

About the only thing that silences humans is hoarseness or laryngitis. Hoarseness can be caused by overworking voice muscles so much that they simply are too exhausted to do their job. In laryngitis, the muscles may be okay, but the cords are too swollen to vibrate.

Sights

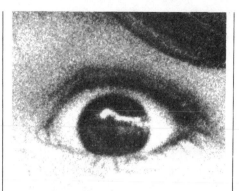

Wavicles

To understand the senses of touch and hearing, you need to know how molecules behave. Molecules can move (you feel the breeze hit your skin). Molecules can transfer the energy of their motion (when they do, you feel warm) and remove it (you feel cool). Molecules can repel (when you stub your toe) and attract (your toe gets dirty). Molecules can, without traveling themselves, transmit energy along a surface or through stuff (when energy reaches you along the surface of the water, you are lifted by a wave and set down in the same place; when the energy reaches you through the stuff of air you hear sound).

All this is mysterious enough. But to understand the sense of vision, you need to think about a more difficult idea. There is such a thing as energy that not only isn't stuff, but gets across space without any help from stuff at all. The energy is light.

Nonstuff energy

Light includes the light you see, and also light you don't see but may know by names such as ultraviolet, infrared, X-rays, radio waves, and microwaves. No doubt you thought these were all different things. They're not. They are all energy made up of a nonstuff called photons. These come in packets of different strengths, vibrate at different frequencies, but all move at the same speed through empty space: the speed of light, 186,000 miles per second. Although photons are particles of energy that can travel without the help of molecules or atoms, they, like sound energy, travel only in wavelike paths. Because they are both wavelike and particlelike, you can call them wavicles.

When you think of light as waves, the differences between the different kinds of light are their wavelengths (and, therefore, their frequencies, or the number of cycles they must repeat to travel 186,000 miles each second. Radio waves, for instance, are very long and have a low frequency. X-rays are very short and have a high frequency.

When you think of light as particles, radio light is low energy packets or photons; X-rays are high-energy photons. In about the middle — medium frequencies, medium energies —

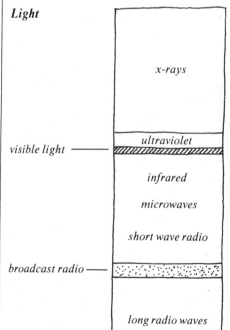

Light

x-rays

ultraviolet

visible light ———

infrared

microwaves

short wave radio

broadcast radio ———

long radio waves

185

are the photons we can see. They are called visible light.

It's no accident that these particular photons are the ones we can see. Our sun, the source of most of the photons arriving at Earth, emits 40 percent of its photons in that range. Perhaps if the sun's spectrum (range of frequencies) were different, the photons we are sensitive to might have been different as well.

And what we can't see

Just beyond our vision, one energy-step higher and at a slightly greater frequency than visible light, is ultraviolet light. Bees see ultraviolet and we feel its effects as sunburn. By using various chemicals that are sensitive to light energies we can't see, we can use nonvisible light to make visible images. The very high-energy photons called X-rays penetrate your body and, like visible light, cast shadows. You probably have seen X-ray shadows as the teeth and bones that show up on X-ray pictures. Infrared light, which is just below the energy levels we can see, is the light that causes our skin to heat up when we sit in the sun (but not to get sunburn which is caused by ultraviolet light), and our toast to brown in a toaster. When infrared is used to make photographs, the image it produces is the pattern of heat radiating from our bodies, our houses, or the surface of the Earth.

The very lowest energy (and slowest frequency) light is radio waves. We think of radio wavicles as noisy things, but they themselves are as soundless as any other light. Just as other wavicles of light can be used to produce visible-light images, radio light can be used to produce sound.

These sorts of light photons radiate out from all the matter of the universe, filling its vast emptiness with energy, crisscrossing space with its paths. But light can't be detected in any way until it interacts with matter. Until a photon of the right energy actually hits your eye, there is no way to know it exists.

What meets the eye

Let's say you are reading this book outdoors. Eight minutes ago, visible-light photons left the surface of the sun, shooting outward in all directions at the speed of 186,000 miles each second. They have been slightly slowed as they hit our atmosphere, but have gotten through its widely spaced molecules quite easily. Now some of them hit an obstacle — the open pages of your book. They sink into the black ink molecules and disappear. The white paper molecules, however, will not absorb them; and so the photons bounce back off the white portions of the page. As they bounce, they hit your eye. They zing through

Cross section of an eye

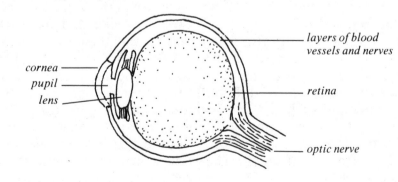

cornea
pupil
lens
layers of blood vessels and nerves
retina
optic nerve

your open pupil, penetrate the transparent lens behind it, and slam against your retina, the rear surface of your eye where visual images form. Photons meet your eye; you see the book.

Follow the dots

Actually, you see the white page, but you do not see the black letters, even though you can read them perfectly well. Picture the surface of your retina as dots crowded closely together. Each dot can either fire a message of impact to the brain when it is hit by a photon, or not fire a message when it is not hit by a photon. The result received by the brain is like the dot pattern that forms the image of a photograph in a newspaper. Empty spaces (the printing on the page) are not seen — they are dark. Filled spaces (the white paper) look brilliant. More widely spaced dots are seen as values of brightness or shadow between the two extremes. When you read, you are seeing the white page with the black areas left out.

A look into the past

If you lift your eyes now to glance at the sun itself (from which these book-bounced pho-tons came), the image that forms on your retina is the sun as it was eight minutes ago. You are look-ing at the past. If the sun were to disappear, you would not be able to sense its disappearance until eight minutes from now.

At night, using the photons of other stars all much farther from us than our sun, you can see great distances — not into space, but into the past. You always see only the photons that meet your eye, not those that are now streaming out from stars millions of miles away. The pho-tons you see, the images they form on your retina, left the stars hundreds, even thousands, of years ago. You may be look-ing at the Milky Way (our own galaxy, in which our sun is a star) and see stars as they were 9,000 years ago. The nearest star in the Big Dipper (Ursa Major or the Great Bear) is, to us, as it was 68 years ago. You have no way of even telling whether our galaxy or the Big Dipper are really there. They have certainly moved and changed since the light now reaching us was first sent out; they may even have ceased to exist altogether. We may be able to believe what our eyes tell us, but the information may be very old.

Newer information

Not all the photons that hit us originated so far away. Mole-cules raised to a high enough state of excitement shed pho-tons. When you send electrical energy through a light bulb, the metal filament (thin wire) inside it sends out photons. That is why you can read this book by lamp-light as well as daylight. These photons, too, take time to reach

Ice cube melting race

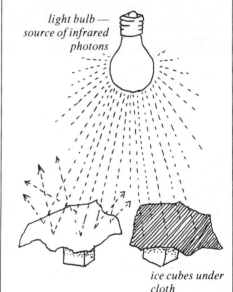

*light bulb —
source of infrared
photons*

*ice cubes under
cloth*

This is a way to see how heat photons, as well as visible light photons, are absorbed by dark surfaces (the black cloth), and bounce off light surfaces (the white cloth). Since more photons penetrate the black cloth, the ice cube under it melts first.

A cat's pupils, like ours, narrow to let in less light. . .

. . . and dilate to let in more light . The first picture was taken outdoors in bright sun, the second in the basement.

Forming images

Photons that get through the pupil hit the lens in your eye. The lens makes the image that you see. Let's say there is light hitting a small arrow. The arrow, like most ordinary objects if you were to see them through a microscope, has an uneven surface. Photons hitting it bounce every which way like ping-pong balls on a bumpy surface. The pattern of photons looks completely disorganized, not like an arrow at all. What you would see, if you could without a lens, is a sheet of light. There is no way to see the arrow because no image of the arrow has formed in space.

our eyes, but the speed is so great compared to the short distance that we see earthly objects virtually in the present.

We can stop most of the photons from penetrating our eyes by shutting our eyelids. We can control the number getting through, even when our eyes are open, by widening or narrowing our pupils. Like the shutter of a camera, the pupil is surrounded by a circle of tissue that can be contracted to close the pupil and relaxed to open it. Closing the pupil so that there is only a small opening cuts off many photons,

keeping the retina from being overwhelmed by too much light.

You can feel the muscles contracting to close the pupil by glancing directly at a very bright light. The fast contraction causes a feeling of tension: an even more sudden contraction can be painful. If you then gaze into shadows, you will feel the relief as the muscles relax. When your pupil is wide open, your eye receives all the photons it can; this helps you to see as well as possible, even in a dark room where photons are relatively scarce.

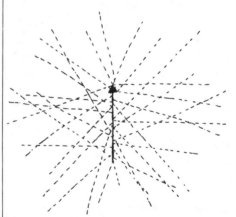

Photons bouncing off an object (the arrow) go in every direction. There is no image. Without a lens you would see only a sheet of light.

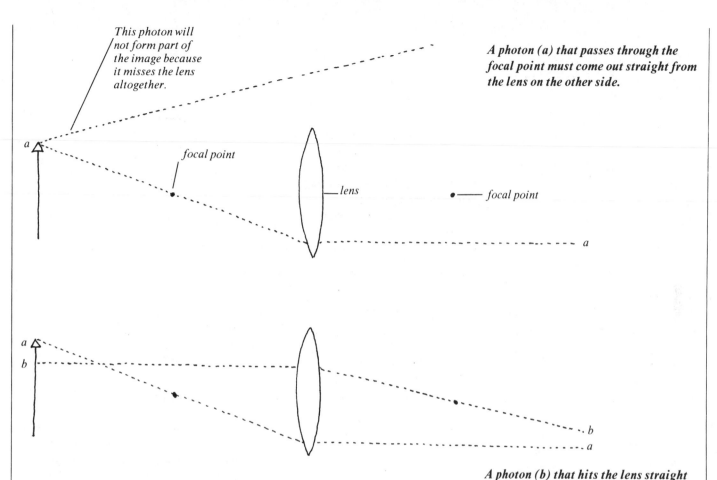

This photon will not form part of the image because it misses the lens altogether.

a

focal point

lens

focal point

a

A photon (a) that passes through the focal point must come out straight from the lens on the other side.

a

b

b

a

A photon (b) that hits the lens straight must come out from the lens at an angle that takes it through the focal point on the other side.

The lens in an eye makes a picture of an object by selecting a group of photons and bending their paths into an organized pattern. The selected group of photons are those that hit your lens. (There are countless photons that aren't aimed in your direction, or that miss the lens.) That selected group is then organized: photons hitting the lens at certain angles, instead of continuing to spread into space, are brought back together again into positions that correspond to where they were when they first left the object. Instead of seeing the photons as they are after having bounced off the object and scattered, you see them as they were a fraction of a second earlier, at the moment they left the object.

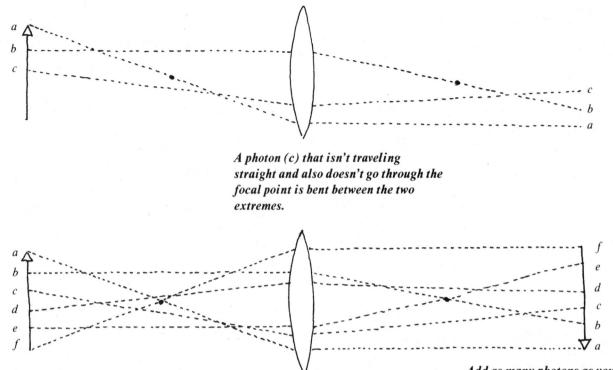

A photon (c) that isn't traveling straight and also doesn't go through the focal point is bent between the two extremes.

Add as many photons as you wish (d, e, f) and they all come out in exactly opposite order from their positions when they left the arrow. They therefore form an upside down, but otherwise perfect image of the arrow.

Changing directions

The paths of photons are bent by any transparent material as the photons enter it and as they leave it. Photons travel fastest (at the speed of light) in empty space where there is no stuff at all to interfere with their motion. They travel somewhat slower through air, and slower still through the molecules of water, glass, or the lens in your eye. As their speed is changed on entering or leaving a substance, so is the direction in which they are traveling. This is something like what happens when you throw a stone at a slant into the water. As it leaves the thinner air and enters the thicker water, it slows, and the drag bends its path somewhat downward.

Lenses, because of their curved surfaces, bend the paths of photons according to exact rules. Both in front and behind the convex lens (one that bulges in the middle like the one in your eye), is a point called the focal point. How far that point is from the lens depends on the curve of the lens. No matter where the focal point is, any photon that goes through that point on one side of the lens must come out straight on the other side, lined up parallel to any other photons that also came through the focal point. Any photon that came straight toward the lens must come out the other side at an angle that takes it through the focal point on the other side. Photons that neither enter through the focal point, nor were traveling straight at the lens, are bent at varying amounts between these two extremes.

What's up is down

Watch what happens as the photons get past the focal point on the far side of the lens: at a certain distance, the pattern they form is identical to the one existing when they left the object on the other side (except that they are reversed — up is now down, and right is left). That's the point where an image or picture of the object forms. In your eyes, that point is on your retina.

The image focused through a lens is upside down because the photons that came from the top of the object are bent so they end up at the bottom of the image while the photons that came from the bottom of the object are bent so they end up at the top of the image. Other experiences in infancy — touching and reaching for objects, walking upright — have taught you that the world is right side up; so, astonishing as it seems, your brain turns the upside-down images right side up to match with your version of reality. Newborn babies probably see the world upside down.

The cells of the retina are connected to nerve fibers. When the cell registers a hit with a photon, it sends an electrical impulse along its nerve toward the brain. The brain interprets the message as light, no matter what actually excites the nerve ending. Close your eyes so no photons can get in and press a finger against one eyeball; you will "see" light. Even a very loud noise, if the impact is enough to excite the optic nerves, can be "seen." All the nerves that connect to the retina meet in a bundle called the optic nerve, which goes from the back of the retina up to the visual center of the brain.

Brain readouts

When the message from the retina reaches the brain, it is not at all in a form you could call vision. For instance, the dots might send a message pattern that shows a very little tree right next to an enormous bug. It is up to your brain to decide on the basis of experience that the tree is far away and the bug very close. It is also up to the brain to compare the image it is presently receiving with images from past experience (the memory of what a bee looks like), including images from just prior to this one (when the bug looked a bit smaller). It must then interpret what is happening now as a bee heading straight for your face. Your brain must also predict you are about to be stung and do something about it. The various ways the brain has learned to construct reality from incoming and stored information are responsible for both correct interpretations and all sorts of illusions.

Blind spot

Close your left eye, and stare at the cross. Move your head toward the page until the dot disappears. The image of the dot is now falling on your optic nerve.

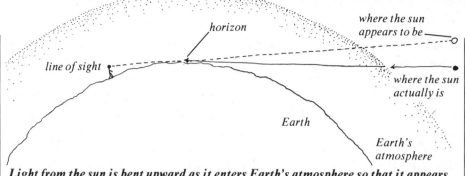

Light from the sun is bent upward as it enters Earth's atmosphere so that it appears to be above the horizon. If you hold a ruler between the actual position of the sun and the viewer's eye level, you will see that the sun is still below his line of sight, and below the horizon.

The sun appears before it rises

When you watch the sun rise, it has not yet risen above the horizon. The sunrise itself is still three or four minutes away. When you enjoy a sunset, the sun has already sunk below your line of sight. The sun sank below the horizon three or four minutes before. All the sunrises and sunsets humans have observed are illusions.

The illusion is caused by Earth's atmosphere. As light speeds from the thinness of outer space into Earth's dense atmosphere, its path is bent. This bending sends the sun's image to our waiting eyes before the sun is actually above the horizon and in our line of sight. The combined illusion-time of sunrise and sunset adds about eight minutes of sunshine to our days.

Creating an illusion

You can create an illusion of a penny by forcing its photons to travel from dense water into thinner air.

Get out a coffee cup, a pitcher of water, and a penny. Put the penny in the middle of the empty cup. Lower your head until the penny just barely disappears from sight below the rim of the cup. Now, without moving your head, fill the cup with water. The penny will appear. The strange event is caused by bending light, this time as it emerged from the water and hit the air.

Bending light accounts also for the twinkling of stars. Stars don't twinkle in outer space; they glow with a steady light. They twinkle on Earth because we are looking at them through our air. Air is a bunchy sort of stuff. In some places, the molecules are closer together; in some places, farther apart. The bunches are always moving here and there. Photons arriving through thicker patches are bent more than photons arriving through thinner patches. Since plenty of photons are coming through from a star, it looks to us as though some bits of the star were coming from one spot in the sky, other bits from slightly different spots. The star twinkles.

By the time you get to enjoy the beauty of a sunset, the sun has already disappeared below the horizon.

Eyeglass guess

As you move your eyes from near to distant objects, your lenses are pulled from a fat shape to a thinner one by the muscles attached to them. As they do so, the focal points move — closer in when the lens is fat, farther out as it gets thin. Because your lenses can change their shape, the image of both distant and very near objects can fall on your retinas. Both kinds of images, therefore, can be seen clearly.

Many humans, however, have retinas that are either too far or too close from the lens for images to be focused properly. For the person whose retina is too far from the lens, the focused image of a distant object, even after the lens has thinned as much as it is able to, forms in front of his retina. By the time the photons hit his retina, their paths have diverged again and the image is blurred. As objects come closer, the image focuses farther back, and hits the retina at the right place. Nearby objects are seen clearly. The person whose retina is too far from his lens is called nearsighted — he or she can see clearly when something is near. Farsighted people have retinas too close to the lens. They have no trouble focusing on distant objects; but for ones close by, the image hasn't formed by the time photons hit the retina.

Both nearsightedness and farsightedness can be corrected by pre-bending the paths of photons before they reach the eye with eyeglass lenses. For the farsighted person, such lenses bend the photon paths inward more; for the nearsighted person, the paths are bent outward more.

A third vision problem has to do with the shape of the lens itself. Some people have uneven lenses which bend light unevenly, forming a distorted image. This problem, called an astigmatism, can be corrected with a lens that is also uneven, but in a way opposite to the lens in the eye.

Amaze your friends by correctly guessing what is wrong with their eyes just by peeking through their glasses. Hold the pair of glasses a foot or so in front of your eyes and look through the lenses. If they make things look smaller, your friend is nearsighted. If they make things look larger, your friend is farsighted. Now rotate the glasses as you look through one lens. If, as you rotate the lens, objects are distorted in shape, that eye has an astigmatism. People can have an astigmatism in one or both eyes, with or without near- or farsightedness.

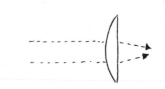

Convex lens bends light inward.

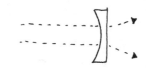

Concave lens bends light outward.

Magnifications

Lenses can help you see details of objects that are too small to form images directly on your retina. Reading lenses and toy-type magnifying glasses are helpful, but if you can, use what is called a hand microscope or field lens. This is a lens or several lenses mounted inside a tube. The usual ones, sometimes available in sporting goods stores or from opticians, are labelled 10X, which means they make an image 10 times larger than normal.

If you prefer an even more detailed image, 25 times larger, resist the temptation to buy an inexpensive school-type micro-scope. The money is better spent on a really high quality hand microscope. Student micro-scopes, which cost about the same, have higher magnifica-tions, but poor lenses that form unclear images. An excellent 25X hand lens is much more helpful and you can carry it in your pocket wherever you go. Write to: Edmund Scientific, 8985 Edscorp Building, Barring-ton, N.J. 08007 for a catalog from which you can order very good lenses.

When using a microscope, a dark background such as black velveteen or felt makes an object stand out better, and an adjusta-ble desk lamp whose light can be directed right at the object will make the image brighter.

Hair: Use a hair you have pulled from your head. The white bulb at the scalp end is the growing portion, which contin-ues to add more material to the strand of hair. The bulb is made of many cells and is alive. The rest of the strand is made of long protein molecules called keratin and is dead. When a hair falls out, the follicle in which it nes-tled makes a new bulb which begins to form a new protein chain of hair. When the follicle itself dies, the result is baldness.

By holding a magnifying glass up to the right side of his face, this boy has tricked the camera lens into photographing that side as much bigger than his left side.

Straight hair is round in cross-section. Wavy hair is round in some places, oval in others. Woolly hair is flattened like a ribbon. Twist hairs between your fingers under the lens to see if you see these shape differences.

Fingertips: Look at your fingertip to see the pattern of ridges separated by valleys. In the valleys, you may see small holes. Each hole is a pore through which sweat or oil oozes from the gland below. The ridge pattern is your fingerprint, and is slightly different from any other fingerprint in the world, even if you have an identical twin. On other skin areas you can see hairs growing from their follicles.

An arch, a loop, and a whorl are the three basic fingerprint patterns. Mixtures are called composites.

Leather: Various kinds of animal skin, even after the chemical treatment that makes them into leather, clearly show the small holes from which hairs once grew. The hair pattern from a pig (pigskin) is different from that of a cow (calfskin).

Corn stalk: Before you prepare a cob of corn for cooking, slice a very thin section from the stalk end with a kitchen knife. Rub a little ink over the surface then turn the slice over and look at the opposite side. The circles you see are the pipes through which water and food once circulated in the stalk.

Bean root: Sprout a bean (page 99) and let it grow until it is several inches long. At this point, you should be able to see, through the lens, root hairs growing from the thick main roots. The root hairs are the only portion of the root that absorb water and dissolved minerals from the soil.

Flowers: Choose blossoms that are fully open. Look at the anthers (page 88). If an anther is smooth, the pollen is still inside it. An older flower should have grains of pollen sticking to the anthers, and you may be able to see that the pollen grains of different kinds of flowers have different shapes. Use a single-edged razor blade to slice through the flower's ovary, and see if you can get a look at the ova as well.

Molds: Look at any mold (page 74) after it begins to look powdery or fuzzy. You may be able to make out the tiny round spores atop short stalks and you will certainly see the tangle of hyphas from which spores will grow.

Spiderlings: Search around cobwebs for round, papery sacs in which spiders keep their eggs. Open them to see if the eggs have hatched. Spiderlings, as the hatchlings are called, and other tiny creatures like aphids, can be watched through the lens even as they move about.

Coins: The portraits on some coins are signed by the artist. Look for the initials "VDB" under Lincoln's shoulder on Lincoln pennies. The initials stand for Victor D. Brenner. John Sinnock signed his initials, "JS," under Franklin Roosevelt's neck on the Roosevelt dime.

Paper money: Under a lens, you can easily make out the red and blue threads pressed into the paper from which American bills are made. The special paper is one way the government foils counterfeiters.

Newspaper and magazine pictures: Both black-and-white and full-color pictures in printed materials are made up of tiny polka dots. With a black-and-white newspaper photo, move your lens around from lighter to darker areas. There are always the same number of dots per square inch, but larger dots make an area darker; smaller ones make it lighter. When you look at a color photograph, you'll discover the picture is made from dots of black, lemon-yellow, turquoise-blue, and magenta.

Crystals: Molecules of many chemicals arrange themselves in patterns. The even shapes that result are called crystals. The crystals of table salt, for instance, will look like cubes under your lens. Some sugar crystals are long, with pointed ends.

Try looking at such substances as boric acid and epsom salts. As these come from the drugstore rather finely ground, you might need to make larger crystals. Pour ¼ cup water into a small saucepan. Add the substance you wish to crystallize, a little at a time, and stir to dissolve. Put the pot on the stove to heat the water (but not boil it) and add still more of the substance. The idea is to get as much as possible to dissolve. When no more will dissolve, prepare a shallow Pyrex plate by heating it under the hot water tap, then drying it. Pour the solution into the warm plate and let it sit.

As the liquid cools, crystals will begin to form. You can actually watch them grow through your lens. Epsom salts form long needle-shaped crystals; boric acid crystals form patterns as lovely as snowflakes.

Mirror, mirror

While your eye is receiving photons bounced off objects, the objects are receiving photons bounced off you, which in turn are bouncing back to your eyes. When the surface of an object is very smooth, even if you were to look at it under a microscope, all the photons bounce back in the same pattern as when they left; you see your own photons returning. That's what happens every time you look at yourself in a mirror.

Photons bounce off the smooth silvery backing of a mirror much as a ball bounces off the floor. You know from experience that when you throw a ball at the floor, it bounces off the floor at about the same angle that you threw it — that is, you wouldn't expect to slant it at the floor and have it bounce back straight up; and you would be surprised if you bounced the ball straight down and it took off at an angle. Photons obey the same bouncing rules when they strike a mirror.

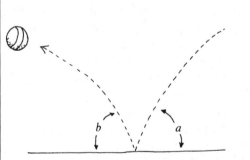

The angle (b) at which a ball leaves the ground is the same as the angle (a) at which it arrived.

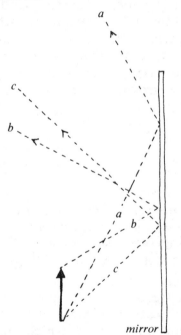

Photons from the arrow bounce off the mirror the same way a ball bounces off a smooth surface.

Through the looking-glass

When your photons bounce from your face to the surface of a mirror and back to your eyes, you see the image as though it were on the other side of the mirror. This is because your eyes don't figure out that the photons have behaved unusually. They assume they are, as usual, coming directly from their source. Follow the photons' paths in the illustration here and you will see that the eye must figure out the image is coming from beyond the mirror.

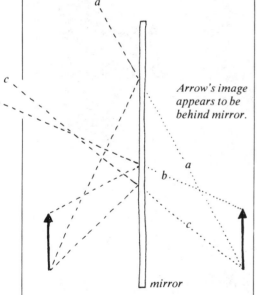

Arrow's image appears to be behind mirror.

The eye, taking no account of bouncing, tracks the photon paths back to their apparent source — on the other side of the mirror.

If you have two large mirrors you are allowed to use for this, you can try the following experiment. Lean the mirrors against opposite walls in a hallway or against two pieces of furniture so they face one another about three feet apart. Stand back and place your hand between the two. Look at the images you see in both the mirrors. You will be able to see your hand repeated over and over again, each time farther away and smaller. (If you don't, fiddle around with the positions of the mirrors until you do.) Looking into one mirror, you will see first the palm of your hand, and behind it, the back of your hand, followed by another palm, then another back, and so on, until the images become too small and dim for you to make out. The material that backs the mirror is grainy, like the surface of your retina. If it weren't, the images would continue into microscopic sizes.

What is happening is this: photons bounce from your palm to one mirror, then back to the other mirror, then back to the first, and so on. Photons from the back of your hand hit the other mirror and also bounce back and forth between them. You see images of images of images.

By setting up two mirrors opposite each other, you can make multiple images of both your front and back side.

If the mirrors are three feet from one another and your hand is exactly in the middle, each palm image will seem to be one and a half feet from the next back image. Move your hand nearer or farther from one of the mirrors to see how the distance in the image also changes.

You'll notice that off in the distance, the image of your hand gets dimmer and dimmer, until it is too dark to see clearly. At each trip between mirrors, some of the photons are entering your eye or being absorbed by your body and the mirror — they are out of the game, so to speak. The fewer photons there are, the dimmer the image. Finally, there are not enough photons still in the bouncing game to register on your retinas.

If, at the moment you place your hand in between the mirrors, you could slow the action down enormously, you would see the first image form, then the second, then another — for it does take time for photons to bounce across that three feet to form the next image. At the incredible speed of light, however, it all seems to happen simultaneously.

Amazing maze

Draw a curvy path like the one shown here, or any other maze you wish, at one end of a piece of paper. Fold up the other end to form a barrier. Sit at a table, with the maze in front of you, and hold a hand mirror beyond the paper so the only way you can see the maze past the barrier is by looking in the mirror. Now try to draw a line all the way through the path without going over the edges. As you will discover, what you see in a mirror is not the same as the object itself. The maze is reversed left to right. Every time you try to turn a corner, your hand, fooled by the reversed image, makes a wrong move.

Visual purple

The molecule in your retina that is responsible for registering the entrance of a photon is called visual purple (rhodopin). Like many large molecules, visual purple is made of smaller molecules. These are named opsin and retinal. The retinal molecule comes in two shapes — a "comfortable," opened-out shape, and an "uncomfortable" one, more like a tightly closed fist. Only the uncomfortable, curled shape can fit within the opsin molecule — like a closed fist inside an open hand — to form a visual purple molecule.

When a photon hits a visual purple molecule, its energy is absorbed by the retinal end of the molecule, and this energy is used to snap it into the more comfortable position. But now, in this different shape, it no longer fits well against the opsin part of the molecule, and the two come apart. The breakage is what releases energy which eventually excites the optic nerve, communicating the fact of light to the brain.

Seeing in the dark

You can prove to yourself that visual purple is constantly breaking apart as it is assaulted by photons simply by walking into a dark room, for example, a movie theater. At first, you can barely see. Many visual purple molecules had come apart in the bright daylight. This was no problem outdoors where photons were plentiful, but the few photons now hitting your retina fall as often on a "blank" spot (one where the visual purple molecule has come apart) as on an active one. You bump into people and have a hard time finding an empty seat. After a few minutes, however, the theater seems to become much brighter; now that you can see clearly, it becomes hard to understand why latercomers are fumbling so. What has happened is this: your eyes have rebuilt visual purple as they always do, but now the molecules are not coming apart so often because fewer photons are hitting them. Gradually the blank spots are filled in, and the retina is covered nearly completely with visual purple molecules.

Where shadows fall

A shadow is an absence of light. It is caused by an obstacle coming between a source of light and a surface on which the light is falling. The darkness of a cloudy day is a shadow, though not a perfect one. Some sunlight is coming through the obstacle of clouds and falling on the Earth's surface. Night is a shadow. The obstacle is the Earth itself. The part of the moon you don't see when it is less than full is a shadow, too; or, if you wish, it is the night of the moon. An object that is completely transparent — photons travel through it without getting stuck inside — leaves no shadow. But you can prove to yourself that glass, transparent as it appears, does trap some of the light falling on it. The next time a glass breaks, carefully hold a piece of it up so the sun shines through it onto a wall. It has a shadow. The shadow is the amount of light that isn't getting through.

Shadow sizes

When the sun is high in the sky, the shadow of an airplane

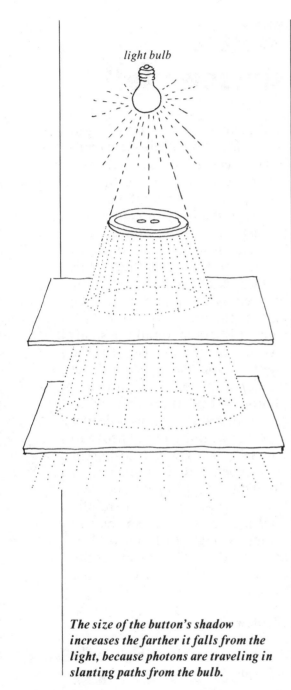

light bulb

The size of the button's shadow increases the farther it falls from the light, because photons are traveling in slanting paths from the bulb.

flying above the surface of the Earth is the same size as the airplane, both when the plane is taking off and when it is a mile high in the sky. You can see that the same is true of your hand's shadow at midday. Measure the width of your hand. Hold your hand over a flat surface (outdoors) around noon to make a shadow. If your hand measured four inches across, so will the shadow — whether you hold your hand a few inches or a few feet from the ground. Yet, when you watch shadows caused by a single lamp in an otherwise dark room, they are smaller when close to the lamp, but grow to gigantic proportions on a far wall.

The difference between the shadow from the sun and the shadow from a lamp is explained by the paths of photons coming from the light source. Photons from the sun that intercept the Earth have traveled straight toward us on parallel paths. A shadow caused by such parallel rays of light is the same size as the obstacle that caused it.

A light bulb, however, is very close. The light from a bulb is composed of photons traveling at every possible angle. Close to the light, their paths have not diverged much, and the area of missing light behind an obstacle is nearly the same size as the obstacle. Farther away, they have diverged more; as they spread, so does the shadow.

This is not the only way in which shadows can change in size. As anyone who has taken a walk early in the morning or late in the afternoon on a sunny day has noticed, when the sun is low in the sky, shadows are much longer than the obstacle that causes them. The same is true of shadows cast on a slanted surface. Put your hand in the sun again, but this time let the shadow fall on a piece of cardboard. Tilt it this way and that to watch your shadow change size — and shape, too.

Changing shapes

A way to understand why this is so is to picture a shadow not as the two-dimensional thing you see lying on a surface, but as the whole, three-dimensional area of missing light. Here, for instance, is the three-dimensional shadow of a round button. The shadow is a cylinder stretching to an infinite distance beyond the button. Now imagine a piece of cardboard cutting through the darkness of the cylinder. If it is held straight, the shadow that falls on it will be a circle that is the same size and shape as the button. But if the

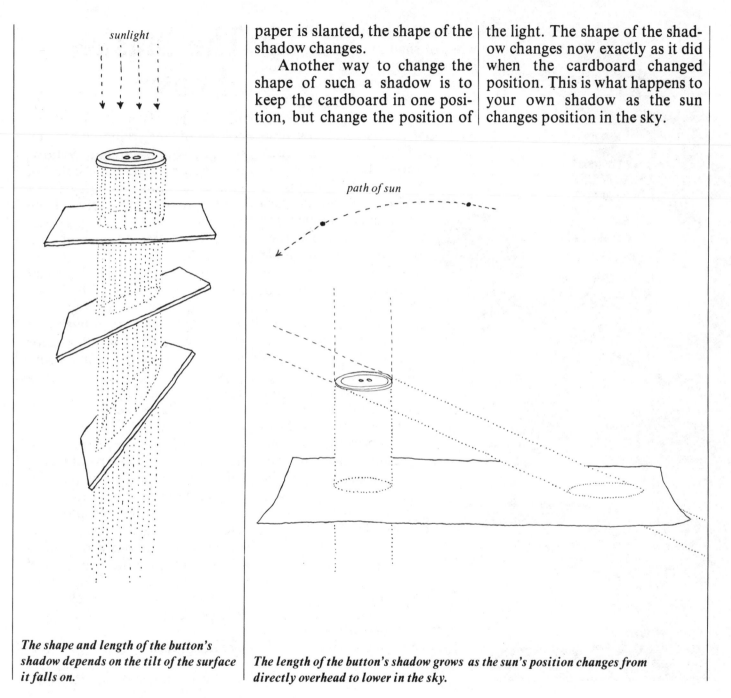

sunlight

path of sun

paper is slanted, the shape of the shadow changes.

Another way to change the shape of such a shadow is to keep the cardboard in one position, but change the position of the light. The shape of the shadow changes now exactly as it did when the cardboard changed position. This is what happens to your own shadow as the sun changes position in the sky.

The shape and length of the button's shadow depends on the tilt of the surface it falls on.

The length of the button's shadow grows as the sun's position changes from directly overhead to lower in the sky.

Even without following the whys of shadows, you can enjoy making them behave in odd ways. For instance, make hand shadows on a wall at night by letting them fall on a big piece of white paper. Use a strong, lantern-type flashlight for the clearest shadows. Bow the paper inward or outward. You can use freezer tape to hold an outward curved sheet against the wall or an inward curved one between two table legs. You can even curve it several times, so that it has a wavy surface, or pleat it. When you cast hand shadows on a bowed, curvy or pleated, surface, you'll find they move in odd ways, too. Parts of the shadow falling on flat surfaces will move just as your hand is moving, but as the shadow dips into a bend and lengthens, it will appear to speed up.

As you move farther away from a close by source of light, the shadow you cast will look much bigger and scarier.

The illusion of color

Visible light is made up of the colors of the rainbow: violet, indigo, blue, green, yellow, orange, and red. Each color of light is photons that carry a particular quantity of energy. Each red-light photon, for instance, carries less energy than a photon of blue light.

Your eye is able to absorb all the photons — each with its particular quantity of energy — in visible light, yet it is only able to send a one-, two-, or three-color message to your brain. From these three color messages (they are red, blue, and green), your brain is able to "see" all the colors you know.

The color you see depends on how many of each type of receptor have been excited by the light hitting your eye. If an equal number of all three receptors are excited, you will "see" white. Mixtures of various proportions of the three give the sensation of all the other colors. When none are excited, you see black — or an absence of color.

Creating green

You can check out for yourself a portion of this color code by playing with colored afterimages. With a crayon, make a large, solidly colored, red polka dot on white paper. Stare at it for a while; try not to move your eyes. After a minute or so, move your eyes to another sheet of white paper. You will "see" a green polka dot. This is what has happened: the color receptors that are most sensitive to red light, and that have sent red messages to your brain, have been excited for some time. They no longer respond well. It's as though they were tired. The light bounced from the white paper contains all the colors. The tired receptors in the circular area of your retina which had been responding to the dot, now fail to react to the red portion of light from the white paper. What you see is white with red subtracted from it, a situation your brain interprets as green.

On your retina where all three types of receptors are functioning well, you see white — all the actual color bouncing from the paper. The opposite would happen if the original polka dot were green. Its afterimage would look red. You can try the same experiment with violet (the afterimage is yellow), or blue (the afterimage is orange). And of course you can do each experiment the opposite way, to produce violet or blue after images.

In fact, you can create a red, white, and blue American flag using the afterimages that result from subtracting certain colors from white. Draw the flag and crayon it with the following col-

The colors of the stripes on this flag are alternating black and green, the stars, black on an orange field. When this girl finishes staring hard at it for about a minute, then looks quickly at a blank piece of white paper, the afterimage will appear as a normal, red, white, and blue flag.

ors: the stripes alternately black and green, with black stars on an orange field. Stare at it as you did the polka dot. When you move your eyes to white paper, the afterimage of the flag will appear red, white, and blue.

Just like magic

Another way to become aware of how the three types of color receptors in your eye encode every possible color for your brain is to watch a photograph from an instant camera developing. The paper on which the photograph will appear after being exposed to light contains three layers of dye — yellow, magenta, and blue — each of which responds to only certain frequencies of light. After exposure to light (when you take the picture), these layers of dye gradually form the color of the photographed objects. You can watch how the color forms (the order in which each dye appears varies with light and temperature conditions) as each dye in turn appears. From the three colors, your brain reconstructs the color composition of the original light that went into the camera, even though those colors are not on the snapshot.

If you don't have a Polaroid, look through a magnifying lens at color printing in magazine ads. The picture is actually four colors of polka dots: magenta, turquoise, yellow, and black. You will find no other colors in the picture, yet when you remove the lens, the sensation caused by the various mixtures of dots is equivalent to any color at all.

Are you sure it's red?

The ability to create colors, rather than record exactly what is really there, means that we can't be sure of what color something really is. For instance, if we are looking at a glass of water in which a red dye has been dissolved, it looks red. But it may look red for either of two different reasons. Molecules of a particular substance can absorb only certain energy packets of visible light. A red vegetable dye, dissolved in water, may be able to absorb all the various energies except that of red-light photons. Those photons cannot sink into the red dye. They bounce back from the unaccepting surface, hit our eyes, and we see red.

There is another way we may see that dye as red. Perhaps, for instance, those particular molecules can absorb only the energy packets carried by green light photons. In that case, all the colors except green are bouncing off the dye molecules and hitting our eyes. In our code, however, white (all colors) minus green equals red — so, again, the dye looks red. When only red light struck our eyes, the actual color of the dye and the color we saw were the same. But when all colors except green bounced back, the actual colors (violet, indigo, blue, yellow, orange, and red) were quite different from the red color we saw.

More confusion

There is still another way a substance can confuse you as to its "real" color. With help from an adult, put several green tree leaves (spinach works too) in the top of a double boiler. Fill the bottom with water, the top with just enough rubbing alcohol to cover the leaves. Set the double boiler on a low heat on the stove. As it heats, lower the flame (or turn it off altogether) so the alcohol gets hot, but doesn't boil (it boils at a lower temperature than water). Within 10 minutes, you will notice that the alcohol has turned a rich green from the chlorophyll in the leaves. Remove the pot from the stove and let the alcohol cool. When it is cool, use a funnel to pour the green liquid into a small clear glass bottle. Throw the leaves away.

When you hold this bottle in the light, you will have no doubt the liquid in it is green. But wait until dark. Now hold the bottle up to a small, bright source of light, such as a candle or a flashlight, in a dark room. The liquid glows ruby red.

Chlorophyll absorbs red light photons. All the other colors bounce off it; the result in ordinary light — white minus red — is green to us. But something quite different happens when a light is shined through the liquid in a dark room. You can't see any photons that are bouncing back — they are all on the other side of the bottle, where the light is (check to see this is so — the liquid looks green over there.) The only light you can see is that which has come through the chlorophyll-dyed alcohol to your side of the bottle. But chlorophyll can only absorb red light. What a molecule can absorb, it can also send out. The chlorophyll-dyed alcohol absorbs only red light from the flashlight and sends out the same: you see red. The odd question is, what color is chlorophyll — green or red?

Optical illusions

What you see, even in black and white, is not the same as how you interpret what you see. The letters in the word "TILT" are not really tipping. To check, hold the book away from you and squint to blur the letters; or take a look at the word from about ten feet away. After you are sure the letters are actually straight, look at the picture normally again. Even though you now know it isn't so, they are still going to look tipsy.

This illusion is the result of the way we move our eyes, and what we expect this movement to tell us. We move our eyes along lines. You can catch yourself doing this when you look at buildings. If the building is tall, you'll find yourself moving your eyes vertically. If the building is low, you'll find yourself moving your eyes horizontally. To look at the leaning tower of Pisa, you would move your eyes diagonally. In each case, the eye movement would tell your brain whether the object was long (horizontal) or tall (vertical) or tilted. Since all the lines that make up the word "TILT" are tilted, your brain interprets the letters as tilted, too. They only appear to stand up straight when you blur the image to get rid of the tilted clues.

To see just how helpless you are to control this tendency of your eyes to follow lines, look at these arrangements of arrows. The first arrangement is rather restful; the arrows seem to be telling your eyes where to stop.

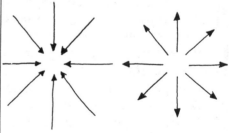

But the second one is downright annoying. There's no place to rest your eyes because they keep trying to follow those arrows in every direction.

Moon mirage

Anyone who watches moonrises has noticed that as the moon appears above the horizon, it is dramatically large; and that as it rises higher over the Earth, it becomes much smaller. That familiar shrinking moon is an optical illusion.

First, remember that the moon doesn't rise higher at all. The Earth is revolving on its axis, and the moon is slowly spinning its way around the Earth, but nothing is jumping up and down. A rising moon is the same distance from your eyes when it "rises" as it will be for the remainder of the night. What is true is that the horizon is quite close to you and the sky above your head infinitely far away. Experience has taught all of us that when an object is close by, it appears larger than when it is far away. When you see the rising moon at the horizon, your brain says, "My, that's quite close!" and exaggerates the image of the moon to suit the logic. By the time the moon is above your head where no trees, hills, or buildings offer distance clues, your brain pays attention only to the actual image it is receiving on the retina of your eye. Now you see the moon's image for what it is — pretty small.

If you doubt that you can be taken in by your own brain — even after its tricks have been explained to you — try this: at moonrise when the moon is full, hold a piece of notebook paper against the window in a dark room. Look through one of the holes, and move your head this way and that, until you can see the moon through it. The moment the moon is "trapped" in the hole, it will lose its illusion of bigness. If you like, you can trap the moon in the hole later at night, and see that it still fits into the hole the same way it did when it was rising. The size of the moon's image on your retina — about the same size as the hole — has not changed at all. The illusion of a big moon at the horizon, by the way, will not change even though you have now shown it for what it is. It's much more important for your brain to keep its own rules.

Eye speed

Eyes don't move equally fast in all directions. They move faster along a horizontal line; slower along a vertical line. This explains why it's almost impossible to draw a perfect square. Try it. When you feel the square is correct, turn the drawing on its side. Now the square will look too high. What you drew was a figure that required equal lengths of time to scan in both directions — a certain amount of time to move quickly along the longer horizontal lines; the same amount of time to move slowly along the shorter vertical lines. When you draw a perfect square using a ruler to measure the sides, your brain will compare time as your eyes scan the lines, and come to the conclusion that the square is too tall.

The eyes' habit of following lines can interfere with seeing shapes correctly. The square is inside a perfect circle, though it looks flattened where it touches the square corners. As your eyes attempt to move around the circle, they are pulled inward every time they get to a corner. The brain interprets the pattern of movement as a round shape flattened or even dented in four places.

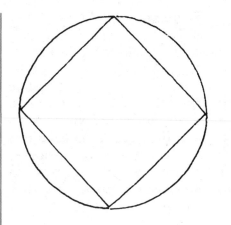

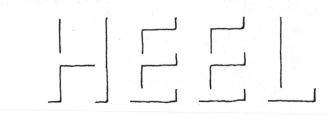

The effect is more dramatic with the wavy checkerboard pattern. Actually, all the lines are parallel. Your eye movements, however, are not. The squares form diagonal patterns. Your eyes may start to track a vertical, then veer into the diagonal motion, and again back to the vertical. Wavering from straight to diagonal and back again is to the brain a perfectly recognizable pattern: waviness.

Some illusions depend on learning; that is, the brain compares an image to others stored in memory, and then makes a decision about it. Here's the word "HEEL" written in block letters. Or at least that's what your brain decides. Look closely and you'll see there are really no block letters at all — only an arrangement of lines. But when the arrangement is compared to memories of block letters, the lines correspond to where shadows would fall. The brain jumps to conclusions with little evidence.

A similar example is the case of the missing slice. To find the slice of cake in the picture, just turn it upside down. The picture is the same either way, but since your brain can't accept a cake held upside down, it prefers to see a slice of cake in a cake pan.

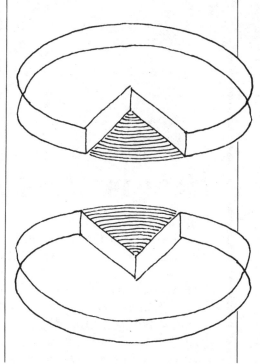

There are other kinds of illusions in which the brain isn't interpreting anything incorrectly, but is having trouble choosing between equally possible interpretations. In other words, there are not sufficient clues to make a firm decision. Take this transparent box, for instance. There are four different ways to get something into it, and they are all equally plausible.

How do you put something into this box? You can find four ways if you concentrate.

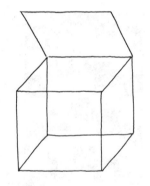

through the back

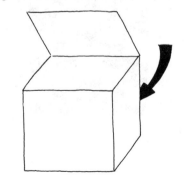

Hole in the hand

Roll a piece of paper into a narrow tube (or use a paper-towel tube). Hold the tube to your left eye, but keep both eyes open. Place your right hand next to the tube, about two inches from the far end. You will see your hand with a round hole right through it. You can look through the hole in your hand to the world beyond. (People who are left-eyed, as tested on page 209, should put the tube to their right eye, and their left hand next to the tube.)

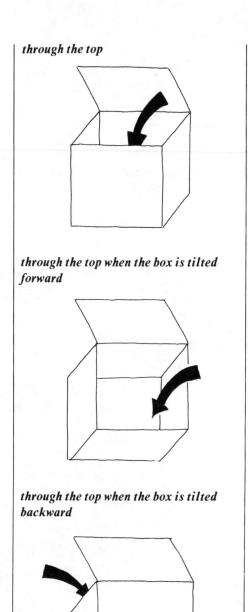

through the top

through the top when the box is tilted forward

through the top when the box is tilted backward

Right- or left-eyed?

Because there is a distance between your two eyes, they each see the world from a different angle. Your brain prefers one of these versions over the other. To find out if your brain pays more attention to the positions of objects seen by your left eye or your right eye, try this experiment. Stand up, and ask someone to make a circle with his thumb and forefinger about three feet in front of you. With both eyes open, move about until some object in the room — a picture on the wall or a lamp — falls just in the center of the circle. Close one eye, then the other, and notice what happens to the image. Through one eye, the picture or lamp will appear to one side of the circle. Through the other, it will be in the center, just as it was when both eyes were open. You are right-eyed if the image you see with just that eye open is the same as what you see with both eyes open; you are left-eyed (much rarer) if it works the other way around.

In a way, you have known for a long time which eye your brain depends on more. Hand someone a sheet of paper with a small hole torn in the middle of it. Tell him to hold the paper in both hands and look through the hole. Right-eyed people place the hole in front of their right eye automatically, while left-eyed people hold the hole to their left eye. The reason you have to ask the person to pick up the sheet with both hands is that some people can be right-handed, left-footed, and left-eyed — or any other combination. If you hand a right-handed person a rolled tube of paper, he will take it with his right hand and hold it to his right eye, even if he is left-eyed. The other movement is just too awkward.

People from families where there are left-handed people are more likely to be left-handed, to have mixes of left and right preferences for eyes and feet and hands, or even to be ambidextrous — good with both hands, able to write or eat with either hand.

Tastes & Smells

Atomic poetry

What you are about to read is wrong. It is wrong in the same way poetry is wrong. When a poet writes, "The moon, like a silver watch . . . ," he does not expect you to look up in the sky and see what time it is. When a scientist says, "The atom, like a sphere surrounded by a cloud of electrons . . . ," he doesn't mean that that is actually the way an atom looks. The "silver watch," the "sphere," and the "cloud" are words that may be helpful to you in forming images, but are not the truth of the matter — as exploration of the moon's surface and experiments with atoms have shown.

With that in mind, here is a description of an atom of hydrogen, the simplest of all the elements. In the center is a nucleus consisting of a single proton. You can picture it as a blob spread out in space. Very far out from the nucleus is a single electron, two thousand times smaller and lighter than a proton. You may picture it as a point. It not only spins on its own axis, but it rotates around the nucleus as well at an average of a certain distance from the nucleus, though at any given moment it is impossible to say where it is; it may be that it is very much farther away or very much closer.

Repelling electrons

The greatest part of the hydrogen atom (or any other kind) is empty space. Atoms are so small that a row of 423 million hydrogen atoms could line up along one inch of a ruler. But, if you were to enlarge one so that a period on this page were the hydrogen nucleus, its electron

The balloons are filled with atoms of helium. Everything else in the picture, and almost everything you know, is molecules formed from atoms bonded to one another.

would be about 30 yards away. That space is never entered by other atoms; electrons are the atom's only communication with the outside world. Not that electrons ever touch one another, either — they repel one another too strongly for that. This means that nothing — not your finger, or your food, or your clothing, or your cat — ever really touches anything else. What feels like a touch is electrons on atoms repelling electrons on other atoms. Empty space surrounds every speck of stuff you know.

A force called the electromagnetic force exists in space around the electron and proton, influencing both of them and acting as a glue. The force carries electrical charge — that from the proton is called a positive charge and that from the electron is called a negative charge. The words positive and negative don't mean the proton has something which the electron lacks. Both have an equal amount of charge, but you can think of them as being in opposite directions. Positive and negative charges exert an attraction between them. Negative and negative, or positive and positive charges exert a repulsion between them.

Superforce

The electromagnetic force is much stronger than gravity. It also has much more to do with your everyday life than gravity does. It is the same force that carries all photons — from radio waves to visible light to X-rays. It is what holds everything — rocks, spaghetti, people — together. It makes sugar dissolve in coffee, matches burn, bleach remove grass stains, and enzymes digest hamburgers. Seeing, hearing, feeling, smelling, tasting, and thinking all require the energy it guides.

To stick together to become molecules, atoms share electrons between them. The sharing is called bonding. Atoms bond, however, only if such cooperation makes for a more comfortable arrangement. For the atom, comfortable means requiring less energy to stick together. Because it would seem relatively easy for hydrogen's one positively charged proton to hold onto its one negatively charged electron, you would think hydrogen was already comfortable, and not inclined to bond with another atom. Comfort, however, has more to do with how electrons fill the space around the nucleus than with how closely and tightly they are held.

Buildings in space

You can think of the space around a nucleus as though it were divided into floors. No more than two electrons fill the first floor. On each of the next two, eight more can fit; on the fourth, 18; and so on, for many floors. What's more, the floors act as though they were further divided into rooms, in each of which only two electrons can be. There are very complicated rules about the order in which an atom prefers to fill its rooms and floors, but whenever the preference isn't met, the atom is uncomfortable, and is more likely to enter into a relationship that will make it more comfortable by decreasing its energy needs.

The simplest comfortable state is two electrons on the first floor. But hydrogen has only one, so it in fact shares its electron willingly so as to gain a partner electron in the deal. Single hydrogen atoms are rare on our planet. For the most part, they exist only momentarily, when they are torn from one molecule and captured by another.

The atoms of all other elements — iron, oxygen, calcium, and others — have additional parts in their nuclei called neutrons. The neutron, unlike the proton, has no charge and affects mostly the weight of an element. Otherwise, all these other elements are similar to the hydrogen atom except in the number of their parts. Hydrogen, with the fewest parts, is the simplest atom. Next comes helium, which has two electrons and two protons (plus two neutrons). Helium is perfectly comfortable because it has two electrons in the space closest to its nucleus, which fill that floor. Because of this, helium rarely bonds, and what helium there is on Earth is in the form of single atoms.

The sum of their parts

Since elements differ from one another, from the simplest and lightest to the most complicated and heaviest, only by the number of their parts, it is amazing that the white calcium atoms that give hardness to our teeth can be so different from the neon gas atoms that light our signs, or the carbon atoms we use to smudge our faces on Halloween.

Yet, these small differences account not only for how the elements differ from one another, but for how they are likely to behave with other atoms to form molecules.

No matter how great the discomfort of an atom, getting close enough to another atom in order to share electrons and to become a molecule is difficult. Both groups of electrons have a negative charge; they strongly repel one another. Extra energy is often needed to push atoms together so they can form a bond. Once a bond is formed, it may be very strong. Again, extra energy is needed to tear it apart.

Almost any form of energy will do to help form or to help break a bond. Light energy, for instance, adds push to atoms already bonded together in your blue jeans. In sunlight, the blue dye molecules break apart; your jeans fade. Heat energy gives the extra push it takes to break old bonds and form new ones when a match is burned or a potato is cooked. Heat energy, in fact, runs the chemistry of your body. Where does all this extra energy come from? From your own muscles, from other atoms in a bottle of bleach or vinegar or alcohol, or from the ends of the universe — in the form of photons.

Tasty smelly

As the smell of bacon drifts through your nostrils, as its salty

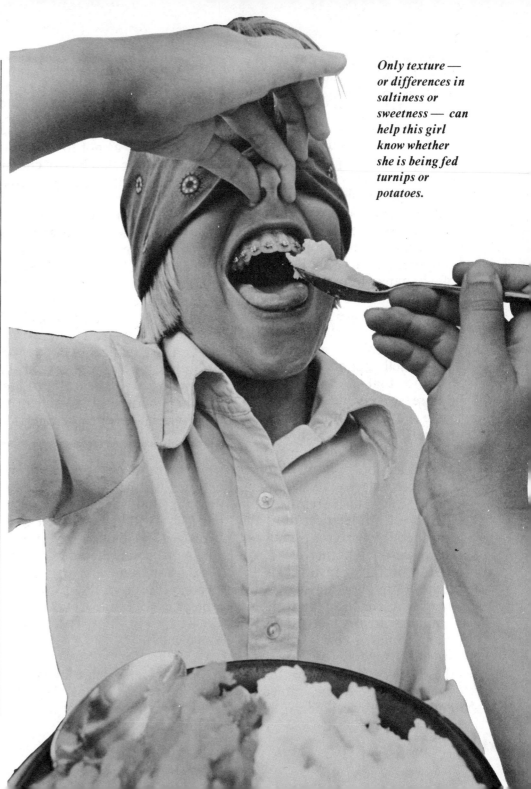

Only texture — or differences in saltiness or sweetness — can help this girl know whether she is being fed turnips or potatoes.

flavor spreads over your tongue, your knowledge of it as bacon depends on identifying molecules. High up within and behind the bony portion of your nose, and scattered over the surface of your tongue, are receptors that are activated by specific molecules. Molecules of salts, sugars, acids, and some chemicals called bases are recognized by receptors on the tongue. Other molecules, like the fragrance of a banana or the odor of bacon (they are constructed of as many as 100 atoms) are recognized by the nose.

We tend to use the words taste and smell quite sloppily. We assume that we smell bacon before it gets in our mouths, taste it after it is in our mouths. In fact, we mostly smell what we are eating. Human tongues send the brain only four different messages: sweet, salty, sour, and bitter. Each taste represents a group of molecules, but the members of the group may not resemble one another at all. All that is sweet, for instance, is not sugar (although all sugars are sweet). A chemical that has no similarity to a sugar may taste many times sweeter than the sweetest sugars we know. Yet the taste buds on the tongue which respond to such molecules and send the sweet message must

What skins can taste

This is a slightly unpleasant experiment and you must do it carefully so as not to hurt yourself. But it does show that the cells of your skin have a chemical sense, too.

Soak a tablespoon of dried hot peppers (the kind that is served in pizza parlors) in a ¼ cup of hot water for 20 minutes. Gingerly, dab a drop of the water on your tongue. You will taste the spicy hotness. Now place a small patch of the soaked peppers themselves on the inside of your wrist. You will "taste" the same hotness there, too. Wash your hands and wrist well with soap and water now because the sensation is even stronger if you happen to get any of the spice inside your nose or eyes. The burning feeling on your tongue will go away in 20 minutes; your wrist will recover soon, too.

The chemical in hot peppers responsible for sensations of hotness on the tongue and skin is one of a group called phenols. Very simple forms of life may sense chemicals over their whole bodies — as you can hot peppers — without the need of special chemical receptors such as taste buds.

find something in common between them. It is currently thought that, perhaps, a very particular distance between two hydrogen bonds on any molecule may be interpreted as sweetness, no matter what the shape or composition of the rest of the molecule.

Taste buds

Such a false sense of sweetness, however, is not the way taste works in everyday life. On the whole, anything you taste as sweet contains a natural or synthetic sugar (the chemical names of all sugars end in "-ose", like fructose, dextrose, sucrose and glucose). Sour foods contain acids, such as vinegar or the citric acid found in citrus fruits. The sour taste of vomit is the hydrochloric acid produced in your own stomach. Both of these chemical sensitivities no doubt helped our ancestors determine which fruits were ripe, which green — and saved them from

Tongue map

Look at your tongue in the mirror. The rosy bumps you see are large pores which protect tiny taste buds, the chemical receptors for the four tastes of sweet, sour, salty, and bitter. Here is an experiment that seems to show that taste buds are not evenly distributed over your tongue. To find out what taste buds are where, mix bottle tops of liquid flavors: sugar water, salt water, water with vinegar added, and another with unsweetened fresh grapefruit juice.

Draw a tongue-shaped diagram on paper. Lay out four round toothpicks. Dip the first in the vinegar solution and touch it to various areas on your tongue. When you taste the sourness at any spot, make a small circle on your diagram at that spot. Rinse your mouth to cleanse it of any vinegar, and repeat with each of the flavors in turn, using a different symbol, such as an X or Y, each time.

This appears to be a real scientific experiment, but it points out a frequent problem in science. Recently, it has been discovered that any taste bud anywhere on the tongue may respond to two or more of the four basic flavors, but that the pattern by which it fires the message to the brain may differ for each taste. A receptor in one location may fire rapidly for sugar, haltingly for salt, while another receptor in another location may do just the opposite. It's up to the brain to put together these varying patterns from different places to figure out what you're tasting. Now scientists have to figure out how come you could make the tongue map you just made. Was the map a tongue map or was it really showing something happening in your brain?

If this experiment is done carefully, rinsing the mouth after each taste of the toothpick, most people find that they taste sweetness most easily at the tip of the tongue, saltiness at both tip and sides, sourness in areas behind the saltiness areas, and bitterness at the back of the tongue.

many a tummy ache.

Bitterness is certainly a warning signal. Most of the plants that contain a bitter-tasting substance are either poisons or irritants to humans. An exception is grapefruit, which has a definite bitterness.

Salty foods all contain salts, usually sodium chloride. Most sodium chloride, or common table salt, is mined from huge salt deposits left behind when vast seas evaporated from our planet millions of years ago.

(The "sea salt" favored by some health-conscious people is misleading — all table salt originally comes from seas.) A fluid similar in chemistry to sea water flows through your body, too. You can taste the salt in tears, sweat, blood, and the clear fluid called lymph that fills a blister.

Smell receptors

Your nose is a much more delicate sense organ than your tongue. It can differentiate between up to 4,000 distinct molecules. The combinations of these molecules, as they drift through the air and into your nose, tell you what's for dinner before you see or taste it. And when you get the food into your mouth, its scent molecules continue to drift up the opening from the back of your mouth into your nasal spaces.

To prove to yourself that the nose knows what you're eating, try identifying food without it. With your eyes closed and your nose held shut, foods that are similar in texture — like mashed potatoes and mashed turnips — may be indistinguishable. Think back to your last cold — a stuffy nose can rob a dinner of flavor.

Many theories as to what it is that the smell receptors recognize have been tried, so far with

Why cats don't beg for cookies

Most dogs will do everything but stand on their heads to get a cookie from you. Cats don't seem to care. The reason for this startling difference in behavior lies in different tongues. Cats have no chemical receptors for sugar. Next time you bake cookies, plan to add the sugar last. Remove a little dough before you add the sugar, and bake that unsweetened dough along with the other cookies. When they're finished, taste an unsweetened one. That's more like what a cat would taste — and that's why it doesn't bother to beg for cookies.

no satisfying answer. One idea, not yet proven, is that molecules of a certain shape and size are smelled by categories such as fruity, flowery, or pungent. Combinations of some seven basic categories would then yield all the different smells an individual can recognize. The trouble is, sniffers can't seem to agree on what the basic smells might be, and the shapes of molecules that smell similar don't all seem to have similar shapes.

A chemical sense

We distinguish between smelling and tasting because of the way our own bodies, and that of many mammals, are organized; some molecules are identified in the nose, others in the mouth. But the ability to recognize molecules, whether by taste or smell, should really be called the chemical sense. The chemical sense is very old and very primitive. Even one-celled creatures like bacteria and yeasts have a chemical sense. That is how they find food and avoid poisons, just as we do. Every cell in every organism, protista, plant, or animal also has a chemical sense that guides its nutrition and survival. Yet this most ancient and basic of all senses is the one least understood.

Kitchen chemistry

When atoms bond to one another to form molecules and when molecules break apart or reattach to another atom or to another molecule, the event is called a chemical reaction. No matter what the original parts were like, the product of a reaction is likely to be enormously different. Take ordinary table salt. Each molecule of table salt is formed by a pair of atoms: one sodium atom and one chlorine atom. Sodium by itself is a corrosive substance that can burn your skin severely; chlorine is a very poisonous gas. Yet when they bond, the substance is not only harmless, but absolutely necessary to life. This is a picture — remember that it really would not look this way — of how a sodium atom bonds with a chlorine atom to make a molecule of sodium chloride, or table salt.

There are a couple of other things to notice about what happens in this simple reaction. Before the two atoms bonded, each had the same number of positively charged protons as they had negatively charged electrons. The positive and negative charges cancel each other out (they are opposite) so each atom, as a whole, had no charge at all. After the bond, the sodium atom, as a whole, has a positive charge because it has given up one negative electron. The chlorine atom, as a whole, has a negative charge because it has taken on an extra electron. Since the two atoms now have opposite charges, and opposite charges have an attractive force, the two atoms are held together by their mutual attraction. That is the meaning of bond.

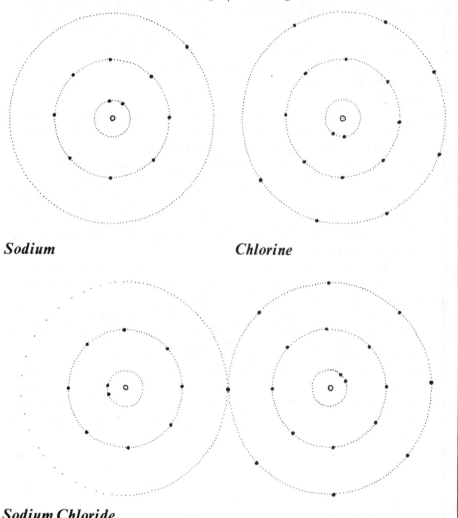

Sodium

Chlorine

Sodium Chloride

Why salt dissolves

When you look at table salt through a magnifying glass (page 196), you can see that it is crystals shaped like cubes. The molecules in each crystal are arranged in neat rows, with each sodium part surrounded by four chlorines, and each chlorine surrounded by four sodiums. When you stir these crystals into water, they disappear — yet the water now tastes salty. Apparently, the salt is still there or its taste would not remain; but something has happened or the salt would still be visible. What has happened is the salt has dissolved.

The salt molecules in a salt crystal are negatively charged on their chlorine ends (because the chlorine has gained an extra electron), and positively charged on their sodium ends (because the sodium has lost an electron). Water molecules, too, are more negative at one end, more positive at the other, though not nearly as much so as salt molecules. When salt is added to water, water molecules cluster around the sodium end of each salt molecule with their negative ends toward it, and around the chlorine end of each salt molecule with their positive ends toward it. Within seconds, the sodium parts of the salt crystals are separated from the chlorine parts by dozens of tiny water molecules. But, though the parts are now farther from one another, they have not changed into another molecule. Nor have they changed back into the sodium atoms or chlorine atoms they once were, to do that, sodium would have to snatch back its electron from chlorine. More spread out through it is, the salt is still salty. If the water is evaporated, you will see that the salt is all still there; it will form into white crystals again as soon as the water molecules get out of the way.

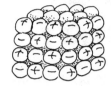

Salt crystal

Positive sodium ends of all molecules lie next to negative chlorine ends in a cube-shaped crystal.

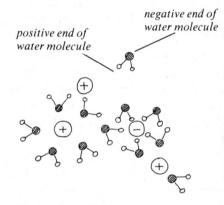

positive end of water molecule

negative end of water molecule

Dissolved salt

Positive and negative parts of salt are now separated by water molecules between them.

---

o   *Hydrogen portion of water molecule*

◑   *Oxygen portion of water molecule*

⊕   *Positively charged sodium portion of salt molecule*

⊖   *Negatively charged chlorine portion of salt molecule*

Chemical potions

Without going into which atoms are doing what in which molecules, here are some reactions you can accomplish using ordinary household chemicals. Some require the extra energy of heat to start up the reactions; others use only the energy already stored in the chemicals themselves; and a reaction may even give off energy which the atoms no longer need as they settle into more comfortable states. Because these chemicals, ordinary as they are, are rather strong or require heating, experiments should be done with adult supervision.

Dancing mothballs: In a two-cup glass measuring pitcher, mix together one cup water, one teaspoon baking soda, and ¼ cup white vinegar. When the mixture has stopped fizzing and looks clear, drop three or four mothballs into it. They will sink at first, then accumulate bubbles on their surface, and rise. Some bubbles will then pop, and the mothballs will sink again, only to rise immediately. The bubbles are carbon dioxide (one carbon and two oxygen atoms). The dancing continues for at least 15 minutes.

Be sure to read the warnings on the package before working

The diaper mystery

The major poisonous substance that kidneys filter out from blood is ammonia. The ammonia is broken down into a safer chemical called urea, responsible for the typical smell of fresh urine. The mystery is, how come when you get the baby up in the morning, and pull down his diapers, your eyes sting, you gasp for breath, and as you hold the diapers at arm's length you smell — ammonia. Various harmless bacteria that are so small they can live in the pores of our skin use urea as food. These bacteria are called anaerobic meaning they can't live in ordinary air because oxygen is a poisonous gas to them. Protected from air by a baby's plastic pants or other diaper covering, and provided with ample supplies of urea, they thrive. But they, like us, must get rid of their waste product — ammonia. It's the ammonia in diapers that causes diaper rash. Now that you know why the urea turns back into ammonia, the solution to curing or preventing rash is obvious: get rid of the plastic covering, so air can reach the baby's skin. Even better in severe cases is no diapers at all.

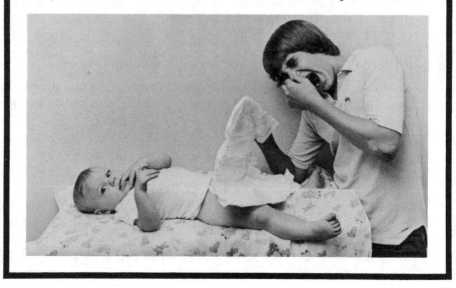

with mothballs. Round mothballs work best because they roll when they hit the surface, and so lose their bubbles more easily. But some mothballs come with edges that prevent them from rolling. Shave these edges down with a paring or pocket knife to make the mothballs rounder.

Clean the silver: People who dislike polishing silver with gooey pastes, oily cotton, or runny liquids need bother with it no longer. Here's an easier way: choose a stainless steel pot (do not use aluminum) large enough to hold the silver. Line it with aluminum foil to completely cover the bottom and sides. Add water to fill the pot, counting how many quarts you use. For each quart of water, stir in 2 teaspoons of bicarbonate of soda (baking soda) available at food stores. When the soda has dissolved, add the silver. Bring the pot to a boil. As you watch, the silver tarnish will disappear, while the aluminum darkens. Within minutes, you can run cold water into the pot to cool the silver, take it out, dry it off, and put it away.

Silver tarnish is silver sulfide, a molecule formed from silver atoms and sulphur atoms. The sulphur is found in air, particularly in industrial areas or in homes with gas stoves. (It is also in egg whites — you can tarnish a silver spoon in moments by eating a soft-boiled egg with it.) The soda in the water undoes the bond between the silver and the sulphur. The aluminum molecules, more uncomfortable than silver, capture the free sulphur molecules, forming a layer of dark aluminum sulfide on the foil surface.

Leaf starch: This is a test that proves that chlorophyll in leaves makes food for plants only when it gets energy in the form of light. The test is for starch, a food made from sugar molecules. Before you begin the test, put a geranium plant in a dark closet for two days (don't worry, this won't harm the plant). During this time of darkness, the plant will use up any sugars or starches that are in the leaves.

As soon as the plant is removed from the closet, wrap one leaf in a piece of aluminum foil in which you have cut a small hole, leaving the leaf attached to the plant. The idea is to let light fall on only the small, round area where the hole is, and prevent light from falling on the rest of the leaf. Now put the plant with the wrapped leaf in strong sunlight for a day. At the end of the day, but before the plant can use up the food in its leaves (as it does at night), get ready to do the test.

Boil an inch of water in a small pot and turn off the heat. Pour an inch of rubbing alcohol into a Pyrex measuring pitcher, snip off the wrapped geranium leaf, unwrap it, and put it into the alcohol. Put the pitcher with the leaf into the pan of boiled water to heat. The soaking in hot alcohol will remove the green chlorophyll from the leaf, leaving it pale. While this is happening, get out a bottle of iodine. Iodine and starch together form a blue-black color, so iodine is often used as a test for starch.

When the leaf has faded, take it out of the alcohol, rinse it, and dab the leaf surface with iodine. Only the round area of the leaf that has received sunlight should turn the blue-black color.

The acid test: Calcium dissolves in acid; and it is calcium that makes tooth enamel hard. An experiment to see what vinegar, an acid, does to calcium-strengthened substances like teeth, bone, and eggshell has rather horrifying results. Put any of these to soak in a glass of vinegar. After a day or so, there will be no eggshell left at all. A

This girl has put one of her old baby teeth in a glass of vinegar. Vinegar is an acid and will, within a few days, dissolve the tooth entirely.

chicken wishbone will lose its calcium in a few days to a week; all that's left is the rubbery stuff called collagen (the same molecules that are in gelatin), so you can bend the bone. It won't look much different, so it can be used as a trick wishbone.

All sorts of innocent drinks contain acid, though they may be ones we can't taste as sour. Try a baby tooth that you saved after it fell out in cola, or in apple cider.

The bacteria that cause cavities in teeth don't actually dine on teeth. Their favorite food is sugar. Acid, however, is one of the waste products a bacteria excretes after digesting sugar. It is that excreted acid which, like vinegar, makes holes in teeth.

Unexpected acid: This is the simplest of all kitchen chemistry experiments and one that happens often in the course of cooking dinner. Peel an onion. You will notice, as you are working, your eyes begin to sting and tear. Molecules drifting through the air from the cut onion meet up with the salty water in your eyes. A chemical reaction occurs. The molecules are changed to sulfuric acid: No wonder your eyes tear!

Spit in the bananas: To see chemicals from your own body — the enzymes in saliva — at work cutting apart starch molecules, spit into a baby food jar of bananas or sweet potato. Leave the jar overnight at room temperature. In the morning, take a look. Your spit, even if it was only a mere drop, will have turned most of the starchy food into a liquid.

How to ripen a tomato: Most tomato fruits are picked green so they won't crush during shipment. Often when you buy them, they are greenish or pinkish, but by no means a good ripe red. Most people put such tomatoes on a sunny windowsill to ripen, but here is a way that brings out a better flavor. Put the tomatoes in a paper bag, along with an apple or two, and keep the bag in a dark, cool place. A gas called ethylene is given off by the apples. Ethylene acts chemically with the tomato cells to speed up the manufacture of sugars that give a ripe tomato its sweetness and the chemicals called esters that give it its fragrance and flavor. Ripening time depends on how green the tomatoes were in the first place; check them every couple of days.

Fire

Is fire a stuff? The answer is yes and no.

Imagine the molecules in the head of a kitchen match. They are not reacting with one another. A match can sit around for years without the molecules changing at all. If someone waves the match quickly through the air, the movement carries energy. You can feel the energy transferred to the molecules in the air as they are pushed into more rapid motion. But the match doesn't light. If a person strikes the head of the match against a rough surface, the energy may be the same, but this time, the energy can't be carried off by moving air molecules. It is transferred to the surface, and to the match head. It lights.

Ready to light

As the molecules in the match head absorb energy, they begin to move about in several ways. Crowded together as they may be, the molecules themselves, always somewhat on the move, move faster and harder. They may stretch, spin, jiggle, wiggle, and bend. Electrons may absorb just the right amount of energy to jump up a floor farther from the nucleus of their atom.

All this wild movement causes molecular discomfort, and increases the chance that the molecules will reorganize themselves. Vibrating molecules of a clumsy shape may break apart. Speeding molecules may hit each other harder, and therefore, get closer to electrons they can use for bonding. Electrons that have jumped farther from their nuclei are easier to capture.

The molecules at the very end of the match, where most of the energy of the striking movement was absorbed, come apart and recombine into new kinds of molecules that require less energy to hold them together. As they settle down into their new forms, they shed the extra energy, some of which is now transferred to nearby molecules. A chain reaction occurs: from the tip of the match down toward its base, each excited area in turn changes to new molecules. You can see it with your own eyes: the pale wood blackens as the reaction spreads down the match.

You also see a flame. The flame is the energy that was once required to hold together the match molecules, but which, in their new form, they can shed. The shed energy is photons: both visible light photons and infrared photons.

The energy that comes from the match is more than the energy you added to it, but no more than what was in the match before it was struck. No atoms have been lost either. The match seems to shrivel, but the missing portion is, literally, going up in flames (in the form of water and carbon dioxide molecules). You don't see them: they are too small. But you see the energy they are shedding in the form of light photons, and feel the energy in the form of heat from infrared photons. The flame is stuff, too, but you can detect only its energy.

Ways molecules move

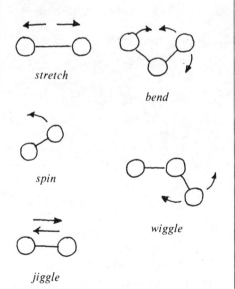

stretch

bend

spin

wiggle

jiggle

Clever snuffer

Ask an adult to try to put out a candle flame using only a 12-inch length of copper wire (16-gauge wire is good for this trick). They're not allowed to dunk the wick in the melted wax. When they give up, let the wire coil, and coil it around a pencil point. Begin at the thick part and end at the point, leaving about four inches of straight wire to grasp in a clothespin (to protect you from getting burned). Remove the pencil, and lower the coil over the flame to put it out.

In case the adult really wants an explanation, this is it: copper atoms can absorb heat energy very easily. When you wind the copper around in a coil, you are simply getting more of its atoms close to the source of heat. The wire, then, can rob the candle of so much of its heat that there is no longer enough energy to continue its chain reaction.

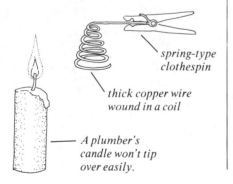

spring-type clothespin

thick copper wire wound in a coil

A plumber's candle won't tip over easily.

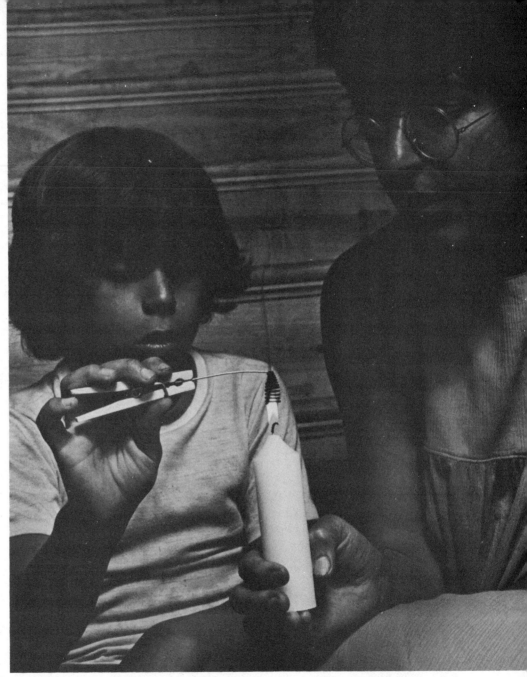

In a moment, the copper coil will rob so much heat from the flaming wick that the chemical reaction of burning will come to a halt; the candle will be snufffed.

Charges

Snap, crackle, and pop

To be on a certain floor above its nucleus, an electron has to hold a certain amount of energy — no more, and no less. It needs the least amount of energy to remain on the first floor, the closest to the nucleus. To get to the next floor, it must absorb a big packet of energy — a photon of ultraviolet will do it. From there on upward through the different floors, it requires less and less energy to hop one floor farther. In outer layers, the smallish energy of infrared photons may let it hop upward. You can understand why this is so by realizing that the farther a negatively charged electron gets from the positively charged nucleus, the less attraction there is between them. This is about the same situation as a rocket leaving the Earth: the farther it gets, the less it is influenced by the force of gravity, and the less energy it requires to move far-ther still.

The farther an electron hops from the positive charge that is holding it back, the more easily it might be attracted by some positive charge beyond its own atom; and there is even a chance it can be grabbed away altogether. This happens all the time. It happens when you brush your hair in winter and it stands out all over the place. It happens when you tumble-dry laundry and the clothes stick together.

The force that holds your hairs away from one another and the force that holds the clothes against one another is the same electromagnetic force that repels electrons from one another and attracts electrons to their nuclei. But you know it under the name of static electricity.

Fickle electrons

This is the way it works. When you brush your hair, the energy from your moving muscles is made available both to the brush and hair molecules. The

A bristle brush, a hard rubber comb or a blown-up balloon can all cause static electricity if you run them briskly through your hair.

looser electrons in hair molecules begin to hop upward at the hair surfaces. As the brush and hair continue to rough each other up, electrons may be energized enough to get to extremely high floors — so distant from the nucleus, in fact, that they can be captured by the other substance, the brush, which holds its electrons more tightly. As that happens, the surface of each of your hairs, now that they have lost negatively charged electrons, will be left with a positive charge. They will repel one another. The same is true of the brush, whose bristles have accepted extra electrons at their surfaces and are now negatively charged. You won't see the brush bristles spread because they are stiffer than hairs.

If you continue to brush, your hair will crackle. (If you were in a dark room, you would see sparks.) The situation has become extreme. So many extra electrons have hopped over to the brush that the electrons already there begin to repel the newcomers violently. And the hair, now left with an even higher positive charge, pulls harder and harder on the wandering electrons. When the repulsion between electrons and the attraction between electrons and nuclei is strong enough, the elec-

Fingertip thunderstorm

Wear leather-soled shoes and rub your feet vigorously across a wool or synthetic carpet (preferably in winter, when the air is drier). Then bring one finger close to a metal doorknob. A spark leaps from the knob to your fingertip. You see a flash of light, hear a crackle of noise, and feel a sensation of pain. You have just been hit by lightning.

Your shoes have been brushing the carpet's hair. This time, though, it is your body that is forced to give up electrons while the carpet gains them. You are left with a positive charge all the way from your feet to your fingertips. Electrons are loosely held in metals. When your charged finger comes close enough, it attracts these loose electrons suddenly and violently. They leap across the gap of air, shedding visible light and infrared photons as they re-enter lower energy floors. You see the spark of light — so high in energy it is often quite blue. You feel pain as energy is transferred to skin sensors and relayed along nerves. You hear the sound wave as air contracts and expands again from the rapid heating and cooling.

A flash of lightning — its electrical shock, the heat that can cause forest fires, and the accompanying thunder — is only a larger version of electrons leaping across a gap of air. The charge, either negative or positive, builds up in the air as warm air rubs against cold air or air laden with water droplets rubs against dry air. When the charge has built to huge proportions, the Earth acts as a doorknob, allowing electrons to violently leap the gap — either from it toward the sky or from the sky to Earth. Of course, if you are standing in the gap, electrons invade you, too. But such a deluge of electrons is lethal: few people recover from the blow.

An interesting chemical reaction occurs whenever there is sparking. Oxygen, which normally clings together as a molecule of two atoms, accepts energetic photons. The extra energy allows it to form a molecule of three atoms, called ozone.

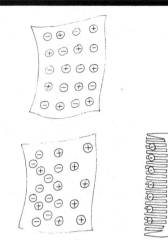

The positive and negative charges on an undisturbed piece of tissue paper are evenly distributed, so the paper is electrically neutral.

As a negatively charged comb approaches, the electrons on the paper are repulsed. They retreat, leaving the edge of the paper positively charged. The comb and paper are now attracted.

Electric wand

Rub a piece of cloth (wool works best) briskly back and forth along a hard rubber comb. In a few seconds, you will have forced many electrons from the cloth onto the comb, leaving it with a negative charge. You can now use the comb as an electric wand for several amusing tricks.

Tear tissue paper into shreds. The comb will pick them up for you. Crumple paper into a ball and hang it on a string. Touch the comb to it to transfer electrons to the paper. Now recharge the comb by rubbing it again. Bring it toward the paper a second time. This time it will repel the paper. The charged comb will attract ping-pong balls and, if you charge it well enough, will bend a stream of tap water toward it, too. A blown-up balloon will be attracted to the comb, unless it too is rubbed, in which case they will repel one another. The best trick is this one: on a plate, sprinkle both salt and pepper and mix them well. Tell a friend you have a magic way of separating the pepper from the salt. Rub your comb well, and hold it an inch above the salt and pepper mixture. The pepper will leap through the air onto the comb, leaving the salt behind.

trons leap back through the air to where they belong. As they return, they can keep only the energy proper to the floor on which they re-enter. They shed photons: high-energy ones you see as light, and lower-energy, infrared ones that are felt as heat.

Strange as it seems, it's the heat that's responsible for the noise. The infrared photons, too few for you to feel, speed the motion of air molecules around the hopping electron. The air heats, which causes it to expand, hits cooler air, which causes it to contract again. The rapid movement is a vibration — the very same kind that sets air molecules into wave patterns of compression and expansion. The compressions hit your ear; you hear snaps and crackles.

You can prove to yourself that the surface of the brush and the surface of your hair after brushing have opposite charges. Hold the brush a few inches from your hair. The two will be attracted; your hair will move toward the brush.

Wash day experiment

Next time there are blankets to be washed and dried in an automatic drier, or a large load of synthetics, offer to do the job.

Schedule it so you will be removing the load from the dryer after dark. Let the dryer go a little longer than it normally would, so the blankets or clothes are subjected to plenty of heat and tumbling. The minute you hear the dryer stop, turn out all the lights and open the dryer.

The scene is peaceful. There are no cracklings or sparks. Are all the electrons where they were when you started the drying? Not at all. During the tumbling, an adjustment has been made. Although heat from the dryer and the tumbling motion has transferred energy to electrons in the fabrics — allowing them to hop off some surfaces and land on others — there has also been plenty of opportunity for oppositely charged surfaces to attract each other and cling together.

Pull them apart to see how disrupted they are. There will be a storm of sparks and crackles as electrons, rubbed off this and glommed onto that, race back to positively charged surfaces. You will find that you have to use a certain amount of effort to pull one thing from another in order to produce the sparks. That's the attraction between negatively and positively charged surfaces — "static cling," as advertisers call it. If there is anything fuzzy in the laundry — a fuzzy sweater or sock — the fibers will be standing on end. This is because, whether that surface is negatively or positively charged, each fiber in it is charged the same way. They are all repelling one another, leaning as far apart from one another as they can get.

Adjacent surfaces of a piece of laundry cling together because one surface has accumulated extra electrons, making it negatively charged, while the other has lost electrons, leaving it positively charged.

Hard candy sparks

Tell a friend you can make sparks inside your mouth. If they don't believe you, invite that person into a dark closet. You come armed with a hard candy (wintergreen Lifesavers work well) or a sugar cube. While they stare into your mouth, crunch hard on the candy or sugar. The energy of your motion, as your teeth break the candy, will produce sparks inside your open mouth.

Drifting electrons

Electrons don't "know" their home atoms. Just as they can be shared between two atoms, they can also move from one to another. They can do this particularly easily in metals like silver and copper. Atoms in these metals form very strong bonds with one another, but at the same time, each atom has one loosely held, more or less extra electron that is as much at home in one place in the metal as another. Such electrons are called "free."

Inside the wires that run through the walls of your home — through every light bulb, toaster, mixer, and doorbell — free electrons race. Their movement is what we call electricity. To get electrons to move, they have to be given a reason. There are many ways to do it, but the one that can be most easily understood is the way it's done in a battery.

An electrical current

In a battery, there are two different substances. One of them gives up its electrons rather easily, the other tends to steal them when it can. So electrons (or sometimes whole charged

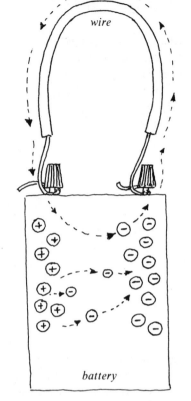

wire

battery

A circuit
Electrons escape from one side of a battery into the wire. As they enter, they nudge other electrons along. At the other end of the wire, electrons are nudged back into the battery and again travel to the other side and back into the wire.

atoms called ions) drift off the substance from which they can get away and go to the substance that pulls them more strongly. There they accumulate, until their negative force is so strong that they repel any new electrons trying to join the crowd. (Meanwhile, the first substance,

now positively charged, becomes harder and harder for electrons to leave.)

At this point, if a copper wire, in which electrons are quite free to drift along, is attached to that negatively charged side, electrons can move into the wire.

The other end of the wire is attached to the positively charged side of the battery, so free electrons can also get out of the wire and return into the battery. Electrons drift in at one end, taking the place of ones already there; these in turn, drift a little farther, until finally the electrons at the end of the wire are crowded. Repelled by electrons coming at them through the wire, they simply leave and enter the battery. As they leave the wire, they go naturally to the substance that lost electrons. Now it has more electrons that are able to leave, and the other side, having given electrons to the wire, has room for new ones. The loop the electrons drift along is called a circuit and the movement of electrons is called a current.

The current from a battery is called a direct current because all the electrons are going in the same direction. In the wires of a house, electrons move through circuits in bursts, or pulses, first in one direction, then in the other. That kind is called an alternating current. But, in spite of this difference, most of how electric currents light a light bulb or heat a toaster can be understood by using the direct current from a battery.

To make the electric devices that follow, you will need some items, which should be available in most hardware stores. (Some you don't really need but may like to include.)

Gadget supplies

Batteries: Lantern batteries (sometimes called dry cells) are both more convenient to use and produce more electricity than flashlight batteries. They are labelled 6V (they give six volts of electricity), and have two terminals at the top to which the ends of wires can be attached. Usually the terminals have little screw caps on them which you tighten to hold the wires in place. A volt is a measure of the energy available (after the battery is hooked up).

Both C- and D-size flashlight batteries are labelled 1.5V (they give one and a half volts of electricity). There is no special attachment for wires; the terminals are the button at the top of each battery and the entire bottom surface. To attach wires to the two terminals, tape the ends in place with freezer tape. If you like, you can increase the strength of flashlight batteries by stacking them atop one another and taping them together. No matter how many you use in the stack, attach one end of the wire to the button on the top battery, the other to the bottom surface of the bottom battery.

You can shorten a wire by winding part of it around a pencil.

Wire: Hardware stores sell insulated bell wire in rolls of various lengths. Buy the shortest roll, as these experiments do not require very much wire. Electrons cannot go through the plastic insulation that surrounds bell wire so, wherever you connect the wire to a battery, bulb, buzzer, switch, or any other part of your circuit, you must remove a portion of insulation at the point of connection. The easiest way to do this is with wire snippers. Grip the insulation lightly with the snippers where you wish to cut it, and pull toward the end of the wire. The short piece of insulation will slip right off. The voltage of batteries is so low that there is no need to protect yourself from shocks by wrapping electric tape around the bare wire. You can touch bare portions even after the circuit is working without feeling a thing. The purpose of the insulation is to keep wires from touching one another in the circuit.

Bulbs and sockets: Bulbs must be matched to sockets as well as to the strength of the battery you are using. Look for screw-type bulbs, not those that simply slip into sockets. For a 6√ lantern battery, use a #502 flashlight bulb, which can take up to six

A bulb and socket

volts. Bulb #14 can take up to three volts, so it can be used with either one or two 1.5V flashlight batteries. If you use a bulb with voltage that is too high for it, it will burn out. If you use it with voltage lower than what it was designed for, it will give only a dim light. After you have chosen the bulb, match it with a screw-type plastic or porcelain socket by checking that it screws all the way down in the socket. Sockets aren't numbered clearly, and, even if you can make out a size, salesmen may not know which bulb it was designed for, since there are so many types of bulbs.

Alligator clips: First the wire is attached to the tube end of the clip (push the wire through the tube then tighten the screw to hold it in place). Then you can simply press the clip open (something like a spring-type clothespin) and clamp it to the terminal of either a battery or a bulb socket. The convenience is

worth minor expense. For most inventions you will need only four, but check the number of connections on the illustrations so you don't run short.

Buzzer: The usual type that runs off batteries has a dome-shaped bell with a clapper inside and a rectangular body. The noise is shrill, so if you use a buzzer, be considerate of other people's ears.

Knife switch: This is a neat switching device; it is more fun to be able to switch things on and off than to have to continually attach and detach wires. The down position is on; the up position, off.

Tools: Use wire snippers for removing insulation. Small pliers, which usually have a wire-cutting area, can be used to cut through wire. Fingers are good enough for bending wire around terminals, but needle-nosed pliers are easier. You will need a screwdriver for tightening screw terminals on bulb sockets, and other parts.

Miscellaneous equipment: Check illustrations to see what else (bolts, wood scraps, boxes, jars) you might need for some of the more complicated inventions.

Wiring

Light circuit: Nothing of great drama is happening inside a copper wire as its electrons nudge one another along. The current itself is not crackling,

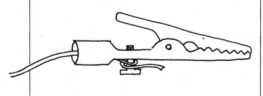

Alligator clip

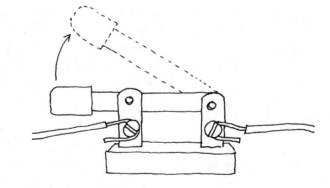

Knife switch

A light circuit

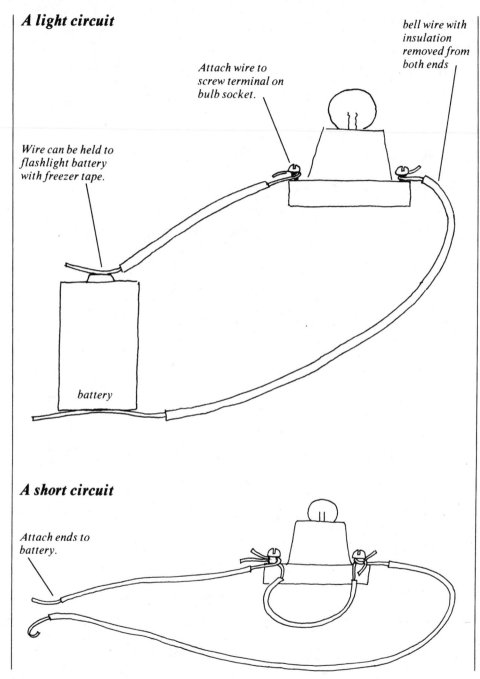

bell wire with insulation removed from both ends

Attach wire to screw terminal on bulb socket.

Wire can be held to flashlight battery with freezer tape.

battery

A short circuit

Attach ends to battery.

sparking stuff. Heat and light are only shed when electrons try to barge their way through materials reluctant to accept them. For instance, the tungsten filament, the thin metal wire, in a light bulb holds tightly to its electrons. When feeling the repelling force of an oncoming electron, instead of simply letting themselves be pushed along, most of the tungsten's electrons stay put because they are held so tightly. In the jostling encounters that result, energy is released. The smaller packets of energy are emitted as infrared photons. The light bulb heats up. The higher energy packets are visible light photons. The bulb glows.

Short circuit: You have probably heard of short circuits — and that they can start fires. The wiring in this drawing is a short circuit. The electrons take the course of least resistance. Since it's hard for them to get through the tungsten filament in the bulb, they'd rather take the easy way through the extra loop of wire. The bulb doesn't light.

Wiring in series and in parallel: Those frustrating Christmas lights that fail whenever a single bulb burns out have been wired in a simple, but annoying, way. The system is called wiring in series, and is shown here. You can see that when the filament in any single bulb breaks, the electrons are stopped at that point, as they would be by an open switch. The second arrangement shown here is called a parallel circuit. You can see that now, even if a bulb were to burn out, the other bulbs would continue to light. The best Christmas lights are wired in parallel.

Light bulb: The filament for this light bulb is made from a single strand of picture wire. Picture wire may come braided rather than twisted; to unravel it, use a needle to tease the strands apart for three or four inches. Coil a single strand by winding it around a bit of the insulated bell wire. Then, pull the coil off the bell wire. Make holes in the lid of the small jar by hammering a nail through it in two places. Insert the two pieces of bell wire through the holes, then tape them to the lid with freezer tape so they don't jiggle as you attach the coil between them. When the bulb is finished and connected to the battery, the filament will glow red for a few minutes before burning through.

Wiring in series

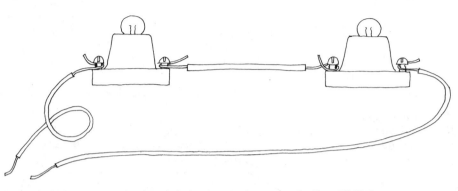

If one bulb burns out, the circuit is broken and no other bulbs will light.

Wiring in parallel

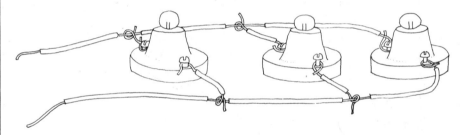

If one bulb burns out, electrons can still drift in a loop to light any other bulbs.

Light bulb

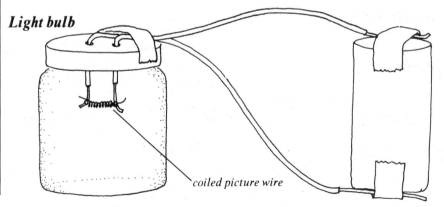

coiled picture wire

Switches

To turn off a light bulb, all you have to do is flick a switch. A switch is nothing more than a device that creates a gap of air in the wire. Electrons travel even less easily through air than through tungsten. Without sufficient energy to force their way through the gap, they simply stop — and so does the electrical current.

One-way switch

This is the simplest switch, made here by using a commercial knife switch. There is an air gap when the switch is in the up position; electrons flow again when the switch is in a down position.

Two-way switch

The switches here are lengths of bare copper wire, one wound around nail 1, the other around nail 2. Both switches can swivel to touch either of the two nails on its block of wood.

The circuit will be completed and the light will be on when the switches are in the positions 1-a and 2-d (as shown), or in positions 1-b and 2-c. You can turn off either switch, then complete the circuit again using the opposite switch, just as you can in a room with a two-way wall switch.

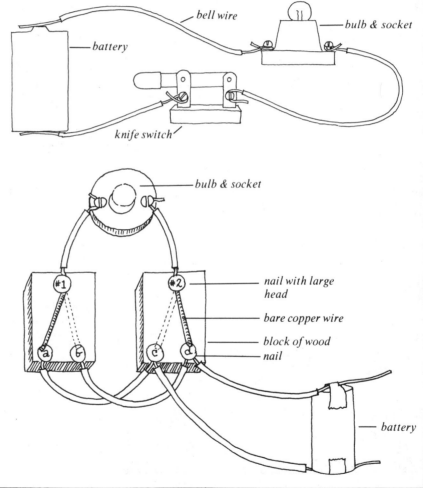

bell wire

bulb & socket

battery

knife switch

bulb & socket

nail with large head

bare copper wire

block of wood

nail

battery

Outside of quiz box

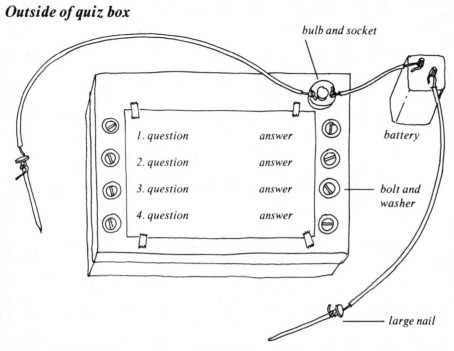

bulb and socket

battery

bolt and washer

large nail

Touch one nail to bolt next to question, the other to bolt next to answer. If answer is correct, the circuit will be completed and the bulb will light.

Inside of quiz box lid

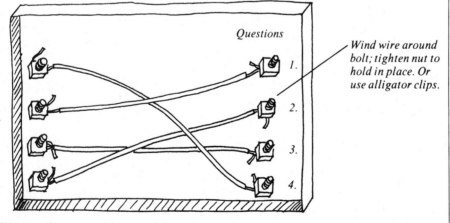

Questions

Wind wire around bolt; tighten nut to hold in place. Or use alligator clips.

Wires go from question to position of correct answer.

Quiz game: The illustration here shows the circuitry needed for this game. You can prepare sheets of paper to cover the top, and they can contain any pairs of questions and answers you wish. The correct pairs, of course, have to correspond to your wiring. Once you have made a sheet of questions and answers, arrange the wiring to conform to it. Whenever a question is answered correctly (by putting one nail to the bolt next to the question and the other nail next to the bolt with the right answer), the circuit will be completed and the bulb will light up. You can change the circuitry to correspond to other arrangements of questions and answers.

The bolts to which the wires are attached beneath the lid must be the kind that are threaded the whole length of the bolt. Length and thickness are not very important, but be sure to get nuts and washers that fit. Glue the bulb socket into place on the box top first, place a piece of paper on the box top so you can mark where the bolts go. How many questions — and therefore bolts — you have room for depends on the size of the box.

With a pointed knife, make holes in the box top where the bolts will go through. When the bolts, washers, and nuts are in place, make as many connectors as there are questions. Measure diagonally, from the first question to the last answer. Cut each piece of wire to that length.

Using bell wire, connect the bulb to the battery and to a nail as shown, and connect the other terminal on the battery to another nail. Make up a question sheet and tape it in place. Connect the wires to the bolts so that the bolt next to each question is wired to the bolt next to its correct answer.

The person playing touches one nail to a question bolt and the other to an answer bolt. If she is right, the circuit will be completed and the bulb will light.

Humans as wires

Though it is always dangerous to take any chances with household current, it can be lethal to do so when you are wet. Normally, human bodies are not as good at allowing electrons to move along them as metal wires are. Pure water isn't a good conductor either. But when your skin is wet, the water on it is not pure at all. It is filled with dissolved salt from your skin. The sodium chloride (salt) molecules, formed from a sodium atom that has given up an electron and is now carrying a positive charge, and a chlorine atom that is now carrying an extra electron and has a negative charge, are only loosely associated. Electrons can make their way along by hopping from one positively charged sodium ion to another. You have become a wire. Because the surface of your skin is continuous, you can be traveled in a loop and act as a short circuit, too.

The tiny spark from a doorknob, even the shock you feel from a battery, does not contain enough energetic electrons to do more than stimulate a few nerves. But when household current short-circuits through a damp mother switching on a can opener, or a wet teenager blow-drying his hair, or a soggy father shaving with an electric shaver, many more electrons are involved. A barrage of electrons going through the person fires millions of nerves in the brain, messing up the ordinary signals that control such processes as breathing and heart beats. The result can be death.

In this quiz the girl on the right is trying to figure out which movie stars appear in some pretty well-known movies. The question column includes a list of the stars' names and the answer column includes the list of movies.

Coordination tester: The piece of wood can be any scrap thick enough to hammer a nail or screw a screw into at each end. Form the coiled wire "path" from 16-gauge, bare, copper wire. Attach each end of the coil to a nail or screw. To one of the nails, attach a short wire that leads to one terminal of the bell. Attach the other bell terminal to one terminal of the battery with another length of wire. To the second battery terminal, attach a long piece of bell wire that ends in a bare loop, not quite closed, as shown.

With this device, the person being tested acts as a switch. The bell will not ring unless the bare loop connected to the second battery terminal comes in contact with the coiled wire to complete the circuit. The idea of the test is to challenge someone to move the loop all the way from one end of the twisted wire to the other end without ever touching it. The more complicated the twists in the wire, and the smaller the loop, the more difficult the test is. Failure is marked by the bell ringing.

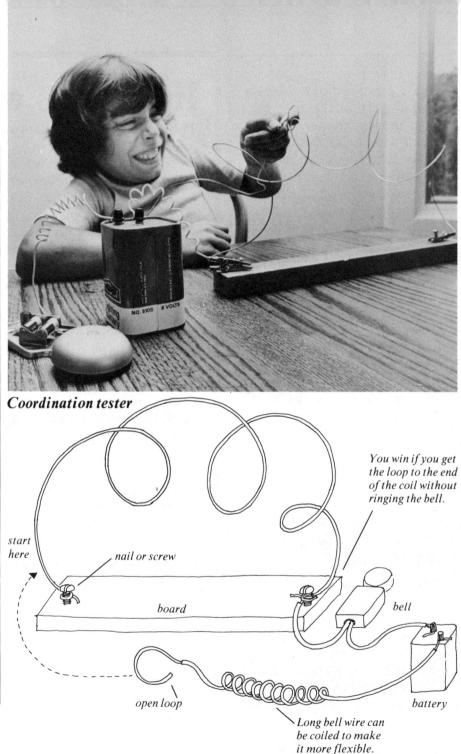

Coordination tester

You win if you get the loop to the end of the coil without ringing the bell.

start here

nail or screw

board

bell

open loop

battery

Long bell wire can be coiled to make it more flexible.

The shape of space

Think of water as it flows through the inside of a garden hose. When you hold the hose up straight, the water flows straight. When you curve the hose this way and that, the water must follow the curves. The space inside the hose has a shape and the water must move within it. All of space, from here to the end of the universe, is also shaped. The movements of photons, electrons — even baseballs or humans moving through space — are as guided by the shapes of space as the movement of water through a hose.

All stuff — the tiniest electron or the largest star — shapes its own space around it, but not by any wall that you can see. Shapes of space are called fields. Although fields guide matter as surely as a hose guides the water inside it, they are invisible. One of the fields that affects our lives is gravity, the shape that large objects, like the sun, Earth, people, and baseballs, create between them. The shape of Earth's field guides your baseball toward the center of the planet, no matter what direction you throw it in.

The other field that has a great deal to do with everyday life is the electromagnetic field. This field is created by charged particles — electrons and protons inside an atom. It is the field that guides electrons when they hop from your hair to your hairbrush, and also the field that guides photons along wave paths from the Milky Way to your eyes.

Fields are not easy to understand, but for those interested in trying to picture the shapes of space, here is an explanation that starts with the shape within and around an atom. A single charge, such as a negatively charged electron or its positively charged proton creates a distortion of space that you can picture, Fig. a.

Fig. a

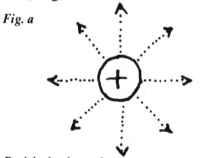

Positively charged proton

Negatively charged proton

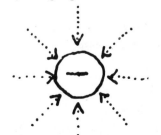

The lines are drawn as arrows to give some idea of the influence the charges have on one another because of the field around each. Actually, the lines

Fig. b

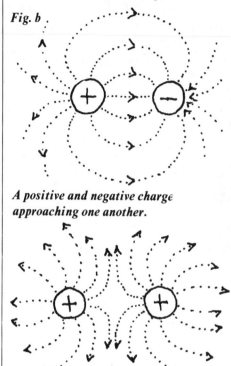

A positive and negative charge approaching one another.

Two like charges approaching one another.

don't "go" anywhere. But the arrows are helpful to see what happens as a negative charge approaches a positive one, or as two like charges approach each other. The arrows are a way to picture attraction or repulsion between charges as their fields come in contact, Fig. b.

If you draw a row of positive charges and a row of negative ones, you can see why two oppositely charged pieces of laundry are guided toward one another, Fig. c. If both rows were negative charges, the lines would bend away from one another — just what happens when you stub your toe against a rock.

Fig. c

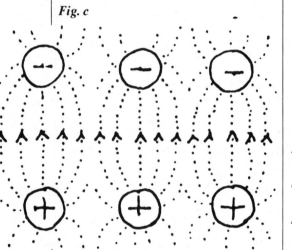

Oppositely charged surfaces approaching one another.

As spinning charges, such as the many electrons in a wire, move along a straight path, the shape of the field they create could be drawn like Fig. d, although actually, there are concentric circles (they have a common center), each farther from the wire than the one inside it.

In the electrical experiments, pages 230-236, the field that forms around the wire is the same as the one below. Take a look at what happens when the wire is coiled into a loop, forcing the charge to move now in a circle instead of a straight path. The field is scrunched together inside the loop and bulges outside the loop, Fig. e.

Fig. d

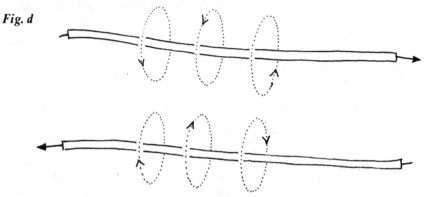

A circular field created by a charge moving in a straight path, as when a current runs through wire. The charges in these two wires run in opposite directions, and so do their fields.

Fig. e

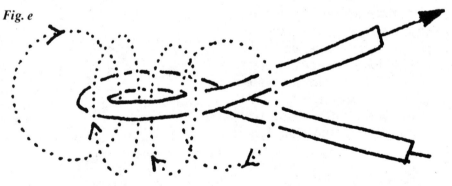

The field around a looped wire
When a charge moves in a loop, its field is scrunched together in the middle, bulges to the outside.

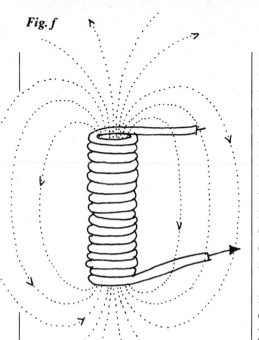

Fig. f

The field around a coiled wire.

If a wire is coiled many times, the field simply stretches, becoming longer the greater the length of a coil, Fig. f.

Take a long piece of bell wire and coil it so that the charge (the electrons) inside it move in a circular fashion. Use a 20-penny common nail (sometimes called a spike) as the core to wind the bell wire around. Leave about eight inches of wire to attach to one terminal of the battery, then wind it around the nail, starting at the head. Wind tightly and neatly to within one-half inch of the bottom, then wind a second layer up to the head. Repeat the winding down and up again so that there are four layers of winding. Leave eight inches of wire at the head end to attach to the other terminal of the battery. When both ends are attached to the battery, the electrons coming through the circuit will be moving around and around, instead of straight, and the field they create will be shaped as it is in an atom.

Touch the end of the wound nail to a heap of pins or paper clips. You'll discover that what you have made is a rather strong magnet. Magnetism is one way in which an electromagnetic field influences objects around it.

Atom magnets

The magnets you may have played with act the same way as this electromagnet because each atom inside them is itself a tiny magnet. In fact, every atom of every substance is a magnet. Electrons can't travel in straight paths around their nuclei — they must circle it, just as you forced electrons to circle in a coiled wire. The field of an atom looks exactly like the field of your electromagnet. In these drawings the north and south poles are shown as they are on an ordinary bar magnet, Fig. g.

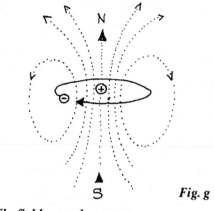

Fig. g

The field around an atom.

In most substances, the atoms are very weak magnets, and their fields have so little influence that they are arranged helter skelter, so their poles don't line up. The fields cancel one another out and you detect no magnetism. If all the atoms are lined up, north pole to south pole, the entire substance acts as magnet, Fig. h.

Fig. h

The field around lined up atoms.

Iron, the usual metal from which magnets are made, tends to align groups of its atoms north pole to south pole. There may be many such magnetic areas in iron, but each may face in a different direction canceling each other out. If you remove the nail from your electromagnet, however, you'll find the nail is now magnetized from its experience inside the coiled wire. Under the influence of the field created by the swirling electrons in the wire, each of its magnetic areas turned to align itself with the shape of the field. Since iron has a tendency to align anyway, the patterns stayed put even after the stronger field was removed. The nail is a permanent magent.

Magnetic influence

When you put a single paper clip to the end of your electromagnet, its atoms line up along the field pattern, and it too becomes a magnet, though a weak and probably temporary one. As long as it remains in the influence of the field, it can pick up another paper clip. But keep adding paper clips, one at a time, and you'll find the force becomes weaker the farther each clip is from the electromagnet. To see why this is so, you have to

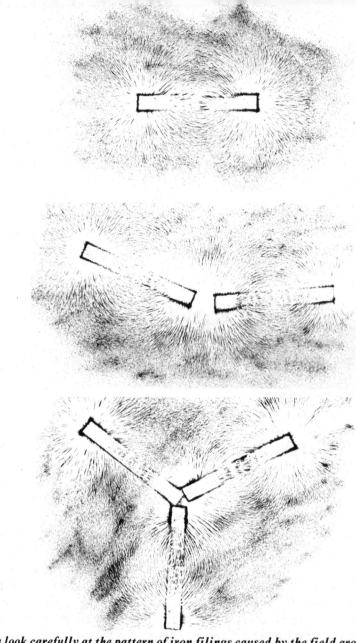

If you look carefully at the pattern of iron filings caused by the field around the single bar magnet, you will see the typical "lines" of a magnetic field. In the second photograph, two like ends of magnets have been brought together, and the fields bend away from one another. In the last photo, two like and one unlike ends have been brought together. See if you can guess which is the unlike one.

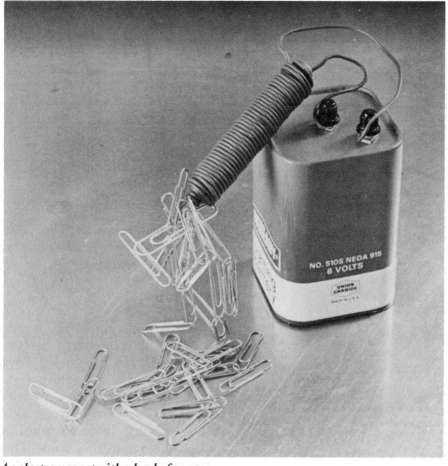
An electromagnet with a load of paper clips.

space itself is strongly distorted, are the portions of the magnetic field that the piece of paper is lying within. Actually, the lines lie not only along the paper but all around the magnet, spreading out in loops that reach from one end to the other. The outermost ones that go off the paper spread all the way to the limits of the universe — and back again — always as loops. The farther they are from the magnet, the more they spread out and the less effect they have on an object — a single atom or the many in a paper clip.

Where the distortion of space is the most extreme, near the magnet ends, the greatest effect is felt. Every object there is creates an electromagnetic field, and space is crisscrossed with a complicated pattern of these lines. You can get a look at more complicated patterns by using several magnets beneath the paper. You can also see the field created by straight-moving electrons if you poke wire through paper and connect both ends to a battery so a charge is flowing through the wire. If the field is not strong enough to influence iron filings to align circularly, try holding a compass near the wire. Its needle will align with the wire's field.

look more closely at the shapes of electromagnetic fields. An easy way to do this is to let iron filings align themselves with the shape of space in an electromagnetic field.

Your school may have iron filings you can use or send to Edmund Scientific (see page 194 for the address) for their catalog, which includes iron filings by the pound.

Sprinkle iron filings on white paper over a bar magnet or your electromagnet. Then, jiggle the paper until the filings form lines over the magnet. Those lines, which are really areas in which

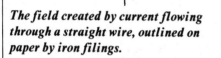

The field created by current flowing through a straight wire, outlined on paper by iron filings.

Although no scientist is sure how stationary electromagnetic fields become incredibly fast-moving electromagnetic waves, it may happen like this: when an electrical charge changes direction, its field becomes disconnected from it. The instant it is free, the field self-propels in the form of waves, radiating out in every direction at 186,000 miles per second — the speed of light. Such moving electromagnetic fields are the guidance system for all the photons. These pictures show how a field is pinched off by a charge that is moving back and forth very rapidly.

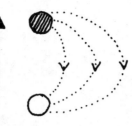

The field created by a charge which has moved from ○ to ◐ .

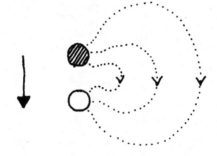

The field is squashed as the charge changes direction . . .

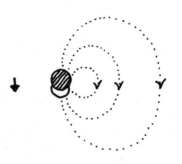

. . . and finally pinched shut.

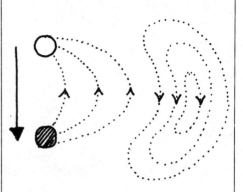

A new field is created, this time in the opposite direction to the first one, which is now free to shoot off as a wave.

This pinching off of a piece of field in an energy-carrying wave happens routinely. These are the waves of radio, light, heat, and X-rays. They are leaving right now from your skin, and guiding infrared photons into the page of this book. They are leaving the book, guiding light photons toward your eyes. They are carrying today's news to radio and television sets around the world. They are bringing twinkling starlight, penetrating X-rays, and even radio messages from tumbling carbon monoxide molecules in dusty regions of galaxies of a billion years ago to the instruments of modern scientists.

Magnetic diversions

A pleasant game to play on long car trips can be made from a paper plate, a magnet, and a few small metal items like a nut, washer, paper clip, or tack. Draw a maze or any complicated path on the plate. Each person takes a turn to see if he can guide a paper clip or nut from beneath the plate with the magnet, down the path to the end without touching any lines.

A more practical invention is a battery tester. Since electrons moving around a coil create an electromagnetic field, the needle of a compass held within the field will turn to orient itself along the lines. Either of these two arrangements — one with the compass held next to an electromagnet; and the other, in which the compass itself is the core of the electromagnet — can be used to see if a battery is still producing current. If the needle doesn't move after the ends of the wire are connected to the battery, the battery is dead.

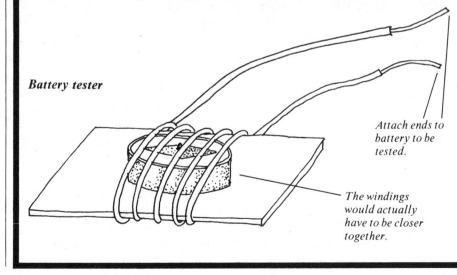

Battery tester

Attach ends to battery to be tested.

The windings would actually have to be closer together.

Thoughts

Gray mush

The gray mush that is inside your skull is an electrochemical organ. Every message of an itch, an odor, a tune, a sweetness, or a flash of light is sent to the brain as a small current of electricity carried in an insulated wire called a nerve. Every message that says scratch, sniff, hum, lick your lips, or blink your eyes travels back along another set of wires to anywhere in you body. If that was all that happened, however, you would be a push button machine: send a signal in, get an action out. Mushy and formless as the brain looks and feels, it is an intricately structured network of nerve endings and nerve beginnings that send messages to one another. Altogether, you are born with about 12 billion nerve cells, most of them in the brain.

You can get a feel of the electrical nature of nerves by fiddling with the place between your elbow bones called the funny bone. That's not a bone; it's a bundle of nerves. When you jiggle the area, it feels something like an electric shock. And that's what it is: an overload of electrical charge caused by firing off too many nerves at once. What you can't feel is that the charge moving along the nerve is caused by a chain chemical reaction.

Brain secrets

Far more chemistry goes on in the brain itself. For instance, painkilling molecules are produced to control awareness of pain. Receptors at the ends of some nerves are shaped to embrace these molecules. When enough receptors are each cuddling a pain-killing molecule, the amount of pain you feel decreases. Some scientists suspect that acupuncture (a Chinese art of twirling very thin needles in the body at various points to relieve pain) works by stimulating certain nerves that release such molecules. Morphine may work as a painkiller because its molecule is so like our natural painkiller that receptors can't tell them apart.

Glands elsewhere in your body produce molecules called hormones that are dumped into the bloodstream. In the course of their travels through the body, they work directly on the chemistry of cells — to make them divide more rapidly during childhood for example — and also in the brain. A hormone called adrenalin not only gives you butterflies in your stomach, but also signals the brain to "feel" frightened.

A territorial map

A great deal is known about how the brain works, but not enough to really answer questions like, "What is thinking?" or "What is a memory?" The answer will probably be a combination of chemical reactions and the wiring patterns inside the brain.

The brain cells that tell us, for instance, where an itch is aren't scattered helter-skelter all through the mush. They are distributed in a particular way, as though the brain could see the nerve cell arrangement as a map. And the number of nerve endings that represent the head portion is very large in comparison to the number of endings that represent other parts. The hands — with very outsized thumbs — are enormous, too. Probably this is no coincidence: in a human, messages from the face as you express yourself to the world, and messages from your hands, as you manipulate objects, are of unusual importance. If dogs were found to have such an organization, the nerve endings representing their front paws are unlikely to be so exaggerated because they don't use them so precisely as we use our hands.

The thinking process

In order to think, an incredible number of nerve connections must be acting on each other all at the same time. As I type, my lips move to shape the words, even though I'm not speaking. Something in my brain is remembering how to spell, how to move my fingers for each typed letter, and even how language works. Something else is deciding between words — one may be too difficult, another not express exactly what I mean. So I am knowing what I mean without words, even as I try to find the words. Then, pictures form of what I'm meaning — even if it is of something I have never seen. I might "image" a molecule snapping back into a com-

A human needs a large skull to contain his very advanced brain.

fortable position, though I have never seen such a thing happen. To do that I'm calling on stored images that make the best "fit" I can manage: textbook pictures of molecules made of round atoms and an image of my left fist fitting into my cupped right hand. As I do that, I vaguely feel my hands "practicing" what happens if I open up my left fist. As though all this were not enough, I'm also worrying that the writing is going too slowly, wondering what others will think of it, and becoming aware that my foot is falling asleep.

And there's more: my eyes are registering what I write, and my brain has the job of noticing that I've mistyped something. To correct the error, I have to realize I should backspace twice and type over. Hovering through everything is an annoying jingle that got stuck in my head at breakfast. And with this huge burden of goings-on inside my brain, I'd still manage to hear it if the dog were to knock over the garbage pail.

These different things all going on in a brain at the same time are quite different from one another. And they happen in different places.

A lizard's skull is quite flat; it doesn't contain much brain.

Three-layered theory

There are many theories about the basic organization of the brain. The one that follows is by no means proven, but there is probably some truth to it, and it is more fun to think about than other, equally unproven, ideas.

According to this idea, the human brain is basically a three-layered affair. Buried deep inside and to the rear of our skulls is a core area sometimes called the R-system. The R stands for reptile because this system represents most (not all) of the brain that reptiles have. Reptiles are known to be short of emotion on the whole: they have plenty of aggression, but little love, and no apparent conflicts. Their behavior is rigid. Each day they do the same things, in the same way, and in the same order. Reptiles never play. It's possible that the R-system in humans, too, is rather rigid, responsible for the urge to hide from the noise of thunder or strike back at the stone that stubs our toe.

The next layer, still quite far inside the brain, is the limbic system. Reptiles have very little of that layer, but all the birds and mammals have it. The limbic system is where smells are processed, and also seems to be responsible for what we think of as "warm" emotions — love, devotion, and altruism. Certain smells can flood us with warm emotions, a hint that the two functions of smelling and feeling good feelings are closely connected with one another.

The newest layer

The third (and, in humans, the vastly largest portion of the brain), is the neocortex (it means new brain, or the portion most recently evolved). The neocortex is what's responsible for the conscious portion of thinking, what we usually call "thought." It can do what no other portion of the brain can do: read words, interpret facial expressions, recognize a piece in a jigsaw puzzle, form speech, solve math problems. Your sense of "me-ness" seems to develop in your neocortex. (A rabbit, with its tiny neocortex, may not be able to think about itself.)

Although the neocortex at birth is potentially able to handle each of these sorts of mental life in any of its parts, it soon specializes. On the whole, the left side (in 90 percent of us) takes on "intellectual" tasks like language, arithmetic, remembering what happened recently, and figuring out problems. The right side takes over "intuitive" tasks, like recognizing patterns, understanding shapes and spaces, memorizing melodies, interpreting people's emotions, and coming up with sudden insights or ideas that don't seem to have

A dog's skull is more domed at the top, and its brain is more advanced than a reptile's.

gone through a figuring-out process.

You can see for yourself that the two sides can act in very separate ways. Within a couple of days, your left brain can learn where the letters of the alphabet are on a typewriter keyboard. But that doesn't seem to help you learn to type. Your right brain, which not only recognizes patterns but oversees how your hands and eyes work together to use the patterns, must then teach your fingers what to do. The process is quite tedious because there can be remarkably little communication between the two sides. Other examples are learning to read music, or to ride a bicycle. The right brain may be able to memorize melodies with ease, but doesn't help the left brain learn to read music. The left brain can understand instructions, but can't help the right brain learn to balance the bike.

One side to the other

Nerves from eyes, ears, and hands cross over from their own side of the body to the opposite side of the brain. Although there are nerve fibers from all of them in both the left and right halves of the brain, the opposite side, for some reason, pays attention to the message. For most people, it is easier to analyze what an object is from sensations arising in the right hand, and interpreted in the left brain. It can be done the other way around, but you get that fumbly, fuzzy feeling that you don't "know" as much from your left hand as from your right (it's often the other way around in left-handed people). Try a similar experiment with two kinds of sound: speech and music. With one ear plugged up by a finger, you should be able to understand what is said to you more easily with your right ear alone than with your left ear alone, and hear music better with your left ear than your right.

Where is dreamland?

Dreaming seems to occur without much help from the neocortex, especially the left side of it. All sorts of illogical things can happen. Sometimes there are words, but they make little sense when you later recall them. Emotions, often more powerful or overwhelming than in "real" life, have free rein. Even attempts to solve intellectual problems are strange.

While you are dreaming, nothing challenges the reality of the dream. Only rarely does some neocortical area say, "Hey, this can't happen," or "This is only a dream." For years, young children are genuinely confounded about the reality of their dreams. One of the greatest disappointments in one of my children's lives was when I failed to produce the tiny live elephant I had given him during the night. But is there, after all, a difference between a dream and other kinds of thinking? All our thinking, conscious or dreaming, is no more than electrochemical activity among those thousands of millions of nerve cells. It should not be surprising that it takes a long time and a lot of effort for a baby to discover that a dream of an elephant, a picture of an elephant, a memory of an elephant, and an actual elephant are real in different ways.

Without a neocortex, mental life might have the quality of dreaming, in which things can happen without reason, emotions are without control, and images form without logical relationship to one another. There is not even a sense of "me" in a dream: you are both inside the dream and outside watching it. Perhaps dreaming is thinking like a rabbit.

The other intelligence

Usually, people think that intelligence is what brains have. All forms of life, however, have intelligence, and most do not have brains. Geraniums and bedbugs know how to make hundreds of different kinds of cells and where each belongs; how to manufacture a multitude of chemicals, when to use them, how to recognize food from poison, how to obtain one, and avoid the other. Such organisms even know how to reproduce their own kind, including how to attract a bee or a mate, and how to provide for the needs of seed or egg. All this and a great deal more can be done without brains.

The basic intelligence of life lies not in brains but in a molecule called DNA.

Beginning of life

DNA was the first molecule of life, the first that could reproduce itself to create a new generation of separate molecules, each one like its parent. That molecule continues, three billion years later, to survive and reproduce itself over countless generations within every living organism there is. A DNA molecule, surrounded only with a thin coat, is all a virus is. DNA molecules, within each of our human cells, are all that genes are. The many million forms of life can all be seen as DNA's way of reproducing itself.

Every molecule of DNA is made principally of four smaller molecules called thymine, adenine, cytosine, and guanine. (They are abbreviated T, A, C, and G.) Different DNA molecules — such as those found in a virus or in a human — differ from each other only in the number of each of these smaller units and in the order in which they are placed. The four units — A, T, C, and G — serve as a four-letter alphabet. These four letters spell out instructions for making every substance and portion of an organism.

Used to a 26-letter alphabet, four letters may seem a stingy number to spell the many thousands of instructions the original egg cell needs to make a complete human. And, DNA's language is further restricted. Words may be only three letters long. There are no more than 64 three-letter words that can be formed from four letters. In DNA, 20 of these words spell out the 20 amino acids of which proteins are made. Two other triplets are periods, marking the end of an instruction. Another seems to mark the beginning of an instruction. The rest appear to be synonyms; they have the same meaning as some other word or punctuation.

Each instruction — made up of perhaps a hundred words read from the beginning mark, in sequence, to the ending mark — tells how to make a protein. C-T-G A-T-A G-G-G C-C-T, for instance, might be the instruction for how to make a protein that is built of four amino acids, which must follow that particular order. Still, to us, who are used to reading thick books of many letters and long words, the amount of information that could be handled by so few letters and such short words seems meager; that is, until you realize that, in the human cell, there are about 20 billion A, T, C, and G molecules to read from. The information in the words they form is probably a good deal more than that contained in your school library.

An unusual library

This library of information is the instructions for all the proteins of which you and every other organism are made. Together, your proteins determine how you are shaped and colored, how you may move and what you must eat, and even the uniquely human way you behave and think.

For most organisms, their DNA library, inherited through genes from generation to generation, is the major intelligence that guides them through their lives. When information is inherited, instead of learned, it is called instinct — or often, "only instinct." The word "instinct" is fine, but to couple it with the word, "only" seems unfair. Our brains have had to tediously learn, over thousands of years, how to navigate by the stars, though birds inherit that complicated information. DNA alone is responsible for a dog's knowledge of how to care for newborn pups, and for our own clever production of just the right enzymes to digest a hamburger. Our brains are quite incapable of making another human being, yet our DNA does that often. DNA, the first molecule of life, is also the basic molecule of intelligence.

Two of a kind

A molecule of DNA is made something like a twisted ladder. The rungs are made of pairs of the smaller molecules — A, T, C, and G. But the shapes of these molecules are such that only an A and a T or a C and a G can fit together to form a rung. The sides of the ladder are other molecules, which simply serve as support for the A-T and C-G rungs.

To reproduce, a DNA molecule unzips down the middle. Each half of a rung now attaches to it, from molecules floating nearby, the only sort that it fits with. An A attaches a T, a G with a C. The free ends of the newly attached molecules then attach the side rungs that complete the DNA. There are now two DNA molecules, each exactly like the original.

Key

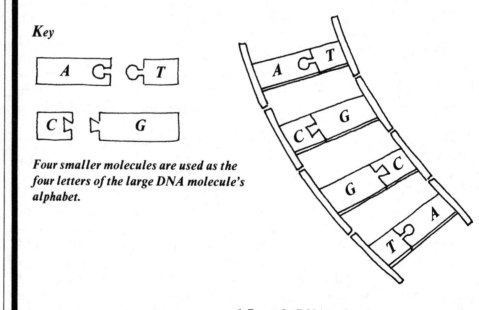

Four smaller molecules are used as the four letters of the large DNA molecule's alphabet.

1. Part of a DNA molecule.

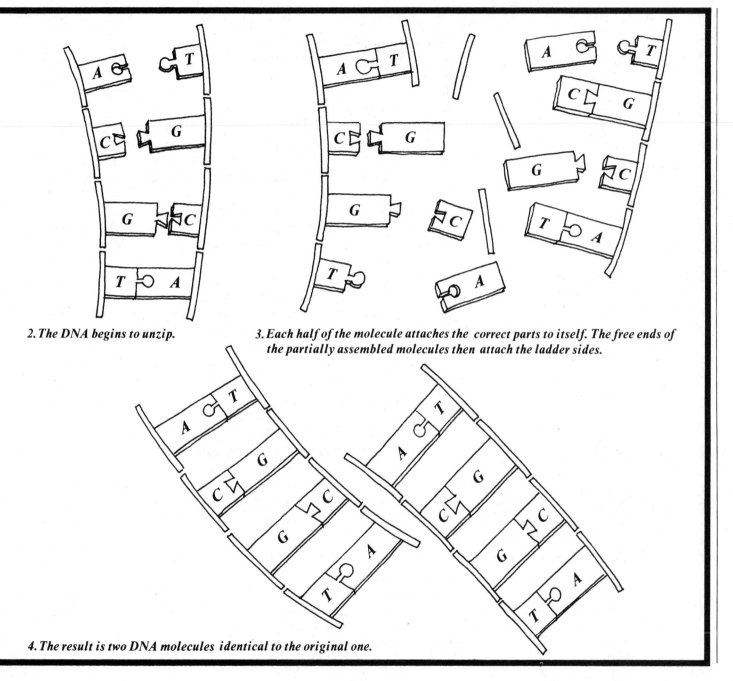

2. The DNA begins to unzip.

3. Each half of the molecule attaches the correct parts to itself. The free ends of the partially assembled molecules then attach the ladder sides.

4. The result is two DNA molecules identical to the original one.

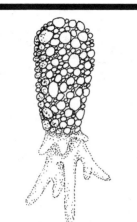

A fortress constructed out of minute grains of sand by difflugia, a microscopic relative of the primitive amoeba. Although it is only a single cell, difflugia builds its fortress by ingesting the particles, expelling them to its exterior, and binding them in place with a secreted glue.

Strange houses

Where there are people, there are houses. but the opposite of that statement is not true: where there are houses, there are not always people. There might easily be termites, bees, birds, or even, a one-celled creature called an amoeba. All these creatures, and many more, build their complicated houses with inherited information written in molecules of DNA.

The difflugia walks about with its house surrounding it. Before it reproduces by dividing, it builds a second house, moves part of itself into the new one, and then divides between the two houses.

Nests of mallee birds are heated by decaying vegetation. The parent birds plunge their long beaks into the egg chamber to feel the temperature. When the temperature rises, they remove sand to let heat escape. When the temperature falls, they heap more sand on top as an insulation.

A nest, made by one of the small birds called titmice, is actually woven together with grass. Other birds stitch their nests together using grass as thread, their bills as needles.

Termites are among the master-builders of the world. The rain-shedding house shown here may stand taller than a person. It is built to withstand a rainy climate.

In hot, dry areas, tall ventilation shafts keep the termite home cool. Some build special rooms in which to raise crops of fungus to eat, and others keep barns of aphids from which they lick a sweet substance called honeydew.

Nests of some titmice are so strongly woven of grasses and tufted with plant down that they are used by humans as slippers and purses. The nest swings on such tiny a branch tip that predators cannot climb out to it.

Nest of a mallee bird, heated by decaying compost. By manipulating the sand layer, parents keep temperature of egg chamber to witin 1 degree of 34 degrees centigrade. Nest is shown in cross-section.

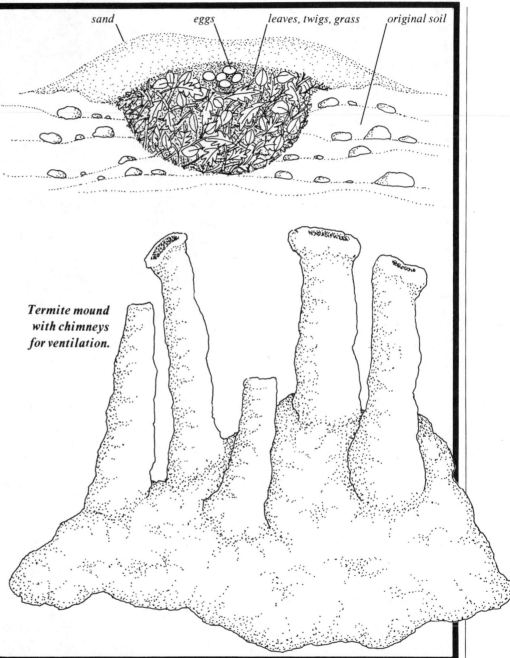

sand eggs leaves, twigs, grass original soil

Termite mound with chimneys for ventilation.

Termite mound with roofs to shed rain.

Your secret face

Here is a photograph of a perfectly nice fellow. As you can see, he is friendly, open, and slightly smiley. Or is he? It depends on which side of his face you're looking at. If you cover the left side of his face with a piece of paper, he's still friendly. But if you do the opposite, cover the right, side you're not so sure.

Apparently, the left side of our face expresses somewhat different, more extreme, or more unpleasant feelings than our right side — especially when our real feelings are not quite so nice as we would like people to know. Yet the left side is a secret side. People cannot read it.

The reason has to do with how the optic nerve is connected with the two sides of the brain. The optic nerve from each eye splits; the half that records the left side of the retinal image crosses over to the right side of the brain. The half that records the right side of the retinal image crosses to the left side of the brain. That means that for anything you see, half the picture is handled by one side of the brain, and half by the other. When you look at a person, the right side of

his face is in the left portion of your retinal image, and crosses over to the right side of your brain. This pleasant image, then, is processed by just the part of the brain that is so adept at recognizing faces and emotions.

The left side of the person's face, which may be expressing less pleasant things, is in the right part of the retinal image, and crosses over to the left brain. The left brain, bright in intellectual matters, is emotionally stupid. It is simply blind to the emotional message it sees — the left face remains secret.

An odd fact is that your own face, as you see it in the mirror, is therefore a different face from the one other people see. Looking at your own mirror image, your left face is in the left side of your retinal image. Able to use your right brain now to process information about yourself, you should be able to interpret your emotional expressions better than others can.

To get a look at the secret faces of your family, place an unframed mirror at a 90 degree angle along the center of a large photograph that was taken straight on. Look along the angle formed by the mirror and photograph to see how the face would look if it were composed of two right or two left sides.

Using two left sides of a face to create a full face turns this friendly-looking fellow on the opposite page into a somewhat more evil looking character.

Making eyes

People have always suspected that you can read love in a person's eyes, but only recently, scientists discovered just what it is about eyes that can convey the message. Humans dilate their pupils when they gaze at people of whom they are very fond. They contract their pupils when they glance toward those they dislike. This gesture is not under anyone's control; and it can't be hidden. It may account for the fact that, no matter what certain people say to you, or how well they control their voices and gestures, you can often sense with certainty that they are really unfriendly to you.

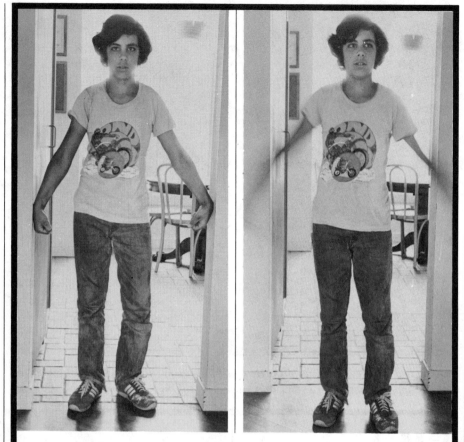

A slow circuit

Stand in a doorway. With the backs of your wrists, push against the door frame on both sides as hard as you can. Keep pressing until you feel your strength give out. Now step away from the doorway and let your arms hang relaxed at your sides. Mysteriously, they will both rise into the air.

Even though you are no longer consciously telling your brain to contract muscles to push against the doorway, there is a lag of several seconds before the brain stops its push signals. Even thought takes time.

Synesthesia

How loud is red? How fast is it? What color is cold? What sound is blue? These may seem like peculiar questions, but no doubt, you can answer them if you think about it a moment. Your answers, moreover, will most likely be these: red is very loud, and it's fast, too. Cold is blue, and the sound of blue is low.

You could also describe sounds by touch: soft, hard, rough. You could describe colors by touch, too. You could probably give the color, pitch, and texture of anger. You might be able to do the same for gloominess. And if you were a very young child, you might even suffer genuine confusion between which sensor — hands, ears, or eyes — is bringing in a message. The confusion, called synesthesia, leads some children to really not see the difference between soft, low, and blue; and to describe what is heard or touched or seen with words that belong to other senses.

The extraordinary thing about this peculiarity is that the sensations, different as they seem in some ways, are actually very like one another in other ways. High-pitched sounds are rapid frequencies; sharp surfaces excite our skin sensors the most; anger is an excited state; and the color, red, although it is a low frequency, is the color registered most quickly in the brain. The color blue is slowest to reach the brain. Low notes are low frequencies; softness energizes skin sensors least; and gloominess is marked by disinterest and inertia.

Long before anyone knew anything about waves, energies, or molecular states of excitement, our sensory equipment and our brains had some basic ability to detect underlying similarities.

Leaf winds and floating islands

Say to a child of about three, "I wonder what makes the wind?" Ask in a truly wondering tone of voice. What you want to find out is how he thinks, not what he has learned he is supposed to think. If you ask with sincerity, the usual answers at that age are that the leaves or the clouds make the wind when they move. He is using, and using perfectly well, the right side of his brain — the one that notices patterns and draws conclusions. The logic is simple: clouds move, leaves move, the wind comes. One must be the cause, the other the effect.

This kind of thinking, in which the left brain fails to act as a critic (it doesn't question the ability of clouds or leaves to move on their own) doesn't go away completely as people grow up. Test adults on their understanding of islands: on a small sheet of paper, draw a line from side to side about a third of the way up the page. Explain that the drawing is like a cross section of the ocean, with the line standing for the surface of the water. Ask them to draw an island in the ocean. Above is a frequent result, even in people who have had a college education.

It's a dog's world

If brains are where we construct our images of reality, and if brains and sense organs are different in different animals, are realities also different? You can't experience another animal's thinking to find out, but you can imagine that it must be so.

Try to get inside a dog's mind. A dog's senses are bringing in information quite different from what you are receiving. Blue and yellow are unknown to it; receptors for the two colors are missing. The sky isn't blue, the butter isn't yellow. The portion of the brain that processes visual images is in the neocortex. Dogs don't have much up front. (Look at the shape of their foreheads!) It's likely that they can't derive much information from what is seen and don't rely on visual images to make judgments.

Our dog often barks at members of the family when she sees them at a distance. She never looks at herself in the mirror. Sight alone doesn't serve to identify herself or us.

Face and finger games

Your intelligent neocortex can make silly mistakes. For instance, it automatically sees a cause-and-effect relationship between two events that happen one right after another. When you perfect the timing of the face and finger games shown here, people watching you will see causes and effects which anyone can tell you are impossible.

Out comes the tongue.

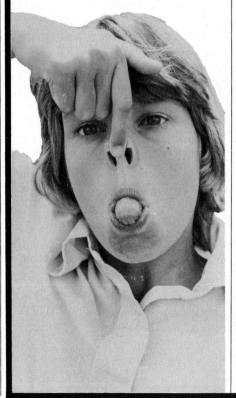

It's tugged to one side . . .

. . . then the other,

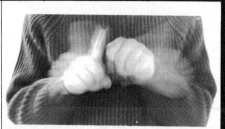

The right hand is about to "transfer" its upright finger to the left hand.

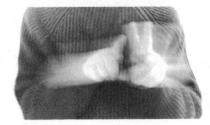

Now the left hand, with one finger already up, has just received a second finger from the right hand.

This boy makes it look as if sticking his finger in his right ear causes his tongue to push out his left cheek.

and pulled back in.

A snake's tongue, flicking in and out so quickly...

Sniffing it out

Compared to vision, the smell portions of a dog's brain are very large. The amount of space given to molecule detection in the nose is fifty times larger than in humans. That's one reason for having a long snout. A dog can smell some substances in concentrations a million times less than we need to smell the same thing. Dogs in doubt about the identity of a human, sniff to decide who he is.

Probably, smelling tells them more than the identity of an individual. Perhaps, a dog knows where that person has been, what emotional state he is in, what sex he is, and much more. Our dog, even though she always barks at a person who has never been to our house before, has on several occasions failed to bark at relatives whom she had never met. Could it be there is a family smell? We can imagine that a dog stores "smell pictures" of individuals, and even categorizes those pictures, just as we do visual images. After all, we are often able to recognize that a stranger is someone's relative by comparing our visual images of other members of the family. People who have been blind from birth dream in sound images. Dogs may dream in smells.

"Silent" dog whistles produce sound in frequencies too high for human ears, but well within the hearing of dogs. Since high sounds also carry farther through the air than low ones, dogs can hear at greater distances than humans. Their hearing, anyway, is far better — that is, they can hear very weak sounds. Also, their ears swivel, helping them both to focus sounds and to locate their source — and each ear can swivel independently. Sound pictures in a dog's brain may be both detailed and "shaped" in three dimensions.

Not much up front

Lacking much in the way of a neocortex, dogs don't have language in the human sense, and seem to have trouble figuring out certain problems. Two of the dogs we've had were determined to hide down the bathtub drain during thunderstorms. The limbic or the R-system can warn of danger from loud noises, trigger an impulse to hide in a hole, and turn on digging behavior. But the next step — saying, "Wait a second; the bathtub hole is too small, and the material is too hard to dig in, and anyhow, I'm already inside the house," is beyond a dog's capacity.

Any emotion we can feel probably can be felt by dogs, too. There is plenty of evidence for love, devotion, altruism, depression, jealousy, mourning, irritation, and rage. The limbic system and the R-system is all anyone needs to feel feelings. Analyzing those feelings and controlling them through logic is another thing altogether. Dogs probably don't wonder, as humans often do, "But does he really love me?"; and they snap at a tiny kitten, who is hardly a threat to their dinner, as violently as if a tiger were about to snatch it all away.

Dogs do dream

Does a dog, like us, have images that are more real or less real? Does it know a dream is only a dream, a thought only a thought? Here's a guess: thoughts and actualities might easily be told apart, depending on whether you did anything about them or not. Thinking about dinner, when you're not really eating (no messages are arriving from muscles or nose or tongue or eyes) is not the same as eating dinner. A dream of eating dinner would be much harder to tell apart from the real thing because the images would, in a dog, almost certainly include smell, and might include a sense of motion, noise, and visual images as well. "Chasing rabbits" is the way my father used to describe a dog's way of making running motions, sniffing, and whimpering as they dream. Yet when you wake a

...the camera failed to catch it here, is used to taste its surroundings ...

dog from a dream, it doesn't seem to look, listen, or sniff about for what was happening in dreamland. Without figuring out what a dream is, maybe a dog can, by certain differences between the two kinds of images, decide at least that dreams happen "there," and real life "here."

Other creatures

Animals less like us than dogs must have even stranger realities. Fish, including a pet goldfish, have pressure-sensitive nerve endings along their sides. Any obstacle, such as a rock or weed in the water, sends a continuous disturbance through the water. So does your finger or another fish. A fish feels all these disturbances along its sides. Most likely, a fish's brain can form an ever-changing image of the shape and motion of the watery space around it. You can vaguely imagine this by concentrating on how the sense of touch in your hands might convey a spatial image if they could be in contact with the entire room around you and all the objects in it. But our spatial images for the most part are visual, not "feel" images. A bat's spatial image is a sound image. The high squeaks they voice all the time bounce back off objects and hit their ears. They hear the shape of the world.

A snake tastes its way along, and a cockroach may do so, too. The snake's "nose" is its tongue, and the cockroach's "nose" is its antennas. Both are organs that identify thousands of different kinds of molecules. A snake's or a cockroach's sense of direction, or even its idea of space, may be a chemical image. For that matter, dogs may have a chemical image of their neighborhoods, too, judging by how they get around with their noses. Humans are so crude in this respect that about the most we can do is recognize when we're driving past the cookie factory. Smell images in a spatial sense are not possible for us. Rattlesnakes do their hunting in the dark, by infrared sensors.

...as a snake makes its way along.

Their sense of space may be built from shades and contours of heat. Probably neither snakes nor cockroaches can dream. Limbic systems, which they lack, seem to be the dreamers.

Familiar realities

Getting back to the more familiar visual realities we are so accustomed to, that reality depends on what the eye sees. Houseflies, with their bulging, many-lensed eyes, can see nearly the entire hemisphere around them — backward, forward, to both sides, and upward. Downward is beyond their vision. Our eyes present our brain with two only slightly different images of the same object. Flies' eyes relay hundreds of images, each from a slightly different angle; and each of only a minute portion of the scene around them. Do they have enough brain to form a single image from these many, or do they see reality multiplied? Whichever way it is, their reality is very small. A fly can only see a few feet of world.

Bees see colors we don't see, and see colors we do see as other colors. What we see as white may be either white or ultraviolet. (It's weird to try to imagine a color that doesn't exist for us.) What we see as orange, they see as yellow-ish green. They are blind to red.

But every creature is blind to every other creature's reality. A dog's world can't be described as anything like a fish's world, or a bat's, or a fly's, or a snake's, or ours. What's real to each is constructed in the brain according to its capacities, and according to what information it has from which to form images. Finding one's way about can be done with heat images, visual images, sound images, or chemical images. Communicating with one's own kind can be done by making scents and smelling meanings, as cats do; or by making gestures and seeing meaning, as dogs do; or by stroking and feeling meanings, as cockroaches do; or by making sounds and hearing meanings, as we do. The argument as to who is "right" is beside the point. Any reality, so long as it keeps us from bumping into walls, lets us say "Hi" to friends, and informs us that breakfast is ready will do.

Glossary & Index

Glossary

A

AC
Alternating current; a back and forth flow of electrical charge such as that in most homes.

Acid
Any of a large group of corrosive chemicals related to vinegar or the hydrochloric acid produced by the stomach.

Acupuncture
Oriental method in which anesthesia is produced by twirling fine needles at the site of certain nerves.

Adenine
One of the four subunit molecules of which DNA is constructed.

Adrenalin
Hormone that regulates some sensations and physical effects of fear and anger.

Aerial roots
Roots that sprout above the soil.

Alga
A one- or many-celled, plantlike protista, such as the green scum in fishtanks, or most seaweeds.

Altruism
Behavior that, while risking the individual's life or safety, tends to protect the safety of others.

Amino Acids
Group of molecules from which proteins are built.

Amniotic Sac
Strong, fluid-filled membrane that surrounds the developing infant within the uterus.

Amoeba
A one-celled protozoa.

Amplitude
Loudness of a sound; or height of a peak when sound is depicted as a wave.

Anaerobic
Not requiring oxygen.

Anesthetics
Chemicals capable of producing unconsciousness, or making a portion of the body insensitive.

Anther
Male, pollen-producing portion of a flower, attached to a petal by the stamen. Together, anther and stamen are the male portion of a flower.

Arteries
Blood vessels through which oxygen-filled blood circulates.

Astigmatism
A defect of vision in which the image formed is distorted in shape.

Atom
Basic unit of all matter, made up of a nucleus of protons and neutrons, surrounded by electrons.

Auditory
Of or related to hearing.

B

Bacteria
A large group of microscopic protistas important in producing certain foods, and as disease-causing organisms.

Base
Any of a large group of corrosive chemicals related to lye and washing soda.

Bicuspids
Double-edged teeth that lie between canines and molars.

Bladder
Sac in which urine is stored.

Bonding
The process by which atoms associate with one another to form molecules; or molecules associate with one another to form more complicated molecules.

Bowel
Intestine; usually used to refer to the large intestine in mammals.

C

Caffeine
Chemical which acts as a stimulant in humans, present in such dilute drinks as coffee, tea, and cola.

Canines
Pointed, often long, ripping teeth to each side of the front incisors.

Capilleries
Very slim, branching ends of veins and arteries, through which blood cells squeeze out to circulate among body cells, and reenter to circulate back to the heart.

Carbohydrates
Group of foods comprising both sugars and starches; such as potatoes, which contain mostly starch, or honey, which contains mostly sugar.

Carnivorous
Meat-eating.

Cartilage
Strong, elastic tissue that provides support for ears and noses, and cushions the ends of bones at joints.

Cell
The basic unit of all organisms except viruses. An organism can be one-celled, as an amoeba, or be constructed of many kinds of cells, such as bone, blood, muscle, and nerve.

Chlorophyll
A green pigment produced mainly by plants, capable of absorbing light energy for food production.

Chromosomes
Strands within the nucleus of the cell, along which lie the genes responsible for inherited information.

Circuit
Closed loop through which a current of electrical charge travels.

Clavicle
Collar bone.

Clitoris
Small organ to the front of the female's urethra, lying between two lobes of flesh. The clitoris, together with the vagina and surrounding tissues, plays a role in sexual sensations.

Clone
Complete individual grown from a single, non-sexual plant or animal cell.

Cloaca
Tube through which waste products from the intestine and kidney, as well as eggs from the ovary, exit from the body. Birds and reptiles have a cloaca, but mammals have separate openings to serve each function.

Clot
Thick plug formed by blood in response to injury, to prevent further blood flow.

Coccyx
Fused vertebrae at the bottom of the spine.

Collagen
Strong elastic tissue that gives bones and cartilage flexibility.

Colostrum
Fluid produced by mammary glands from shortly before birth until milk production begins after birth.

Compressing
Bunching or squeezing together particles or molecules so that they are closer to one another.

Concave
Curved or dipping inward.

Concentric circles
A series of circles, having a common center, lying outside one another.

Convex
Curved or bulging outward.

Crustacean
Usually a water-dwelling animal with a segmented shell, such as a shrimp, crab, or crayfish. The pillbug is a land-dwelling crustacean.

Crystals
Regular and repeated formations of molecules, such as salt or ice crystals.

Current
A flow of charge, such as that caused by electrons drifting through a wire.

Cytoplasm
The fluid within a cell.

Cytosine
One of the four subunit molecules of which DNA is constructed.

D

DC
Direct current; a one-directional flow of electrical charge, such as the current produced by a battery.

Dermis
Inner layer of skin, made up of living skin cells and supplied with blood vessels, sensory nerves, sweat and oil glands.

Dextrose
A glucose molecule of a particular shape.

Digestion
The process of cutting food molecules into pieces small enough to be absorbed by the body.

Dissolve
Separate or disconnect, as when water molecules come between the portions of a salt or sugar crystal, separating the parts from one another, and dispersing them within the liquid.

Diuretic
Medicinal substance used to relieve swelling from accumulation of water in tissues.

DNA
Long, twisted ladder-shaped molecule made of the four subunits thymine, adenine, cytosine, and quanine, which encodes inherited information in all forms of life.

Dominant
Commanding. Dominant is used to indicate genes whose message will be obeyed to produce a characteristic such as eye color.

Dormant
In a temporary state of inactivity, such as a hibernating animal, or a leafless tree in winter.

Dug
Nipple containing a single hole through which milk is drawn from the mammary gland.

E

Earphone
A device that focuses sound at the ear to improve hearing.

Ecology
Relationships between organisms and their environment. Ecology includes not only the effect of climate and terrain, but all the effects local plants, animals, and protistas have on one another within the environment.

Electricity
Charge; a basic property of electrons and protons. Electricity is usually used to mean the effect of charge, as when it is put to work to light a lamp or heat a toaster.

Electromagnetic force
The force associated with charged particles, and independent of the force of gravity. Electromagnetism holds electrons to their protons in an atom, and guides energy transfer.

Electron
A particle outside the atomic nucleus that carries a unit of negative charge.

Embryo
A stage in the development of both plants and animals that begins when the fertilized egg cell begins to divide and ends either when the animal embryo takes on the recognizable form of its species, or when the plant embryo sprouts roots and leaves.

Endocrine
Internally secreting directly into the blood stream. Endocrine organs include the pancreas and adrenal glands.

Endorphin
Brain chemical, believed to lessen the sensation of pain.

Enzymes
Body chemicals that cut molecules into smaller ones, or splice them together into larger ones in such processes as digestion and cell repair.

Epidermis
Thin, outer layer of skin, made up of dead skin cells.

Erection
Enlargement and stiffening of an organ, particularly the male penis, female clitoris and surrounding tissue.

Ethylene
A colorless gas that has a ripening effect on fruits.

Euglena
A protista that has plant characteristics, such as chlorophyll, and animal characteristics, such as the ability to swim freely.

Evaporation
The process by which a substance, usually a liquid, becomes a gas.

Excrete
Get rid of damaging or unneeded waste products, such as by exhaling, urinating, or defecating.

Expanding
Spreading out particles or molecules so that they are farther from one another.

F

Fallopian tubes
Oviduct, in mammals.

Farsighted
A defect of vision in which the eye forms a clear image of distant objects, but a blurred image of nearby ones.

Feces
Solid waste material, mostly undigested food, excreted through the bowel.

Femur
Upper leg, or thigh bone.

Fertilization
Joining of male and female sex cells; in plants, pollen with ova; in animals, sperm with ova. Also, adding chemicals to soil for plant nourishment.

Fetus
A stage after the embryo stage but before birth in mammals and some other animals. In humans, the embryo is called a fetus beginning at about three months, when obviously human characteristics have developed.

Fiber
Thin strand of material such as a muscle fiber or the fibers formed in clotting blood.

Fibroblast
Body cell capable of migrating to the site of an injury, and dividing rapidly to start the repair process.

Fibula
Small bone of the lower leg.

Fields
Areas in which space is distorted. Fields influence matter, as gravity and electromagnetic fields; and guide energy, as light waves.

Filament
A very thin thread or wire, such as that in a light bulb.

Focal Point
A spot before and behind a convex lens. Light entering the lens at a right angle to the lens converges at the focal point and emerges behind it, at a right angle to the lens.

Follicle
A pit or pocket, such as that from which a hair grows, or that which contains an egg cell in the ovary.

Frequency
Number of vibrations per second in light or sound.

Fructose
A sugar found in many fruits.

Fungus
One of a group of protistas that include the molds, mushrooms, and yeasts, as well as the shelf fungi found on trees.

G

Gas
A state of matter, such as fumes, air, or water vapor, in which atoms or molecules are very spread out from one another. A quantity of gas spreads to fill whatever contains it, so has neither a shape of its own nor a definite volume.

Gelatin
Substance obtained from collagen, and used to gel or stiffen foods such as jelly desserts.

Gender
Sex, male or female.

Genes
Sites of DNA molecules along the chromosome in the nucleus of a cell, responsible for inherited information.

Germ
Plant embryo, the portion of a seed that will develop into a plant. Also a common word for disease agents such as viruses and bacteria.

Germinate
To sprout roots, stems, and leaves, as when the germ or plant embryo in a seed sprouts.

Gland
Organ whose main job is to secrete.

Glucose
Simple sugar used by the body for heat and other energy needs.

Gravity
Force by which all objects, outside the atom itself, exert an attraction on one another.

H

Heart
Organ which pumps blood.

Histamine
A body chemical used as a defense, and responsible for the itching of bites and rashes.

Hormones
Body chemicals circulated in the blood, which regulate such processes as growth, fertility, and some emotions.

Host
An organism whose body provides nourishment to other organisms, usually to its injury or even death, and never to its benefit.

Humerus
Upper arm bone.

Hybrid
The offspring of crossbreeding a male of one variety with a female of a different variety, such as the offspring of dogs of two different breeds, or many crossbred fruits and vegetables.

Hyphas
Threads that grow from mold spores into an organic substance to digest and absorb food.

I

Ilium
Front, upper blade-like bone of the hip.

Immune
Not susceptible to an illness or disorder.

Immunize
Make unsusceptible to illness, as by a polio vaccination or german measles inoculation.

Incisors
Blade-shaped biting teeth, at the front of the mouth.

Infection
Invasion and multiplication within an organism of a disease agent such as a virus, fungus, or bacterium.

Infrared light
Medium-energy, non-visible light, capable of penetrating soft body tissues.

Ingests
Takes into the body, as when an animal swallows food, or a macrophage cell engulfs a bacterium.

Instinct
Behavior governed by inherited rather than learned intelligence.

Insulin
Hormone, which regulates the use of sugar in the body, secreted by the pancreas.

Intercourse
Reproductive act, during which the male's penis is inserted into the female's vagina.

Interferon
Body chemical believed to have a role in fighting virus infections.

Intestine
Long tube leading from the stomach to the rectum, which absorbs food during digestion.

Ions
Atoms that carry a charge either by the loss or gain of one or more electrons.

Ischium
Rear, lower, "sitting" bone of the hip.

K

Keratin
Protein molecule of which hair and nails are made.

Kidney
Organ which, through a filtering process, removes waste products and excess water from the blood, and empties the resulting urine into the bladder.

Kinesthetic Sense
The sense that informs the brain of the position and location of body parts, or movement, and of effect.

L

Larva
Wormlike form, such as the caterpillar, which is the first stage after hatching in the development of many insects.

Laryngitis
A swelling or inflammation of the vocal cords that interferes with sound production.

Lens
A piece of curved, transparent material which forms a visible image by focusing light.

Lichen
Two organisms, a fungus and an alga, that live as a unit, each supply the other with essential functions such as food manufacture and water absorption.

Ligament
Tough tissue band which connects muscle to bone, bone to bone, or holds organs in place in the body.

Limbic system
Middle layer of the brain.

Liquid
A state of matter such as water, molten lava or mercury in which the atoms or molecules flow easily around one another. A quantity of liquid takes the shape of the container that holds it, but unlike gas, has a definite volume.

Liver
Organ which, among other functions, converts harmful chemicals in the body into non-harmful ones.

Lungs
Organs which fill with air, and provide an extensive spongy surface through which oxygen can enter the blood.

Lymph
Clear, salty liquid similar to blood but lacking red blood cells. Lymph circulates between cells throughout the body.

M

Macrophages
Large body cells capable of migrating to the site of an injury, and engulfing or digesting invading bacteria or dead cells.

Mammary gland
Milk-producing gland such as that within a woman's breast or a cow's udder.

Metacarpals
Hand bones.

Metatarsals
Foot bones.

Membrane
Thin sheet or layer, such as that which surrounds the cell.

Menstruation
Monthly flow of blood from the uterus lining of human females.

Methane
Gas composed of carbon and hydrogen, produced by decay.

Molars
Relatively flat-surfaced grinding teeth in the rear of the mouth.

Mold
A protista of the fungus group, often fuzzy in appearance, that grows on damp organic matter such as leather, food, and wood.

Molecule
Two or more atoms associated with one another, and forming a substance with properties that are different from the atoms of which it is made.

Mycelium
Mass of all the hyphas growing from a mold spore.

N

Nearsighted
A defect of vision in which the eye forms a clear image of nearby objects, but a blurred image of distant objects.

Neocortex
Outermost layer of the brain.

Nipple
Protuberance on the surface of the mammary gland through which the infant sucks milk.

Nucleus
The massive central portion of an atom; also the portion of a cell that contains the DNA molecules.

O

Octave
A range of eight musical notes. The pitch of the lowest note has a wavelength exactly twice as long as that of the highest note in an octave.

Opsin
A small molecule that, together with retinal, forms the visual purple pigment of the retina.

Organ
A part of a plant or animal, made up of various types of cells, that performs a certain job such as the heart, which pumps blood, or the skin, which protects the body.

Organic
Containing substances that originated in living organisms.

Organisms
Forms of life, such as protistas, plants, or animals.

Orgasm
In both sexes, orgasm (rhythmic spasms) marks a peak of sexual feeling, followed by relaxation. In the male, semen is expelled from the penis.

Ova
Female sex cells of both plants and animals. An ovum, when it joins with a pollen grain or sperm, contributes half the information to a plant or animal embryo.

Ovary
Female organ in which eggs are matured in preparation for fertilization, both in plants and animals.

Oviduct
Tube through which eggs, or ova, leave the ovary. In mammals, the oviducts are called fallopian tubes.

P

Pancreas
Endocrine gland which secretes the hormone insulin, and several digestive enzymes.

Patella
Kneecap.

Penicillium
A group of blue molds commonly growing on bread, from one member of which the antibiotic penicillin is derived.

Penis
Male organ lying in front of the testicles and containing the urethra, serving both for passage of urine and semen.

Phalanges
Toe and finger bones.

Phenols
Any of a large group of chemicals such as the one that causes the burning sensation from hot peppers.

Photons
Particles of light energy.

Pigment
Colored substance, such as the green pigment chlorophyll, the red pigment in red blood cells, or the brown pigment in human skin.

Placebo effect
Relief of symptoms by a substance that has no actual medicinal effect.

Placenta
Large, soft organ inside the pregnant uterus, by which the developing infant obtains oxygen and nourishment through its mother's blood supply.

Planaria
Flatworm; a small, non-segmented fresh water worm.

Pollen
Male sex cells of a flowering plant, comparable to sperm cells in animals. A grain of pollen, when it joins with the ovum, contributes half the genetic information to the plant embryo.

Pollination
The fertilizing of a plant ovum by a pollen grain.

Protein
Any of a large group of complicated molecules made up of amino acids. Proteins are the basic molecules of all life.

Protista
Kingdom of organisms that are neither plant nor animal. The protistas include viruses, bacteria, algae, and fungi.

Proton
A particle in the atomic nucleus that carries a unit of positive charge.

Protozoa
The most primative group in the animal kingdom, including many one-celled organisms.

Pubis
Front lower bone of the hip.

Pupa
Legless form, such as that inside a cocoon, which is the second stage in the development of many insects. The adult insect emerges from the pupa.

Pupil
Opening at the front of the eye through which light can pass to the interior.

Pus
Collection of dead cells, bacteria, and lymph that accumulate in injuries infected with bacteria.

Q

Quanine
One of the four subunit molecules of which DNA is constructed.

R

R-System
Innermost layer of the brain.

Radius
Outer bone of forearm.

Recessive
Subordinate. Recessive is used to indicate genes whose message, while present in each cell, will be ignored in favor of the message carried by a dominant gene.

Rectum
Lower end of the bowel ending in a muscular opening through which undigested food exits the body.

Reflexes
Muscular reactions, often protective, such as eye-blinking, that are quick and automatic.

Regurgitate
Throw up; usually used to mean expel the contents of the stomach only, to rechew food or feed young.

Resonate
Vibrate in the same rhythm as a sound, thereby increasing its loudness.

Retina
Light-sensitive inner layer of eye.

Retinal
A small molecule that, together with opsin, forms the visual purple pigment of the retina.

Rhodospin
Visual purple.

Root
The bottom portion of a plant, usually growing into the soil. Roots both support the plant and absorb water and minerals from the soil.

Rootlets
Small roots that branch out from larger, supporting roots.

S

Saliva
A liquid produced by glands that empty into the mouth. Saliva contains enzymes that digest starch.

Scab
Hard, dry crust formed to protect an injured surface.

Scapula
Shoulder blade.

Scrotum
Bag-shaped container in which the pair of testes are suspended outside the body in male animals.

Secrete
Produce, separate out from other products, and emit a substance. Both individual cells and whole organs secrete a variety of substances.

Semen
Milky, thick fluid in which sperm are protected.

Seminal Vesicle
Sac in which semen is stored.

Sepals
Leaflike parts that cover flower buds or, when the blossom opens, lie beneath the petals.

Solid
A state of matter, such as rock, wood, or ice, in which the atoms or molecules are close together and more or less rigidly attached. Solids maintain a shape of their own, and have a definite volume.

Soundscope
A device for visualizing sound waves.

Spasm
Strong, involuntary muscle contraction.

Sperm
Male sex cells of animals. A sperm, when it joins with the ovum, contributes half the genetic information to the embryo.

Stamen
Thin stalk in a flower bearing the anther. Together, stamen and anther are the male portion of the flower.

Sternum
Breastbone; connects the ribs at the front of the chest.

Steroids
Body chemicals that reduce redness and swelling, among other effects.

Stigma
Sticky tip of a flower pistil to which pollen grains adhere.

Sucrose
Sugar obtained primarily from sugar cane and sugar beets.

Synesthesia
A sensation, such as that of a color, stimulated by a different sense, such as hearing a sound.

T

Teat
Nipple containing many holes through which milk is drawn from the mammary gland.

Testes
Male glands in which sperm are produced.

Testicles
Male reproductive organ, made up of the testes, and the scrotum that contains them.

Thymine
One of the four subunit molecules of which DNA is constructed.

Tibia
Large, or shin bone of lower leg.

Tissue
Group of cells, of one or several kinds, that make up a body material such as skin, bone, blood, or muscle.

Toxin
Substance, such as certain bacterial waste products, that are irritating or poisonous to humans.

U

Ulna
Inner bone of forearm.

Ultraviolet light
High-energy, non-visible light, capable of causing sunburn.

Umbilical cord
Tube containing blood vessels through which blood circulates between the developing infant and the placenta within the uterus.

Ureter
Tube connecting each kidney to the bladder.

Urethra
Tube through which urine is emptied from the bladder.

Urine
A liquid, excreted by the kidneys, consisting of water in which waste products are dissolved.

V

Vagina
A body opening in the female mammal through which the young are born from the uterus.

Vapor
Gas.

Vas deferens
Tube through which sperm leave the testes.

Veins
Blood vessels through which oxygen-emptied blood circulates.

Vertebrae
The separate bones that make up the backbone.

Vessels
Tubes through which fluids, such as blood, circulate.

Vibration
A regular back and forth motion, as that of a stretched rubber band when it is plucked.

Virus
An organism unlike other forms of life in that it is not a cell. Viruses must penetrate another organism's cell in order to reproduce.

Visual purple
A light-sensitive pigment formed in the retina.

Voicegram
A visual pattern, produced by voice vibrations, that is different for each individual's voice.

Voltage
A measure of electrical current. A current of high voltage can do more work than one of low voltage.

W

Weaned
No longer obtaining milk from the mammary gland. In humans, weaned can also mean no longer obtaining milk from a bottle.

X

X-rays
Very high energy non-visible light, capable of penetrating soft body tissues.

Index